"This book makes a valuable contribution, not only to the discussion about the why and how of nonviolent peacemaking, but also to the development of an ethic of virtue that has relevance for public policy. In a rare and important synthesis, McCarthy shows clearly how virtue ethics and human rights discourse can be brought together fruitfully in the midst of a religiously pluralistic society."

—LAURIE JOHNSTON
Emmanuel College

"Engaging and clearly written, Becoming Nonviolent Peacemakers draws upon an impressive range of sources to turn questions of violence towards virtue theory. What sets the book apart is McCarthy's case for understanding nonviolent peacemaking as a particular virtue distinct from and central to other virtues. The treatment of thinkers and practitioners from faith traditions other than Christianity is an added bonus. Highly recommended."

—TODD DAVID WHITMORE
University of Notre Dame

"Over the past generation, nonviolent movements have transformed the way in which oppressed peoples fight injustice. Now, McCarthy's Becoming Nonviolent Peacemakers promises a transformation in how nonviolence itself is conceived—namely as a virtue, a way of life. And McCarthy has the temerity to take this virtue to the site where it is most needed: United States foreign policy."

—DANIEL PHILPOTT
University of Notre Dame

Becoming Nonviolent Peacemakers

Becoming Nonviolent Peacemakers

*A Virtue Ethic for Catholic Social Teaching
and U.S. Policy*

ELI SASARAN MCCARTHY

With a Foreword by William O'Neill, SJ

PICKWICK *Publications* · Eugene, Oregon

BECOMING NONVIOLENT PEACEMAKERS
A Virtue Ethic for Catholic Social Teaching and U.S. Policy

Pickwick Publications
An Imprint of Wipf and Stock Publishers
199 W. 8th Ave., Suite 3
Eugene, OR 97401

www.wipfandstock.com

ISBN 13: 978-1-61097-113-3

Cataloguing-in-Publication data:

McCarthy, Eli Sasaran.

Becoming nonviolent peacemakers : a virtue ethic for Catholic social teaching and U.S. policy / Eli Sasaran McCarthy ; foreword by William O'Neill, SJ.

xviii + 260 pp. ; 23 cm. Includes bibliographical references and index.

ISBN 13: 978-1-61097-113-3

1. Peace — Religious aspects — Christianity. 2. Religion and international affairs. 3. Virtue. 4. Ethics. 5. Catholic Church — Doctrines. I. O'Neill, William R. II. Title.

BT736.4 .M40 2012

Manufactured in the U.S.A.

I dedicate this book to my four-year old son Lazarus

May you spread your Wings!

Contents

Foreword

Becoming Nonviolent Peacemakers

WILLIAM O'NEILL, SJ

"So many in these days have taken violent steps to gain the things of this world—war to achieve peace; coercion to achieve freedom; striving to gain what slips through the fingers. We might as well give up our great desires, at least our hopes of doing great things toward achieving them, right at the beginning. In a way it is like the paradox of the Gospel, of giving up one's life in order to save it."[1]

S O WROTE DOROTHY DAY, founder of the Catholic Worker Movement, in September, 1957. Surely at the heart of Christian faith lies the God of peace, *shalom* (Rom 15:33)—the God desiring peace for all people far and near (Ps 85:8; Is 57:19). Yet in a world of terror and casual slaughters, walking "in the way of peace" (Lk 1: 79) remains a hard grace.

The great 16th Century British physician, Thomas Linacre, it is said, first opened the New Testament only late in life. Chancing upon the "hard sayings" of Matthew's Sermon on the Mount, e.g., "turning the other cheek" (Mt 5:39), he was horrified: "Either this is not the Gospel," he exclaimed, or "we are not Christians." Linacre, his biographer tells us, "flung the book from him, and resumed his medical studies."[2] Even if

1. Dorothy Day, *The Selected Writings of Dorothy Day*, ed. Robert Ellsberg (New York: Knopf, 1988) 280.

2. R. W. Chambers, *Thomas More* (Maryland: Westminster, 1949) 84.

apocryphal, the story bears a grain of truth. For then, as now, how read-ily the "things that make for peace" (Lk 19:42) slip through the fingers!

Eli Sasaran McCarthy's splendid new book takes up Day's challenge of living "the Gospel of Peace" (Acts 10:36; Eph 6:15) today. Wise and passionately argued, *Becoming Nonviolent Peacemakers* offers a novel as-sessment of nonviolent peacemaking from the emerging perspective of virtue ethics. McCarthy's virtue-based approach is itself irenic, incorpo-rating not only the wisdom of Ghandi and Abdul Gaffar Khan, but the mediating discourse of human rights in public policy.

The significance of such an interpretation becomes apparent against the backdrop of our regnant political rhetoric of war and violence—the belief, in Michael Walzer's words that war remains a "rule-governed ac-tivity, a world of permissions and prohibitions–a moral world," even "in the midst of hell."[3] Pacifism, by the same token, is assimilated to what McCarthy describes as "rule-based" or "strategy-based" alternatives, so that our thinking about nonviolent peacemaking turns on the regulative logic of just war.

And yet, as McCarthy persuasively shows, the logic itself is decep-tive. For even disciples espousing the *justum bellum* can never forsake the primacy of *shalom*, incarnated in the "Gospel of Peace." Thus for Augustine, war was a tragic necessity, the consequence–and remedy–of fallen nature. Indeed, the "love of enemies" admits "of no exceptions," yet the "kindly harshness" of charity does not "exclude wars of mercy waged by the good." Inspired by the "severity which compassion itself dictates," such "wars of mercy" presumed that those inflicting punishment had "first overcome hate in their hearts." Neither Ambrose nor Augustine permitted violent *self*-defense; for only defense of the innocent neigh-bor could satisfy the stringent claims of charity.[4] Thomas Aquinas, too, recognized the normative primacy accorded *caritas* in-forming justice, posing the *quaestio* in the *Summa Theologiae* II-II, Q. 40 "whether it is *always* sinful to wage war?" Harking back to their Thomistic heritage, the Renaissance Spanish schoolmen Francisco de Vitoria and Francisco Suárez fashioned the just-war tradition in the law of nations or interna-

---

3. Walzer, *Just and Unjust Wars*, 36.

4. Cf. Augustine, *Epist.* 189, and 209, 2; *De Civitate Dei*, XIX, 12-13, XXII, 6; *Quest. Heat.* VI, 10, SEL., XXVIII, 2, p. 428, IV, 44, CSEL, XXVIII, 2, p. 353; *De Libero Arbitrio*, V, 12, Migne, PL, XXXXII, 1227; *Contra Faustum*, XXIII, 76 and 79; *Epist.*, 138, ii, 14. Cited in Bainton, *War and Peace*, 91ff.

tional law–law ordained, in Vitoria's words, to "the common good of all," including that of one's enemies.

Still further variations emerge in the seventeenth century, with the doctrine's progressive disenchantment. In the Prolegomena of his magisterial *De Jure Belli ac Pacis* (1625), Grotius writes that the "manifest and clear" precepts of natural law retain their validity *"etiamsi daremus non esse Deum"* (even were God not to exist)."[5] For Grotius, the impious premise "cannot be conceded"; yet for his successors, the speculative hypothesis soon became "a thesis." For Pufendorf, Burlamaqui, and Vattel the self-evidence of natural law increasingly left God a supernumerary in Creation.[6] Under the spell of modernity's disenchantment, Grotius' heirs thus treat the validity of the just-war rules as logically independent of the religious tradition that bore them. And with the corresponding eclipse of the Thomistic ideal of the common good (the medieval's virtue-based *bonum commune*), the sovereign self's natural rights reign supreme.

In Hobbes's militant rhetoric, for instance, the "state of nature"—no longer naturally pacific–is aptly "called war, as is of every man against every man." And in that inglorious "tract of time" we call history, "wherein the will to contend by battle is sufficiently known," we have but *one* right, that of "self-defense"—the very right Ambrose and Augustine denied."[7] For stripped of Grotius' natural sociability, it is only "the foresight of their own preservation," that leads "men who naturally love liberty, and dominion over others" to submit to "that restraint upon themselves, (in which we see them live in commonwealths)."[8] Violent self-preservation, no longer a "stain upon our love for neighbor" in Ambrose's words, is our natural right, writ large upon the "artificial person" of the state. Neither does Leviathan sacrifice this right, even if it is tempered by the rule of international law. For Hobbesian realism legislates for self-preservation in the form of laws of nature, the force of which depends upon general compliance. In a state of partial compliance, governed by weak inter-

5. Hugo Grotius, *De Jure Belli ac Pacis, Prolegomena*, trans. F. W. Kelsey (*The Classics of International Law*, Publication of the Carnegie Endowment for International Peace 3, 1925) par. 11.

6. A. P. D'Entrèves, *Natural Law: An Introduction to Legal Philosophy*, 2nd. ed. (Hutchinson: London, 1970) 55.

7. Thomas Hobbes, *Leviathan*, ed. C. B. Macpherson (London: Penguin, 1968) 185–86.

8. Ibid., chap. 17, 52.

national law, reason will abide by the laws of nature, e.g., of the *justum bellum*, if, and to the degree, they promote national security. There are, in this sense, theoretical limits to Hobbesian realism, underwritten by realism itself.[9] And so, the "violent bear it away" (Mt 11:12)—less by abjuring the rules of just war per se, than by incorporating them within the realist narrative.

A great divide thus appears between the rules of "just" war and pacifism, itself viewed as a "rule-governed activity." Indeed, we seem to face a Hobson's choice between peace, whether rule-based or strategy-based, and justice as legitimate self-defense. Inspired by Lisa Cahill's critique, McCarthy's recovery of a virtue-based assessment of pacifism belies such a simple dichotomy, for the demands of biblical shalom are never less than just. In the Psalmists words, "justice and peace shall kiss" (Ps 85:10).

The turn to virtue, moreover, permits McCarthy to incorporate human rights claims under the rubrics of the global common good as elaborated in modern Catholic Social Teaching. For basic human rights generate structural imperatives that seek to redress the systemic causes of violence. Finally, McCarthy's rapprochement of virtue and rights underscores the family resemblance of religiously inspired nonviolence peacemaking, e.g., the rich affinities of Christian pacifism, Ghandi's *ahimsa*, and Abdul Gaffar Khan's theory of nonviolence.

In the midst of polemics more indebted to Machiavelli and Hobbes, than Augustine and Thomas, McCarthy gives us reason for hope—our hope of "doing great things" as together we live "the Gospel of peace." In the words of Dorothy Day, whom Machiavelli would deride as un-armed prophet: "Yes we go on talking about love. St. Paul writes about it, and there are Father Zossima's unforgettable words in the Brothers Karamazov, 'Love in practice is a harsh and dreadful thing compared to love in dreams'. What does the modern world know of love, with its light touching of the surface of love? It has never reached down into the depths, to the misery and pain and glory of love which endures to death

9. Cf. Walzer's citation of Hume: "The rage and violence of public war: what is it but a suspension of justice among the warring parties, who perceive that this virtue is now no longer of any *use* or advantage to them?" Nor is it possible, according to Hume, that this suspension itself be just or unjust; it is entirely a matter of necessity, as in the (Hobbist) state of nature where individuals "consult the dictates of self-preservation alone." *Just and Unjust Wars*, 76, n.

and beyond it. We have not yet begun to learn about love. Now is the time to begin, to start afresh, to use this divine weapon."[10]

10. Dorothy Day, "Love Is the Measure," *The Catholic Worker*, June 1946, p. 2.

Acknowledgments

I THANK THOSE WHO have inspired and guided me through this book, particularly the graciousness, patience, wisdom, and devotion of my doctoral advisor and friend William O'Neill, SJ. I also thank scholars Michael Nagler, Jim Donahue, Sr. Marianne Farina, and Jim Keenan, SJ for their commitment and expertise during my studies. A special thanks to the passion of my professor Kevin Burke, SJ for lighting my theological flame at Weston Jesuit School of Theology. I deeply thank Mike Campos PhD, Mark Miller PhD, and Alan Goulty, who was the former British Ambassador to Sudan, for taking the time to read over my work and offer constructive feedback. I thank Holy Trinity parishioners Charlotte Mahoney and Jean Johnson for their continued inspiration and support as they live out the practices of nonviolent peacemaking in parish life. I have had many mentors in nonviolent peacemaking along the way. I particularly thank Bob Cooke, Mary J Park, David Hartsough, and Fr. Emmanual McCarthy. I also give thanks for some of the more famous nonviolent peacemakers for weaving this thread through history and inspiring my personal journey—Jesus, St. Francis, Gandhi, Abdul Ghaffar Kahn, Dorothy Day, Martin Luther King Jr., Thomas Merton, Thich Nhat Hahn, Cesar Chavez, and Oscar Romero.

However, I must also thank the many poor and marginalized persons, whom I have encountered and have oriented my vision. These include the orphans lying on dirty cement floors in Haiti, the homeless persons I worked with in Boston, such as Rick, Joe, and Chuck, and the elderly who opened their arms in friendship, such as Shelia, Adrienne, Dorothy, and Ed. To those doing the exhausting work of teaching me how to grow in love, so that I am less of a resounding gong or clanging cymbal (1 Cor 13:1), I thank you for your everlasting patience and love: Joy and Lazarus. And ultimately, I thank the God who created us out of love, walks with us in love, and draws us toward love.

Introduction

SOME THINK "NONVIOLENCE IS simply a rule against violence, or a rule against violence but under some conditions violence is justified based on national security or 'just' war criteria." Others think, "Ok, we will try nonviolence if it will work. If not we will use the tool of violence." My journey indicates a 3rd way of orienting "nonviolence" and "peacemaking."

My present social context is Washington DC, although I grew up in a small rural town in western Pennsylvania, later lived in Boston, Massachusetts for five years, and then in Berkeley, California for five years working on my doctoral degree. I have experienced conflict during different stages of my life, out of which my passion for peacemaking in part arose. My experiences with the people and the poverty in Haiti, of my first teaching opportunity being shaped by 9/11, and the subsequent wars in Afghanistan and Iraq function as core moments in my movement toward the offering in this book. My five months in Haiti during the spring of 1999 particularly transformed my life as I finally began to ask some of the questions of social justice. How were some people so happy in Haiti with so little things? Why were resources so inequitably distributed? What is my role as a U.S. citizen and the role of the country I live in? Where is God in all this? I have experienced the structural and cultural privileges of being a middle class white male in the U.S., which is upper class relative to the global scene. I also practice Catholicism, with a love for Jesus that has continued to orient my life since my undergraduate days.

In the midst of this journey, this book explores two interrelated questions that grow out of the common ways of thinking about nonviolence mentioned above. First, what is a more adequate way to assess nonviolent peacemaking compared to the more common rule-based or strategy-based assessments? Second, what is a more fruitful way to mediate or persuade others in public discourse to implement nonviolent peacemaking practices not only in our daily life but also particularly in public policy?

My thesis is that a virtue-based assessment of nonviolent peacemaking enhanced by aspects of human rights discourse largely resolves key limits of rule-based and strategy-based assessments of nonviolent peacemaking for public discourse and policy.

For clarification of terms, my virtue-*based* approach does not exclude the use of rules and strategy in nonviolent peacemaking, but it does uplift and shift the emphasis to virtue. Further, by "nonviolent peacemaking" I mean in general a family of practices, but I elaborate on this later. For this project, I use "peacemaking" in a broad way to include the practices often distinguished in the terms peacekeeping, peacemaking, and peacebuilding. By "public discourse" I mean the discourse of persons intended to influence public deliberation about public policy, and to arrive at consensus on such policy in the midst of different conceptions of the good or basic political differences.[1]

The broader context and significance of this book consists in the following elements. The Catholic context of this project plays an important role. The people of the Catholic Church live in the midst of significant transformations, and at times contestations elicited by Vatican II in the 1960's. Vatican II explicitly acknowledged the call to holiness for lay and religious, rather than merely the religious, i.e. clergy, religious brothers and sisters. In this spirit, the Church also opened up more deeply to the broader world as a partner for dialogue and a source for wisdom. Vatican II encouraged ecumenical and inter-religious dialogue. Catholic Social Teaching framed the notion of the common good less in terms of human flourishing and more in terms of human dignity and basic human rights, which more easily resonates with public discourse. At the same time, recognition grew of the Bible as a key source for moral theology. Along with the call to holiness, this re-turn to the Bible sparked increasing attention to virtue in Catholic circles. The relationship between human rights and virtue has slowly been unfolding in official Catholic Social Teaching. This book aims to contribute to this unfolding, specifically around issues of acute conflict.

1. Especially in light of feminist critiques, I do not understand "public" as signifying a public/private dichotomy. I particularly do not subscribe to the reduction of religious belief to some "private" realm. For more insightful discussion on the public/private framing see Butler, *Precarious Life*.

This particular contribution to Catholic Social Teaching is significant for the following reasons. First, Catholic Social Teaching intends to not only guide Catholics, but also to persuade the thinking of all "people of good will" in public discourse and policy. Second, the use of Catholic Social Teaching on issues of war and peace, especially by most U.S. Catholic leadership in my opinion has not adequately challenged U.S. political and military leadership on a) the preparation for war, i.e. being by far the largest spender on and seller of arms in the world, and on b) the use of war, i.e. the atomic bomb in WWII, and wars in Vietnam, Iraq, and Afghanistan, etc.[2] Third, the documents of Catholic Social Teaching have been strengthening the presumption against war and recognizing the increasing importance of nonviolence for public policy. Fourth, religious communities usually entail cultivating a way of life or set of practices, which in turn function significantly to impact religious and even non-religious persons' responses to conflict.

The U.S. context of this book includes the election of President Barack Obama. He premised his campaign on "change." However, this "change" entailed both moments of stirring great hope and moments of simply repeating past patterns. A deep economic crisis remains with us, although the U.S. still remains the dominant economic power on the globe. Our relations with many other countries have been strained over the past decade, but Obama has been working somewhat to restore these relations. The continuing presence and exercise of our military dominance and our explicit national security strategies aiming for global strategic dominance represents one of the key reasons for this strain. These get expressed in our global dominance in military spending and arms sales, in our unmatched nuclear arsenal, in the enormous presence of our military bases spread around the world, in our wars within Iraq and Afghanistan/Pakistan, in Guantanamo Bay and the use of torture, and for some, the extent of our military aid to Israel. Obama planned to broaden our methods of responding to conflict and not to rely primarily on military power. The gradual, yet still slow, development of the Civilian Response Corps within the new Bureau of Conflict and Stabilization Operations in the U.S. State Department represents one positive sign. But the entrenched military power in our culture, public discourse and policy has and will continue to make this initiative

2. Notably, the historical origin of the U.S. Conference of Bishops resides in the National Catholic War Councils of WWI.

quite difficult, as we saw with the increase of troops in Afghanistan, the continued drone bombing in Pakistan, the military efforts in Libya, and the disproportionate levels of our military spending.

In the U.S., the political theories of realism, which emphasizes military power, and liberalism, which emphasizes economic power, dominate public discourse and policy. However, undergirding *both* of these dominant political theories is a kind of western, philosophically liberal moral framework. In this framework of moral reasoning, the moral options primarily shift between obligation-based approaches, with categories such as principles, rules, duties, law, and human rights, or consequences-based approaches, particularly utilitarian versions that focus on strategy and interest/preference satisfaction. This framework of moral reasoning has played a significant role in cultivating our present U.S. context, particularly regarding our responses to acute conflict, such as terrorism, Iraq, Afghanistan, Sudan, and Libya. Further, this framework of moral reasoning has led to the prevailing assessments of nonviolence being primarily understood as a *rule* against violence, or primarily a *strategy* or technique to use under certain conditions. These rule-based or strategy-based assessments show up in Catholic Social Teaching, the public discourse about policy, the academic discourse in ethics, political science, and peace studies, and even more in popular discourse.

The broader U.S. society also indicates alarming patterns of violence that exist in the midst of these policies, prevailing moral frameworks, and assessments of nonviolence. For instance, violence shows up often in children's toys, especially those given to boys, in cartoons, television shows, and movies. Many of our major cities and their public schools continue to struggle with gun violence. Domestic violence and rape continue at alarming rates even though these often go unreported. The U.S. suffers the largest incarceration rate in the world and remains one of the few economically advanced countries to use the death penalty. Our political rhetoric too often draws on violent imagery.

I recognize violence in the broad types of direct, structural (systemic), and cultural as Johan Galtung describes. By cultural he means the symbolic sphere of existence, such as religion, ideology, language, art, etc. that can be used to legitimate direct and structural violence. He more specifically defines violence as "avoidable insults to basic human needs," which include survival, well-being, identity, and freedom needs.[3] Michael Nagler deepens this by highlighting the dehumanization, or discord with human dignity aspect of violent activity for all parties involved.

In light of these patterns of violence, this book analyzes the prevailing moral frameworks in the U.S., particularly through the common assessments of nonviolence. The significance for the particular discipline of ethics consists in a critical elaboration of virtue ethics and human rights discourse with respect to nonviolent peacemaking. I also discuss how to understand the relationship between religion and public discourse with respect to nonviolent peacemaking. This research offers political significance regarding the approach to policy formulation and the content of our policies, particularly regarding our responses to acute conflict. Yet, I do not make a systematic analysis of "just" war approaches, nor do I thoroughly engage the question about the relationship between nonviolent peacemaking and "just" war approaches. However, this research does have important and at points more obvious implications for this question.

I begin the engagement with these key questions through an exposition and critical evaluation of the rule-based and strategy-based assessments of nonviolent peacemaking. In this evaluation, I identify key limits of each approach. I use major components of official Catholic Social Teaching and moral philosopher James Childress to illustrate rules-based assessments. I use Gene Sharp and Peter Ackerman to illustrate strategy-based assessments.

Toward addressing these limits, I initially unfold a virtue-based assessment from a Christian perspective and argue that nonviolent peacemaking represents a distinct and central virtue. This virtue uplifts and qualifies other key virtues, including their core practices. I offer examples of three contemporary Christian theorists' virtue-based assessments of nonviolent peacemaking, namely Bernard Häring, Stanley Hauerwas, and Lisa Sowle Cahill. I explain how a virtue-based approach specifically addresses the key limits of the rules and strategy-based assessments identified earlier. I end by raising some questions about the limits of such a virtue assessment of nonviolent peacemaking from a Christian perspective. For instance, do these arguments translate within

---

3. Galtung, "Cultural Violence," 291–92.

other religious frameworks? Even if they do, how persuasive is a virtue-based approach in U.S. public discourse and policy?

I address these virtue-based limits from a Christian perspective by using analogy to show how these practices of nonviolent peacemaking extend to and get enhanced by those beyond the Christian community. First, I explore Gandhi's theory of nonviolence and corresponding practices, as a representative figure of Hinduism. Second, I explore Abdul Ghaffar Khan's theory of nonviolence and corresponding practices, as a representative figure of Islam. Both representative figures also illustrate how a virtue-based approach engages and impacts public discourse and policy. However, I do not assess the whole religious traditions of Hinduism and Islam in this project.

Moving toward questions about U.S. public discourse and policy, I offer an analysis of the prevailing moral frameworks that undergird public discourse in the U.S. Without intending any disrespect to the U.S. military or individual soldiers, I use the U.S. military to exemplify both a key player in forming the culture from which arises our public discourse and policy, and in illustrating the effects and limits of U.S. public discourse and policy. Finally, I use the example of Dr. Martin Luther King to offer some initial contributions which a virtue-based assessment brings to U.S. public discourse and policy regarding issues of acute conflict. However, I also acknowledge three key limits of a virtue-based assessment for U.S. public discourse and policy.

I address these limits by analyzing the contributions that certain aspects of human rights discourse offer a virtue-based assessment for U.S. public discourse and policy. I begin by describing some general characteristics and types of human rights theory, as well as some key limits of human rights discourse. I analyze the contributions by drawing primarily on Martha Nussbaum, William O'Neill, John Dear, and Catholic Social Teaching.

I analyze the fruits of merging a virtue-based assessment of nonviolent peacemaking supplemented by these aspects of human rights discourse. I use Catholic Social Teaching to illustrate a trajectory of thinking that integrates virtue and rights. However, I offer key contributions to developing this integration in Catholic Social Teaching regarding nonviolent peacemaking both in terms of a) shifting to a virtue-based assessment, and b) a set of seven core practices, which also have implications for U.S. public discourse and policy.

Finally, I initiate a conversation about how these core practices could potentially be applied in a situation of genocide or mass atrocity, such as Sudan.

The application of these practices to this case is significant because Sudan typifies a situation that often yields a broader consensus for armed intervention, such as the use of "peacekeepers." I primarily raise questions and suggest a repertoire of possible responses, which would also potentially hold for other similar situations, rather than making a detailed proposal for the particular situation in Sudan. Further research and closer on the ground contact would be required to make a detailed proposal for this ongoing conflict.

I hope the reader enjoys and is challenged by this book about becoming nonviolent peacemakers. I look forward to the ongoing dialogue about these ideas and opportunities. I hope this book inspires and offers a way for all of us to move significantly further into the life of peacemaking and justice-making as well as to King's "Beloved Community." Together, let us engage and rejoice in the adventure!

PART ONE

Common Assessments
of Nonviolent Peacemaking

1

Representative Types of Rule-Based and Strategy-Based Assessments

INTRODUCTION

WHAT ARE SOME COMMON assessments of nonviolence? For many people nonviolence is *primarily* about avoiding all violence as a rule, duty, or obligation. Thus, some will simply protest against war, the military or police that use guns and brutality. Using the same assessment, others will say such a rule can simply be trumped by other rules or duties. Another assessment entails saying that nonviolence is *primarily* a strategy to use if we suspect it to "work." Thus, nonviolence is a tool alongside the tool of violence. Some think nonviolence will "work" more often than others do, but the point is only to use nonviolence if the immediate objectives seem to call for it.

In this chapter I am asking the question: what limits exist in common assessments of nonviolent peacemaking? I identify two primary common assessments, which entail important limits: first, the rule-based assessment, usually expressed as primarily a rule against using violence, and second, the strategy-based assessment, usually expressed as primarily a strategy or technique. I first give an exposition of type one and then assess its limits. Next, I follow the same approach to the second type. This sets the stage for my argument that a virtue-based appeal is more adequate to assess nonviolent peacemaking practices.

In Christian terminology, the spectrum of responses to violence generally entails nonresistance, nonviolent peacemaking, limited war theories, and the crusade.[1] My focus is on assessments of nonviolent peacemaking, or what is often merely called nonviolent resistance.

PRIMARILY A RULE: DEONTOLOGY

The first common assessment explains nonviolence as primarily a rule against violence. This approach resonates with a rules-based or deontological moral reasoning. Key representatives of this assessment are much of official Catholic Social Teaching and moral philosopher James Childress.

Rules can be understood as absolute or as prima facie, i.e., relative. Accepting nonviolence as an absolute rule can be grounds for categorically rejecting violence. Those who understand nonviolence as a relative rule argue that we can apply criteria to determine when to override this prima facie duty of nonviolence. For instance, such criteria often include the limited or "just" war theories, and sometimes simply the criteria of national security or national interests.

In general, most of the earlier documents of Catholic Social Teaching from *Rerum Novarum* in 1891 through *Pacem in Terris* in 1963 utilized a deontological model of ethics. Since 1963, this model continues to hold significant sway even as other models receive more attention.[2] Charles Curran argues that the tendency to focus on structures and institutions has also contributed to inadequate attention to the person and development of virtues.[3] In this context, Catholic Social Teaching often represents the rule-based assessment of nonviolence. Lisa Sowle Cahill points to *Pacem in Terris* as an evolution in official Catholic thinking about pacifism, but still articulated in terms of rules. This version of pacifism coheres with "just" war theory as a caution about whether the "just" war criteria can be met in our nuclear age.[4] Two years later at Vatican II, *Gaudium et Spes* maintained this rule-emphasis by arguing that pacifism, like "just" war theory, aims at self-defense along

---

1. The theory called *Just Peacemaking: The New Paradigm for the Ethics of Peace and War* (edited by Glen Stassen, 2008) is certainly another point along this spectrum, most appropriately set between nonviolent peacemaking and limited (just) war theory. I will discuss Stassen's theory more directly later on, pointing out its many similarities and some key differences with my argument for nonviolent peacemaking.

2. Curran, *Catholic Social Teaching*, 81–82.

3. Ibid., 121.

4. Cahill, *Love Your Enemies*, 212.

with individual and communal rights. The difference resides simply in the means to these shared ends. Disagreement on the means is confined to individuals, such that war against aggression is a duty incumbent on those responsible for the common good.[5] Cahill explains that most recent official "pacifist" manifestations really amount to a development of a rule-based "just" war theory in the modern context.[6]

In the 1983 document "Challenge of Peace," written by the U.S. Bishops, Cahill suggests that as far as the U.S. Bishops "portray pacifism as aiming at defense of the common good and human rights, they tend to assimilate pacifism to the natural law just war model."[7] Richard Miller claims that the pacifist ethic remains hedged in by a theory of rights and justice. He argues that the U.S. Bishops maintain the basic teachings on the pacifist ethic as found in *Gaudium et Spes*.[8]

Although the 1993 document by the U.S. Bishops called "The Harvest of Justice is Sown in Peace," develops more of the role of virtue, rules-based language in the form of human rights has a significant, if not primary role. The term "virtue" is only used thirteen times, while the term "rights" is used over fifty times. In the vision of a peaceful world, all three components are defined in terms of human rights. Humanitarian intervention, i.e., using lethal force, is permitted in exceptional cases as a right and duty. Seriously considering nonviolent alternatives by national leaders is described as a moral obligation, or what Drew Christianson calls a "*prima facie* public obligation."[9] Further, in the 2004 Compendium of the Social Doctrine of the Church, the priority of rights is even more pronounced and there is no longer mention of "peaceable virtues" as found in the 1993 U.S. Bishops document.[10]

In terms of specific thinkers, Cahill gives the example of Brian Hehir, who is a major contributor to U.S. Catholic social thought. For him, the presumption against war becomes an absolute rule in the pacifist position rather than a relative rule. Hehir is troubled by the possibility

---

5. Miller, *Interpretations of Conflict*, 82–84.

6. Cahill, *Love Your Enemies*, 237.

7. Ibid., 6; see also U.S. Bishops, "Challenge of Peace," par. 74.

8. Miller, *Interpretations of Conflict*, 84.

9. Christianson, "Catholic Peacemaking," 23.

10. Pontifical Council for Justice and Peace, *Compendium of the Social Doctrine of the Church*, C.11, par. 494, 496.

of pacifism becoming a non-minority position in the Catholic Church, and argues that this would be inconsistent with "just" war assumptions.

Philosopher James Childress illustrates the rules-based assessment to the extent he categorizes nonviolence as a *prima facie* duty not to injure or kill, i.e., nonmaleficence. This *prima facie* duty implies a presumption against the use of violence understood as the direct, intended physical attack on other humans. He explains that the just war tradition includes a similar *prima facie* duty of acting justly and pursuing justice. Thus, when these duties conflict, the just war theory indicates when the former can be overridden or outweighed by the latter.[11] Yet, Childress admits these criteria are variously interpreted and weighted.[12]

Further, using this rule-based frame, Childress claims that nonviolent movements often work because their opponents respect the just war criterion of noncombatant immunity from direct attack. The nonviolent resistors trust that the opponents will follow the rules or criteria governing the just use of force. Meanwhile, the resistors will be trustworthy by not "crossing the line" or the rule against using violence.[13]

Another example of a rules-based assessment of nonviolence in pubic discourse is that of some politicians, who framed the more recent conflict situation in Iraq as a choice between maintaining lethal force or cutting and running.[14] The implication is that the alternatives are violent force or passivity. Thus, nonviolence is portrayed again as primarily a rule against the use of violence, which results in passivity or flight during conflicts.

LIMITS OF RULE-BASED ASSESSMENTS

Rule-based assessments face three core limits, which entail various secondary components. A central premise, which often integrates these core limits with their own internal logic, is the notion that nonviolence is primarily the absence of violence or even conflict. First, this is a serious truncating of the imagination in terms of practices of nonviolent peacemaking. A secondary component of this limit is that the limited ("just") war criteria often become the standard of moral reason-

11. Childress, "Nonviolent Resistance," 216–17.

12. Ibid.

13. Ibid.

14. Fletcher, "Bush Attacks Party of 'Cut and Run.'" McCain, "Not Tet: Iraq is Not Vietnam."

ing about acute conflict. Second, in Christian tradition, the rules-based assessment often gets played out in a tendency to blur the boundaries between nonresistance and nonviolent peacemaking on the one hand, and nonviolent peacemaking and limited war theory on the other. Third, a character, which simply develops the knowledge of the rule(s) and the will to obey them, risks becoming the standard of maturity or human excellence. Thus, the virtues are narrowly conceived and limited in number. I will now elaborate on these three core limits and their secondary components.

Truncated Imagination

With its rules-based assessment, Catholic Social Teaching since Augustine has too often been limited in its ability to imagine and promote practices of nonviolent peacemaking. Conscientious objection was officially endorsed only in the 1960's and the possible vocation of nonviolent peacemaking only for an individual remained the position in the 1983 U.S. document called a "Challenge of Peace." Only in the 1993 document called "The Harvest of Justice is Sown in Peace," do the U.S. Bishops seriously acknowledge the rising legitimacy of a public role of a range of nonviolent peacemaking practices in acute conflicts by civil society, governments, etc. Significantly, this shifting of imagination about nonviolent peacemaking occurs in the context of greater attention to the role of virtues in the 1993 document. Nevertheless, this document still appears to suffer from lack of exposure and even respect among numbers of Catholics and the general public.[15]

One secondary component of the truncated imagination is that the limited ("just") war criteria often become the standard bearer of moral reasoning about acute conflict. For instance, Cahill argues that just war theorists often "grapple with pacifism by posing it as an absolute rule against violence."[16] This way of assessing nonviolence is congenial to the rule-exception premises of most just war theories. Cahill wonders if this rule-based version also underlies the inclusion of pacifism as an uneasily aligned option within the natural law strand of just war thinking in Catholic Social Teaching.[17]

---

15. Christianson, "Peacebuilding in Catholic Social Teaching," 2.

16. Cahill, *Love Your Enemies*, 210.

17. Ibid., 211.

In response to Hehir's concern about pacifism understood as an absolute rule being inconsistent with just war assumptions, Cahill suggests
that the "real potential for inconsistency lies in the distinctive view of
the Kingdom and role of the Christian community in relation to culture,
not in an endorsement of a possible pacifist outcome of just war based
analysis."[18]

Cahill argues that this rules-based approach still assumes that
"moral obligations can and should be best articulated in rules about
permitted and excluded varieties of specific conduct."[19] She suggests that
biblical pacifism did not revolve around an absolute rule or value but
around a converted life in Christ, and thus, about a transformation in
character and imagination oriented to Christ. [20]

Blurring the Boundaries

The cultivation of an insufficient imagination for nonviolent peacemaking practices arises from and perpetuates a blurring of important
boundaries. In Christian tradition, the rules-based approach to nonviolence tends to blur the boundaries between nonresistance and nonviolent peacemaking on the one hand, and nonviolent peacemaking and
limited ("just") war theories on the other. I have shown how much of
contemporary Catholic Social Teaching exemplifies this blurring of
nonviolent peacemaking and limited ("just") war theory. Drawing on
Augustine, Reinhold Niebuhr is a good contemporary example of blurring nonresistance and nonviolent peacemaking.

The blurring of nonresistance and nonviolent peacemaking occurs
in part because as far as nonviolence is understood as primarily a rule
against violence, then it more easily perpetuates the nonresistance interpretation of Jesus' ethic, and vice versa. The nonresistance interpretation
of Jesus' ethic is exemplified in Reinhold Niebuhr, who was a, if not the,
key Protestant thinker on war and peace issues in the twentieth century.
He argued that Jesus counseled nonresistance, i.e. Niebuhr's interpretation of Jesus saying to "turn the other cheek." Thus, Niebuhr concluded
that "nonviolent resistance was no more faithful to the Gospel than violence—after all, it *did* resist."[21] Yet, he still affirmed that a pacifism, which

18. Ibid., 213.

19. Ibid., 212.

20. Ibid., 210–13.

21. Niebuhr quoted in Paul Elie, "A Man for All Reasons: The Sage of Nonviolence."

explicitly disavows the political task and responsibility for social justice could act as a good witness of the limited norms of social justice and coercion within history.[22] Niebuhr strongly critiques the forms of pacifism that claim to arise from a sense of political and social responsibility. He calls such political pacifism a heresy, particularly for absorbing the renaissance faith[23] and liberalism's optimism in the goodness of the human, along with liberalism's presupposition about history as progress.[24]

One of the secondary components of this limit is that some Christian groups trying to be faithful to the nonresistance interpretation of Jesus' ethic often withdraw from society as much as possible and neglect some of the larger structural violence or social justice issues around them. By primarily assessing nonviolence as a rule against violence, they often fail to connect the practice of nonviolence with its constructive component. Not all, but some types of Anabaptists, such as some Amish, fall into this category.[25]

The nonresistance interpretation not only yields pragmatic problems but also entails an inadequate interpretation of the Christian scriptures and the person of Jesus. I have already referred to Cahill's argument that biblical pacifism is more conversion-governed rather than rule-governed. Other key figures argue that the more adequate interpretation of Jesus' way of love is a way of nonviolent resistance to injustice rather than nonresistance understood as passivity.[26] A nonresistance assessment often leaves the Christian with little motive, creativity, or wisdom for addressing social injustices, particularly in a nonviolent way. This kind of moral formation struggles to co-exist with the character of Jesus who proclaimed the dawning Reign of God, continually uplifted the poor and outcasts, and creatively challenged the religious, political, and economic powers of his time.

The central premise that integrates the three core limits of rules-based assessments arises more clearly in how the nonresistance interpretation of Jesus' ethic often yields an understanding of nonviolence as the absence or reduction of conflict. For instance, this has manifested

22. Niebuhr, *Christianity and Power Politics*, 5.

23. Ibid., 6.

24. Niebuhr, *Love and Justice*, 261.

25. PA Dutch Country Welcome Center, "The Amish and the Plain People."

26. For instance, see Pope Benedict XVI, Martin Luther King, Walter Wink, Bernard Haring, Simon Harak.

itself in some contemporary Catholic Social Teaching, which theoretically seeks to prioritize nonviolence with its strong presumption against war. Curran argues that in Catholic Social Teaching there tends to be an inadequate appreciation for the pervasiveness of conflict and for the alternative kinds of power one might harness with conflict, i.e. a kind of constructive conflict.[27] Instead the emphasis tends to be on order and harmony. For instance, Catholic Social Teaching has tended to focus on the nonviolent practice of dialogue, with insufficient attention to the role of collective nonviolent struggle exemplified more recently by Martin Luther King and Gandhi. However, in the 1993 document by the U.S. Bishops, the value and possibilities of this kind of nonviolent peacemaking start to receive attention, though as yet they remain underdeveloped.

Another example of this non-conflict understanding of nonviolence was found in opponents of Martin Luther King. Many Christian leaders criticized him for stirring up conflict rather than being patient and working primarily through legal channels. King responded by suggesting the "Negro's great stumbling block" is the "white moderate who is more devoted to 'order' than to justice, and who prefers a negative peace which is the absence of tension to a positive peace which is the presence of justice."[28] He argued that there is a type of constructive, nonviolent tension, which is necessary for growth.[29] He used methods that revealed the destructive type of conflicts in order to expose deeper wounds in the community, which needed healing for a more lasting peace and justice. Thus, King's assessment of nonviolent peacemaking corresponds with those who emphasize the practice of conflict transformation rather than mere conflict resolution, which often rests on the assumption that all conflict is destructive or to be quickly ended.

Similar to King, Stanley Hauerwas claims that peace is not the avoidance of conflict. Hauerwas argues that virtues make it possible to sustain a society committed to risking conflict and working out differences short of violence. However, he claims that U.S. society has largely failed to cultivate the virtues and corresponding practices, which can risk, transform, and be transformed by conflict.[30] The historian and former WWII bomber Howard Zinn makes a similar claim about U.S.

27. Curran, *Catholic Social Teaching: 1891–Present*, 86.

28. King, "Letter From a Birmingham Jail," in *Peace Reader*, 226.

29. Ibid., 222.

30. Hauerwas, "Christian Critique of Christian America," 479.

culture and particularly how our writing of history has suffered from a strong tendency to "avoid controversy." For instance, he argues that we often leave out of our history books important social change movements, and the times our country has perpetuated injustice.[31]

The blurring of boundaries limit also often entails the tendency to exclude parts of humanity from the life practice of nonviolence. This takes various forms. For instance, one form is the argument that nonviolence is only required for those in religious lives, such as clergy, rather than for all Christians. This assessment is found in Thomas Aquinas, who tended to follow the nonresistance strand of interpretation.[32] A second example is the claim that nonviolence is only for Christians.[33]

A third example is the argument that nonviolence is only for individuals and interpersonal relationships. For instance, Terry Nardin describes nonviolence as primarily a rule against violence or the taking of human life, and thus, finds it inadequate for a strategy for international relations. He explains the logic of Christian pacifism as a Christian duty to obey God's laws. Nardin argues that this implies the fortune of any person or community should not trump obedience to God's laws, otherwise, we would enter into a kind of idolatry. Thus, with his absolute rule or duty-based assessment, Nardin concludes that the pacifist ethic offers no practical ethic or strategy for international relations.[34] Versions of this are also found in Reinhold Neihbuhr and the U.S. Bishops 1983 letter, "Challenge of Peace."

A final example of this tendency is the argument that nonviolence is only for the extraordinary heroes or saints. This arises not only in Christian circles, but also in popular society. So, exceptional people like Gandhi, Martin Luther King, or even Jesus are called to follow this rule, but it is not for everyone and probably not even for most.

In these examples, those excluded or devalued in their human capacities to practice nonviolence include lay people, non-Christians, groups, communities, corporations, governments, and ordinary people. The restriction of nonviolence to clergy or Christians has been reassessed for the most part in Catholic Social Teaching, drawing on the examples of Dorothy Day, Cesar Chavez, and Gandhi. But the restric-

---

31. Zinn, *Passionate Declarations*, 62.

32. Aquinas, *Summa*, II.II, q. 40, a. 1–2.

33. Stassen and Gushee, *Kingdom Ethics*, 168.

34. Nardin, *Ethics of War and Peace*, 261.

tions of nonviolence to individuals or to extra-ordinary heroes continue to have significant traction in key sectors of Catholic thinking and society in general. Therefore, these restrictions also perpetuate the first core limit regarding a truncated imagination for practices of nonviolent peacemaking in society as a whole.

Inadequate Attention to Virtue

The third core limit of rule-based assessments is the inadequate attention to virtue, especially the narrow conception of the virtue of prudence as a habit to follow the rules. Both James Childress and key parts of Catholic Social Teaching suffer from inadequate attention to the persons who interpret and apply rules. For instance, Childress initially acknowledges that the criteria for overriding the *prima facie* duty of nonviolence are variously interpreted and weighted.[35] Recognizing the significance of the kinds of persons and groups who do the interpreting and weighing of the criteria raises questions about character, but this is underdeveloped in Childress' assessment. This functions as a limit of some rule-based assessments.

A more adequate assessment of nonviolence, and potential acts of violence, would seem to require attention to the kind of dispositions, habits, and practices that cultivate one's character. For instance, our character entails our capacity to perceive the morally relevant features of a situation, and particularly to exercise the virtue of prudence in interpreting and weighing rules. As Hauerwas explains, rules cannot interpret and apply themselves.[36] Yet, the virtue of prudence also entails enabling us to develop the moral virtues and directing these toward their corresponding end. Prudence reflects not only on the end of a specific act, as in whether the act fittingly follows some rule, but also on how all of one's acts as a whole fit into the end of human life.[37] Catholic Social Teaching does a better job with attention to virtue in general, but only in the 1993 document does this become significant, especially for nonviolence.[38] Nevertheless, nonviolence remains embedded in a rules-

---

35. Ibid., 217.

36. Hibbs, "Interpretations of Aquinas's Ethics," 416.

37. Pope, *Ethics of Aquinas*, 40.

38. U.S. Bishops, "The Harvest of Justice is Sown in Peace," section 1.

based framework, which leaves the attention to and function of virtue underdeveloped.

Further, Childress does not adequately include character development and human excellence in his assessment of how and when nonviolence works. For instance, this inadequacy arises when he argues that nonviolence often depends on the opponents following just war criteria, especially noncombatant immunity from direct attack, in order for nonviolence to "work." However, this argument yields a narrow understanding of "work." It implies that "work" cannot occur if the nonviolent actors were to get killed. In turn, "work" is limited to physical survival or immediate effects, rather than imagining and attending to the deeper and long-term transformations of both character and structures. Thus, Childress' argument in his assessment of nonviolence limits its activity to less dangerous situations or merely against apparent weak oppressors, which again limits the imagination for nonviolent peacemaking practices.[39]

Finally, most contemporary rule-based assessments of nonviolence, such as key parts of Catholic Social Teaching, tend primarily to measure the success of such practices by their protection of basic human rights, with inadequate attention to character development and human excellence. A common conclusion drawn from this measurement is that nonviolence is incapable of adequately protecting these rights, and thus, violence is often or sometimes necessary to meet this standard. This approach raises further questions about a rule-based assessment in terms of the sufficiency of human rights as a standard of measurement, and the conclusion drawn about the inadequacy of nonviolence to protect human rights. I will expand on this argument when I discuss human rights theory in chapter six.

In sum, the limits of the rule-based assessment are significant and numerous. As primarily a rule against violence, the implication is that nonviolent peacemaking has little to do with a practical way of life, a mature kind of character, or a set of virtues to cultivate. First, there is a serious truncating of the imagination in terms of practices of nonviolent peacemaking. Nonviolence is often portrayed as having little constructive to add beyond refraining from violence. Therefore, nonviolence is often associated with lacking a practical ethic for conflicts, especially be-

---

39. For elaboration on this myth of only working against weak oppressors, see Nagler, *Is There No Other Way*, 244–46.

tween groups, or with passivity. Further, the main question in rule-based assessments of nonviolence tends to be about whether to use violence or not, rather than what practices might serve to guide our peacemaking initiatives and to indicate a genuine commitment to peace. Thus, merely following the rules often means that the limited ("just") war criteria become the standard of moral reasoning about acute conflict.

Second, in Christian tradition, the rule-based assessment often gets played out in a tendency to blur the boundaries between nonresistance and nonviolent peacemaking on the one hand, and nonviolent peacemaking and limited war theory on the other. This blurring often yields an understanding of nonviolence as the absence or reduction of conflict. Such a notion of conflict often creates an overemphasis on dialogue and a devaluing of nonviolent struggle, especially if the aim includes transforming structural violence. Further, this blurring often excludes parts of humanity from the life practice of nonviolence, i.e. only for individuals or for extraordinary persons.

Third, in the rule-based assessment, a character, which simply develops the knowledge of the rule(s) and the will to obey them, risks becoming the standard of maturity or human excellence; and thus, there is an inadequate attention to virtue. Cahill argued that the rule-based approach assumes that "moral obligations can and should be best articulated in rules about permitted and excluded varieties of specific conduct,"[40] rather than focusing on developing character or a course of action over time. The virtues are often limited in number and narrowly conceived, particularly regarding prudence. The narrow conception and neglect of virtue also entails inadequate attention toward the significance of the kinds of persons or groups interpreting and applying the rules.

PRIMARILY A STRATEGY: CONSEQUENTIALISM

The second common way of assessing nonviolence is to view it as primarily a strategy or technique. This entails understanding nonviolence as a technique that will work under certain conditions, while under other conditions violence may still conceivably be considered appropriate or even necessary. Violence is not categorically ruled-out as if nonviolence were an absolute rule against violence. In contrast, this assessment tends to use consequences-based moral reasoning. Sometimes called

40. Cahill, *Love of Enemies*, 212.

the "pragmatic" approach, it sees conflict as normal and the rejection of violence as an effective way of challenging oppressive power.[41] Key representatives of this type are Gene Sharp and Peter Ackerman.

Gene Sharp is arguably the most prolific contemporary writer on nonviolence. He is the founder and a Senior Scholar at the Albert Einstein Institute in Boston, which promotes the strategic uses of nonviolent struggle. He has been called "the Clausewitz of nonviolent warfare" and "the Machiavelli of nonviolence."[42]

Sharp is arguing against those who understand nonviolence as a mere witness, as prioritizing a search for believers or converts, and as impractical, especially politically. He argues that nonviolence has been used and should be used primarily for pragmatic reasons rather than "merely" religious or principled ones. According to Thomas Weber, nonviolence has a mere instrumental value for Sharp.[43] Arguments about principles and the deeper relationship between means and ends tend to fade in his work, while being overtaken by arguments solely based on effectiveness.[44] Sharp explains that the question is not about "morally right or morally wrong, justified or unjustified," but rather about the "consequences."[45]

A key feature for Sharp is power rather than ethical principle. Thus, the emphasis is on wresting power from the oppressor to the oppressed. Sharp describes nonviolent action as a technique by which the population can restrict and sever the sources of power of their rulers or other oppressors and mobilize their own power potential into effective power. This technique is based on understanding political power as depending directly on the obedience and cooperation of the population.[46]

He often refers to nonviolence as an alternative weapons system, a means of combat like war, a waging of battles, and needing soldiers. For Sharp, conflict is viewed as a relation between antagonists with incompatible interests.[47] The "opponent" refers to an adversary, who could be

41. Weber, "Nonviolence Is Who," 250.

42. Sharp, *Waging Nonviolent Struggle*, end of book 'About the Author.'

43. Weber, "Nonviolence Is Who," 252.

44. Ibid., 261.

45. Quoted in ibid., 256.

46. Sharp, *Waging Nonviolent Struggle*, 39.

47. Weber, "Nonviolence Is Who," 258.

a group, institution, regime, invader, or at rare times an individual.[48] A primary goal is to defeat the opponent[49] by redistributing power rather than to seek unity with them.[50] In this sense, he maintains the political realist emphasis on the balance of power, and begins to indicate a utilitarian version of consequences-based reasoning. For instance, he describes four mechanisms of change in the opponents: conversion, accommodation, nonviolent coercion, and disintegration. He argues that an opponent's conversion or change of view rarely occurs, and thus, the nonviolent struggle should not emphasize such an approach.[51] Rather, the emphasis should be on increasing the costs for and taking power from the opponent in order to maximize the good for the majority.

By way of contrast, a Gandhian approach that relies more on a religious rejection of violence is concerned with re-establishing communication rather than imposing defeat or seizing power. The method of self-suffering is uplifted and the emphasis is on action and even pressure towards conversion more than a coercion against the opponents will. The opponent is viewed as a partner in the struggle to satisfy the needs of all.[52] In turn, the primary adversary is the unjust or violent actions of some persons or groups rather than the persons or groups themselves.

Sharp appears to go through a key transition stage in his thought.[53] In his earlier years he emphasized a more Gandhian approach, such as a personal belief in nonviolence as a way of life and personal transformation. However, during the 1970's and early 1980's he seems to wrestle more with Gandhi and transitions his emphasis to what he refers to as a more pragmatic nonviolence, being "realistic," and to the strategy of nonviolent sanctions. Sharp describes nonviolent sanctions as punishments, pressures, a means of action to penalize, thwart, and alter the behavior of other persons, groups, institutions, or States.[54]

An example of this wresting occurs in his 1979 book *Gandhi as Political Strategist*. Here he lays out different types of principled nonviolence and affirms his personal belief in nonviolence as a principled way

48. Sharp, *Waging Nonviolent Struggle*, 40.

49. Weber, "Nonviolence Is Who," 258.

50. Sharp, *Waging Nonviolent Struggle*, 28.

51. Ibid., 46.

52. Weber, "Nonviolence Is Who," 258.

53. Ibid., 225.

54. Sharp, *Social Power*, 326.

of life. Sharp explains Gandhi's *Satyagraha* as both a norm (principle) and a technique.[55] Then he spends considerable time working on the relationship between morality and politics, as well as means and ends. Sharp argues that the practical technique approach is necessary to solve pressing political problems, such as war and tyranny, as well as a particularly pressing problem in moral philosophy, i.e. the relation between principle and practical effectiveness. He suggests that the principle (moral) and practical approaches are really not so different.[56]

For instance, Sharp locates a key error in the common assumption that power must be violent. In contrast, he argues that the power found in nonviolent technique could provide a way to unify morality with politics, principles with action, nonviolence with political effectiveness.[57] Many have distrusted the practicality of nonviolence, and thus, have found it difficult to affirm a universally binding principle of nonviolence. He admits that some may reason from a principle of nonviolence to practice, but suggests that most people need to experience the practice and effectiveness in order to lean towards affirming such a principle.[58]

In turn, he argues that people of principled nonviolence ought to work with pragmatists to make nonviolent struggle more effective and to sustain the nonviolence. However, Sharp insists that such people should not try to convert pragmatists into "believers," since this will not increase effectiveness and likely will solidify the pragmatist's support for violence. Sharp is pushing for wise strategy and competent planning, which he suggests are "*not* matters of the depth of one's convictions about principled nonviolence, nor are they the application of empathy, love, intuition, and emotions."[59] Rather, such wise strategy requires the intellect, which both main camps must exercise together. As this alternative of strategic nonviolent struggle develops, the basic principles of moral or religious nonviolence will reveal themselves as the basis of the highest pragmatism.[60]

55. Sharp, *Gandhi as Political Strategist*, 219.

56. Ibid., 252.

57. Ibid., 267.

58. Ibid., 300.

59. Sharp, "Principled Non-Violence," 8–10, my italics of "not."

60. Ibid., 10–11.

Another example of his transition in thought is how Sharp reflected more adequately in his earlier work on the effects regarding the kinds of people and society we become in nonviolent struggle. In *Social Power and Political Freedom* (1980), he considers the kind or character of society one cultivates via violent sanctions versus nonviolent sanctions. With violent sanctions, Sharp argues that the human personality becomes coarsened and hardened, as sensitivity to suffering withers. Legitimated acts of violence may also unintentionally contribute to non-legitimated violence by individuals and groups.[61] In contrast, those using nonviolence may lead persons to become more respectful of life, more able to think through problems and to adhere to their decisions in difficult circumstances.[62]

However, the emphasis is shifting away from nonviolence as a way of life that cultivates a certain type of character and toward the use of nonviolent sanctions to wield power. For instance, Sharp argues that violent sanctions contribute to increased centralization of power in decision-making, in structures of the political system, and in control of the capacity to apply the sanctions.[63] In contrast, nonviolent sanctions contribute to decentralizing and diffusing effective power, which empowers the oppressed. Sharp also suggests that the society will experience growth in non-State institutions as a part of the diffusion of effective power. Society will become more resistant to oppression and more able adequately to meet human needs, which include physical, psychological, social, and political needs.[64] Such needs entail developing certain qualities or capacities, such as the capacity for power and the capacity to relate to others.[65]

According to Sharp, liberation must be primarily self-liberation, such that one becomes unwilling to accept being oppressed. Also, liberation must occur by means that strengthen the subordinate group, in order to prevent future oppression. His vision of a better society lands primarily on the approximation of political freedom, rather than adherence to the search for truth as with Gandhi. He argues for the means that will end unjust conditions and establish lasting control by people over

61. Sharp, *Social Power and Political Freedom*, 346–47.

62. Ibid., 345.

63. Ibid., 327.

64. Ibid., 369.

65. Ibid., 310–11.

their own lives and society.[66] Popular empowerment enables freedom from a number of key social problems, and freedom for the capacity to control our own destinies.[67]

One of Sharp's more intriguing points is about being "realistic" with the society we live in. He explains that as long as violent sanctions are accepted as the only possible or most effective way, then violence cannot be removed from political societies by witnessing against it or denouncing it on moral grounds. To assert the necessity of a full belief in nonviolence as an ethic or norm is insufficient to remove violence from such a society. Further, public education, negotiation, and forms of dialogue are not sufficient substitutes for violence in acute conflicts.[68] Thus, Sharp argues that first nonviolence must be seen as an alternative form of sanction.[69] Once that has occurred or is well developed, political ethics will have a different character. In turn, we can then consider the finer ethical problems that arise in the application of nonviolent sanctions and make refinements in their tactics. In other words, start with what is most easily achievable.[70]

Peter Ackerman also represents the primarily strategy-based assessment of nonviolence. He argues that nonviolent strategies have somewhat better success rates than violent strategies. Most contemporary nonviolent actors simply find nonviolent strategies to be more effective and less costly. For instance, he suggests that civilian based defense may be an appealing option to small countries with no realistic hope of military defense. Ackerman says the reality is that history-making nonviolent resistance is not usually taken as an act of moral display. In other words, "it's not about making a point but about taking power."[71] He rejects the claim that true nonviolence must be understood as a transforming activity and philosophy. Ackerman calls Gene Sharp the great theoretician of nonviolent power. In turn, he argues that the pragmatic approach is nonviolence.[72]

66. Ibid., 360–62.

67. Ibid., 376.

68. Sharp, "Principled Non-Violence," 5.

69. Sharp, *Social Power*, 326.

70. Ibid., 395–96; Weber, "Nonviolence Is Who," 258–59.

71. Quoted in Claire Schaeffer-Duffy, "Regime Change without Bloodshed," *National Catholic Reporter*.

72. Weber, "Nonviolence Is Who," 264.

Ackerman describes the nonviolent popular movements of the 20th Century as disruptive actions used as sanctions, as aggressive measures to constrain and punish opponents and to win concessions.[73] He understands sanctions as instruments of power, which function to create costs for the opponent and create a shift in the relative power of the contestants. Examples of sanctions include strikes, boycotts, defiance campaigns, creation of parallel institutions, civil disobedience, etc. Sanctions bring pressure to bear without killing or direct physical injury to the opponents or their agents.[74]

Conflict is described as adversarial, involving sanctions, and inflicting costs to the opponent in order to change their behavior.[75] This view of conflict sounds strikingly similar to the common view exemplified in the U.S. prison system, which tends toward retributive justice in order to change behavior. For Ackerman, waging conflict entails acting unilaterally to overcome the opponent and secure outcomes of one's own interest. Since the objectives must be achieved at the expense of the opponents, he explains that the corresponding strategy of nonviolence will perpetuate a view of conflict as adversarial.[76] In order to control the contest, the nonviolent movement must exploit concessions, threaten with penalties,[77] punish the opponent for refusal to grant its demands, and minimize the punishment that it absorbs in return.[78] Hence, they came not to make "peace" but to "fight."[79]

Ackerman claims that most of the nonviolent movements of the twentieth century used nonviolent action because military or physical force was not a viable option.[80] In turn, he surmises that the object of nonviolent conflict is not to avoid violence except in so far as it damages that cause or the movement, which he admits violence often does. Rather, the purpose of the technique is to end oppression, check invaders, secure human rights, or establish democracy.[81] Thus, Ackerman im-

73. Ackerman and Duvall, *Force More Powerful*, 3.

74. Ackerman and Kruegler, *Strategic Nonviolent Conflict*, 3–4.

75. Ibid.

76. Ibid., 6.

77. Ibid., 37.

78. Ackerman, *Force More Powerful*, 497.

79. Ibid., 5.

80. Ibid.

81. Ibid., 492.

plies that if violence seemed viable to a movement, then he apparently would permit it.

However, Ackerman does point out how adding violence to nonviolence would very rarely be helpful. He quotes Judith Steim who remarks about the strategist contemplating the use of violence, "because the possibility of using violence is always in a person's mind, there is an inhibiting effect upon his ability to explore fully the possibilities of nonviolence or to take the risks inherent in serious struggle. His [her] imagination, his [her] persistence, and his [her] capacity to accept suffering are likely to be so impaired as to prevent his [her] utilization of nonviolence in any but its most obvious and safest form."[82] Ackerman suggests not pushing this argument to "extremes," but given the tendency to overestimate the effectiveness of violence, it is worth keeping in mind.[83]

Further, he does emphasize that nonviolent sanctions used effectively can end oppression and liberate nations and people with less risk and more certainty than resorting to violence and terror.[84] For instance, nonviolent action measures the potential gains in taking power and delivering justice against likely losses in lives, property, and human dislocation. Ackerman claims the failures of nonviolent resistance do not "jeopardize as greatly [as violence does] the flower of generations and the fate of movements on which freedom, human rights, and democracy may depend."[85] Regarding democracy, he sees nonviolent movements as incubators of democratic skills. They teach people how to assume responsibility, make consensual decisions about the substance of goals and the process for reaching them,[86] insist that laws and leaders derive from the people's consent, and thus, nonviolent power becomes the first line of defense for a society's most sacred values.[87]

Ackerman places emphasis on consent or choice, and participation versus hierarchy in his analysis. He explains that the nonviolent paradigm of action is not based on fear or taking lives but on reclaiming power taken away without the people's consent.[88] Such movements are

82. Steim, "Contemporary Theories of Non-violent Resistance," 17.

83. Ackerman, *Strategic Nonviolent*, 44.

84. Ibid., 8.

85. Ackerman, *Force More Powerful*, 466–67.

86. Ibid., 468.

87. Ibid., 491.

88. Ibid., 489.

participatory not hierarchical, so that they become what they want their country to become, i.e. open in form and democratic in function. The rule of law, resting on the power of the people, shall put an end to the rule of persons over persons.[89]

LIMITS OF STRATEGY-BASED ASSESSMENTS

These strategy-based assessments face three core limits, which entail various secondary components. Two central premises integrate these limits with their own internal logic. These premises are viewing means as merely instrumental to ends, and viewing conflict as an adversarial struggle between persons or groups. The first core limit is an overemphasis on consequences, and leans toward utilitarian moral reasoning. This method of moral reasoning yields an inadequate attention to integrating a virtue ethic, which results in a narrow view of prudence and insufficient attention to the formation of kinds of communities needed to envision, strategize, and sustain nonviolent struggle. The second core limit is the emphasis on wresting power from the other, which entails a lack of resistance to humiliating the other and a de-emphasis on empathy, healing, and reconciliation. The third core limit is their embeddedness in western liberalism's framing of moral reasoning options and view of the person, which entails an emphasis on self-interest, choice, procedural skills, and negative freedom.

Overemphasis on Consequences: Utilitarian Moral Reasoning

The first core limit of both Sharp and Ackerman's approaches is an overemphasis on consequences, which assumes we can adequately know them in order to determine our strategy. This would require a vantage point to examine the consequences of all or most available options. Yet, it seems quite difficult for anyone to enjoy such an epistemological vantage point. In the rare case one could enjoy such a vantage point, that person or group would also need to be able to claim a breadth of experience. In turn, Gandhi claims that consequences cannot be adequately known in advance and thus, the means, which we have control over, must be kept as pure as possible.[90] Further, how far down the road of consequences does one look in their weighing of strategic outcomes? How do we know

89. Ibid., 503, 505.
90. Weber, "Nonviolence Is Who," 256.

what consequences are "good" or "better"? Again, we return to the point about what kinds of people do the perceiving of the situation, imagining of the options, and weighing of the consequences. Something more than consequences is required to assess the practices of nonviolence.

Their overemphasis on consequences and utilitarian reasoning yields an inadequate attention to virtue ethics. Sharp wrestling with Gandhi and more precisely with the relation between moral reasoning based on principle or on practical effectiveness indicates an important opening in his thought. He is trying to move "step by step toward resolution" of this apparent conflict in moral reasoning or between "nonviolent ethic" and "political practicality," with hopes of a more "advanced thesis."[91] Thus, the opening calls for a moral reasoning that more adequately integrates convictions, practices, effectiveness, and moral growth. One way to step into the opening could be a virtue-based moral reasoning. Such reasoning would entail cultivating dispositions and habits, which move us toward convictions about an approximate human *telos*; correspond to paradigmatic practices and feelings; integrate virtuous persons and relationships into the measuring of effectiveness; and locate the appropriate tension for personal or group moral growth.

However, Sharp has not addressed this possibility of virtue ethics. When he does mention virtue in this work, he simply says that "if Gandhi only preached the virtues of the morality of nonviolence," then he would likely have had little influence on political events. Instead, he offered "a practical course of action."[92] So, Sharp proposes to offer the action without reference to the virtues. Sharp appears to be limiting his understanding of virtue to inner attitudes or intentions, which is an inadequate account of virtue and even more of a virtue-based moral reasoning. He does argue that nonviolent struggle will help us develop certain qualities or capacities, such as the capacity for power and the capacity to relate to others.[93] However, the capacity to relate is still a far cry from developing virtuous relationships and human excellence.

Further, he suggests that wise strategy or practical reasoning is neither a matter of convictions nor of applying emotions, empathy, or love. Rather, he calls it an exercise for the intellect. Would not our degree of empathy for others, such as the oppressed and particularly the op-

---

91. Sharp, *Gandhi as Political Strategist*, 303, 306.

92. Ibid., 303–4.

93. Sharp, *Social Power*, 310–11.

ponents, shape our objectives and the kind of strategy we devise? Is this distancing between the emotions and intellect an adequate account of an integrated human person, and of moral reasoning? Our desires shape our objectives, yet our emotions arise from and indicate our desires, as well as the kind of people we are becoming.[94] Thus, shouldn't we attend more to how our emotions direct, and can enhance, action or strategy? Virtue-based moral reasoning would value the role of emotions in the exercise of practical reasoning. On the one hand, Sharp wants to raise the value of wise strategy, but on the other hand he has not adequately attended to the key habit or excellence of such practical reasoning, i.e. the virtue of prudence and the corresponding significance of emotions. In turn, he leaves undeveloped a potentially instructive and fruitful corresponding virtue ethic.

His argument about using nonviolent sanctions as a first realistic step resembles a kind of moral development approach, which resonates more with a virtue ethic. However, improving behavior does not necessarily entail virtuous activity. In a virtue-based ethic, virtues are habits oriented or responsive to an attraction to the good rather than merely dispositions to act from duty or fear of punishment. For instance, to entrench a moral character that simply responds to fear of sanctions or punishments, whether violent or nonviolent, enshrines a limit on our moral development as individuals and societies. To emphasize this motive of fear of sanction or punishment indicates that Sharp seems to maintain and perpetuate the vision of humans as self-interested calculators, such that when our costs sufficiently increase then we may change behavior or at least re-distribute effective power. Thus, by using his nonviolent technique it would seem we risk limiting our development to becoming self-interested calculators. For instance, Sharp illustrates this developmental limit further when he suggests that giving up violence for nonviolent struggle can be done quickly since his version of nonviolence does not require moral maturity.[95]

The limited attention to moral development and virtue arises in part due to how Sharp's earlier work integrated many Gandhian insights, but his later work transitioned more and more away from these insights. For instance, in his more recent work on civilian defense, Gandhi is

94. For more research on the importance of emotions, see Goleman, *Emotional Intelligence*.

95. Sharp, "People 'Don't Need to Believe Right.'"

rarely mentioned.[96] In turn, the attention Gandhi brings to personal integration and transformation gets minimized. In one of his more recent works, *Waging Nonviolent Struggle* (2005), Sharp only briefly points to the potential increase in self-confidence, liberation from fear, discipline, courage, organization, and sense of responsibility in the practitioners of nonviolent struggle.[97] However, there is even less attention in any of his work to the kinds of people oppressors may become as they encounter nonviolent struggle. This lack of attention tends to reinforce practices that humiliate the opponent. Weber argues that Sharp's attention has faded away from the deeper relation between means and ends, such as the kinds of people and society we become practicing and encountering nonviolence. In his early scholarly years, Sharp emphasized the "way of life" and the method of love to integrate and transform both people and society.[98] However, his thought over the last twenty-five years or so has taken a more realist-pragmatic turn, which has included more frequent marginalizing of the Mahatma.[99]

Sharp's brief reflections on the kind of people and society we become using nonviolent methods, i.e., more free, less centralized, etc., indicate the value of developing a virtue ethic. However, Sharp rarely refers to virtue and neglects the possibility of developing and integrating a virtue ethic into his assessment of nonviolence. Instead, he maintains an emphasis on consequences and leans more toward a utilitarian version. In turn, Sharp tends to reflect more on the end(s) of specific acts, and less on how all of one's acts as a whole fit into the development of virtuous persons, human excellence, and a possible end of human life.

Related to this neglect of virtue and formation is the structural critique of Sharp's theory of power from sociologist Brian Martin. He first describes how Sharp has enormous currency in the field of activists, but has had considerably less influence in policy or scholarly circles. Martin says, "for most policy makers, who deal in the nitty-gritty of practical politicking and its assumptions of top-down decision-making and the ultimate reliance on violence, Sharp's commitment to non-violence and diffusing power is far too radical and hence is dismissed as impractical or utopian. Furthermore, training populations in methods of non-vio-

---

96. Weber, "Nonviolence Is Who," 256.

97. Sharp, *Social Power*, 424–29.

98. Weber, "Nonviolence Is Who," 253.

99. Ibid., 257.

lent action would make the task of 'governing' society—that is, maintaining the reality and legitimacy of inequalities in power, wealth and status—immensely more difficult, and would jeopardize the positions of the policy makers themselves."[100]

Further, Martin explains how "Sharp's focus on consent is individualistic and voluntaristic in orientation, as shown by his attention to psychological reasons for obedience." A structural critique implies that certain types of social interaction are so regular and entrenched that they take on a dynamic of their own. Thus, Martin argues that Sharp gives insufficient attention to core patterns in our communities such as capitalism, patriarchy, and bureaucracy. Capitalism is not taken up by Sharp as a system of power, which divides workers. In a bureaucracy nearly everyone has superiors and subordinates, and thus, Sharp's ruler-subject dichotomy is of limited value. Patriarchy is intertwined in the State and the military, which are the focus of Sharp's analysis. Martin explains that the withdrawal of consent cannot turn off patriarchy as a structured set of social relations.[101] In other words, Sharp offers insufficient attention to the formation of the kinds of communities, which can envision, strategize, and sustain nonviolent struggle.

Like Sharp, Ackerman begins to open the door to the significance of virtue when he discusses critical "qualities" a nonviolent conflict strategist must possess. However, Ackerman also gives inadequate attention to virtue. He merely points to the importance of premeditation and foresight. Each of these could be components of a robust discussion of practical reasoning and the virtue of prudence. Yet, Ackerman merely describes premeditation as molding behavior to conform to his principles of strategic action, with the purpose of seeking an optimal result.[102] The optimal result consists of meeting the objectives, which Ackerman describes as the interests of the nonviolent struggle party over against one's opponent, and the taking of power from the opponent in order to move toward a fuller democracy. Thus, Ackerman appears to understand prudence either as a mere habit to obey the principles or rules of strategic action, or as a mere means to more external ends, i.e. the immediate objectives of the strategy. A virtue ethic would enrich the understanding of prudence as a habit that directs the moral agent(s)

100. Martin, "Gene Sharp's Theory of Power," 213–22.

101. Ibid.

102. Ackerman, *Strategic Nonviolent*, 337–38.

toward moral virtues and human excellence, and a habit that more fully integrates the means and ends.

In general, understanding nonviolence as primarily a strategy or technique often implies that the means, in this case the practice of nonviolence is instrumental but not constitutive of the proximate or ultimate ends of action. James Douglas describes our modern culture as technique saturated. In turn, he argues we seek technical solutions that seem to provide an effective response to immediate problems of life while distracting us from most of life's overarching questions. We inadequately get the degree to which the means form the more distant ends of life. Thus, we can use the strategy of nonviolence or violence when we suspect one to work or meet our more immediate and visible objectives. In contrast, Gandhi sought the means that corresponded to the end of Truth or reality, and rediscovered that means are end-creating as a seed is to a tree.[103] The disconnect of means and more distant or less visible ends found in the strategy-based assessment of nonviolence yields both a de-emphasis on the kind of people we become in our practices, and an easier slippage into strategies of violence.

Ackerman's inadequate attention to virtue and communities of formation impacts his assessments of particular nonviolent movements. In his analysis of the people power movement in the Philippines he gives little mention of the years of nonviolent training many of the people received during the 1970s and early 1980s. Nor does he mention the development of consumer collectives similar to Gandhi's ashrams that began in the mid 1970s.[104] Such training illustrates how individual and community formation is a key aspect, which a strategy or technique approach can miss or de-value in its assessment of nonviolent peacemaking. Ackerman also leaves out the *alaydangal* orientation coined by some of the Filipinos to describe their active nonviolence as "offering dignity."[105] This term resonates with the official social teaching found in the significant Catholic influence of that movement. Thus, he gives insufficient attention to the kind of healing and transformation a significant number of them sought for the whole community. In turn, he fails to assess how this orientation gets embedded in certain concrete practices, and the kinds of consequences or ends such practices tend to

103. Douglas, *Nonviolent Cross*, 40–44.

104. Zunes, *Origins of People Power*, 133–34.

105. Ibid., 139–40.

yield. Instead, he primarily focuses on the levers of control and power in his analysis.

Another example of Ackerman's inadequate assessments of nonviolent movements is the Polish Solidarity movement of the 1980s. Related to the above case, Ackerman gives little attention to the role character formation plays in the kind of people and communities enabled to practice nonviolence. A key indicator of this limit is his 1994 book that briefly mentions religious celebrations as merely reinforcing "the unity of the strikers,"[106] and his claim of the opportunistic use of religious places.[107] In his 2000 book, Ackerman gives a bit more attention to the election of Pope John Paul II and his visit to Poland, which made the Poles "braver" in terms of independent organizing.[108] However, he leaves unexplored the broader range of particular kinds of character virtues and the kind of community cultivated by religious practices. Further, he tends to limit such practices to "reinforcement" rather than considering the significance of their power in creating something new in persons and communities, such as patience, perseverance, humility, imagination, a willingness to suffer for justice, and an orientation toward reconciliation.

Wresting Power from the Other

The second core limit is the emphasis on wresting power from the other, which promotes an "us vs. them" framing and experience of the situation. By concentrating so much on nonviolence as a strategy, their approach seems to put a premium on "winning" something that an opponent must "lose." What is important for social change in their approach is that the oppressor no longer has the ability to impose his will.[109] Ackerman says that, "it is not about making a point [i.e., new insight] but about taking power."[110]

The framing of their arguments and proposals resembles closely the framing and language of military strategy. For instance, Ackerman admits that much of the conceptual content for his principles comes from the literature on military strategy. He gives the example of using

---

106. Ackerman, *Strategic Nonviolent*, 290.

107. Ibid., 311.

108. Ackerman, *Force More Poweful*, 131–33.

109. Bing, "Albert Camus: *The Plague* and An Ethic of Nonviolence."

110. Schaeffer-Duffy, "Regime Change without Bloodshed."

"offensive" and "defensive" dimensions to conflict.[111] In the forward to his book, Thomas Shelling explains that the style of reasoning found in strategic violence and strategic nonviolence is necessarily similar.[112] For instance, Ackerman explains that nonviolence works like violence in one sense by identifying an opponent's vulnerabilities, and then taking away his ability to maintain control.[113] Further, he suggests that the nonviolent movement increases the punishment for the opponents when they refuse one's demands, and minimize the punishment the movement absorbs in return. In contrast, Gandhi would suggest that the nonviolent movement be prepared and expect to take on the suffering in the situation in order to expose the deeper rupture in human relationships, and to cultivate the soil for a healing, which leads to a more lasting justpeace. In Ackerman and Sharp, the emphasis placed on punishing, overwhelming, and increasing the costs to the opponent, while also basing the objectives on serving the interests of the nonviolent protagonist maintains the military style zero-sum, utilitarian reasoning.

Such adversarial posturing affects the kinds of people we become and kinds of relationships we cultivate. For instance, this will cultivate relationships structured by competitiveness more than cooperation, "us" versus "them," "winners" and "losers," and a zero-sum view of the world more than a non-zero-sum that recognizes our deep interdependence and interconnections. These are precisely the kinds of conditions that risk perpetuating practices of injustice and violence. For instance, when Bush used language like the "Axis of Evil"[114] or said, "you are either with us or against us,"[115] he perpetuated divisive and hostile relations that expressed themselves in a lengthy war with Iraq and Afghanistan, in torture, and a lack of due process in Guantanamo Bay, etc. The ongoing struggles for civility in U.S. political discourse, particularly in light of the attempted murder of a U.S. Congresswoman and killing of several people in Arizona, is another example of the violence such adversarial posturing too often perpetuates.

With the emphasis on wresting power from the other in an adversarial conflict, humiliating the opponent finds little resistance in their

111. Ackerman, *Strategic Nonviolent*, 21.

112. Thomas Shelling, forward to Ackerman, *Strategic Nonviolent*, xvi.

113. Ackerman, *Force More Powerful*, 494.

114. Bush, "State of the Union Address."

115. Bush, "Bush Says it's Time for Action."

approach. In part, humiliation more easily occurs because non-violent action" is understood as waging conflict with the absence of mere "physical violence."[116] Ackerman's claim that waging conflict nonviolently means one comes not to make peace, but to fight seems to indicate a narrow view of peace as the absence of fighting or conflict.[117] More importantly, this may also indicate why Ackerman seems to be operating with a simple distinction between aggression, i.e., "fighting," and passivity, i.e. making "peace," rather than making a distinction between aggressive and assertive measures. In this context, aggression implies a concern with taking from another with little regard for their dignity or possible truth they may offer, and thus, being at ease with humiliating the opponent. Rather than identifying an opponent's vulnerabilities, and then simply taking away their power,[118] assertion implies the asserting of one's dignity while maintaining a capacity to sense the dignity and hear the truth of the other, i.e. identify their strengths or potential contribution. For instance, Gandhi speaks of identifying not only vulnerabilities for setting up strategy but also and primarily of identifying the other's strengths or sense of truth they may have to offer. Gandhi would recommend appreciating concessions rather than exploiting them as Ackerman recommends. This practice of appreciation acknowledges the dignity and truth the other offers and cultivates the soil for a more lasting justpeace. Also, as previously mentioned, some Filipinos in the people power movement in the Philippines referred to their nonviolent action as *alaydangal*, which meant to offer dignity rather than a simple focus on taking away the other's ability to control.

A striking example of Ackerman's logic arose in a statement by President Bush who said that, "some seem to believe that we should negotiate with the terrorists and radicals, as if some ingenious argument will persuade them they have been wrong all along."[119] An assumption in this statement is that the other *is* wrong all along. Our discursive engagement with them could only be about us exposing their falseness or vulnerabilities. They have no part of the truth to offer us. Bush apparently resorts to lethal violence more easily than Ackerman, however each seems to be functioning with assumptions about the "opponent," which

116. Sharp, "Technique of Non-Violent Action," 88.

117. Ackerman, *Force More Powerful*, 5.

118. Ibid., 494.

119. Stohlberg, "Bush Speech Criticized as Attack on Obama."

arguably could be classified as violating their dignity and functioning as a kind of "cultural violence."[120] Thus, even Ackerman's nonviolent strategies could leave society with very unhealthy and volatile relationships, and far from a justpeace.

The inattention to or willingness to permit if not advocate for humiliation, cultivates the kinds of conditions, which maintain the distrust, fear, and alienation that often lead to practices of injustice and violence. In contrast, a Gandhian approach emphasizes non-humiliation of the opponent, since nonviolence includes care for the fuller psychological and spiritual aspects of all persons, such as human dignity.

Along with little resistance to humiliation, neither Sharp's "realist-pragmatic" turn nor Ackerman's approach emphasizes becoming more loving, empathetic, compassionate, merciful, humble or forgiving, etc. by participating in nonviolent struggle. Nor do they emphasize healing and reconciliation. A de-valuing of these qualities or bracketing of them as unrealistic, sets important limits on the kinds of people we become, relationships we cultivate, and society we engender. Thus, their analysis and emphasis on power and self-determination sets limits on the kind of peacemaking one may cultivate and the endurance of such peacemaking.

Western Liberal Framing

The third core limit, particularly for critics of western liberal moral reasoning, is that both Sharp and Ackerman indicate an ethical framing, which resonates with western liberal societies.[121] The moral options seem to be between obligation-based approaches, with categories such as principles, rules and duties, or consequences-based approaches, particularly utilitarian versions, which Sharp and Ackerman favor. Hauerwas claims this opposition is often seen as the only choice left for philosophical liberal ethical thinkers, thus often excluding the possibility of a virtue-based approach.[122] Hence, this limit reconnects us to the first core limit mentioned above.

Ackerman acknowledges his utilitarian thrust of strategic nonviolent conflict. He describes critics of this thrust as diverting attention from his point. Ackerman simply points out that his description

120. Galtung, "Cultural Violence," 291.

121. I'm referring to the philosophical liberal tradition that impacts many in Western societies, not the political liberals or "left-wing" of U.S. politics.

122. Hauerwas, *Peaceable Kingdom*, 20.

of nonviolence is how most people have done it. Further, he claims that neither a "principled nor a pragmatic orientation, in itself, constitutes a prior determinant of, or constraint on, overall strategic performance."[123] A number of questions arise. First, is it accurate that most people have been using utilitarian reasoning for nonviolent action? Second, even if we grant that as true for the sake of argument, is this the most adequate way to assess what is actually happening to people and what could happen in the practices of nonviolence? Third, why are the options only principled or pragmatic? Ackerman seems hedged-in by the same common framing found in philosophically liberal societies around moral reasoning as either obligation-based or consequences-based.

Servais Pinckaers argues that people in philosophically liberal societies often envision the person as self-centered. In turn, he claims that liberal justice aims at the equality between rights of individuals to satisfy their needs. Society primarily gets viewed as a collection of self-interested persons that justice tries to organize in order to maintain a balance of power and contribute to the well-being of the majority. He argues that philosophically liberal societies at times view persons as morally either good or evil, rather than acknowledging the good and evil *within* each person.[124] He is not arguing that these characteristics are true of all persons or theorists of philosophically liberal societies. However, as far as Sharp and Ackerman describe nonviolent struggle as aiming at the redistribution of power in the second core limit, as victory over against an adversary, and as a mechanism of sanctions, which implies primarily motivating self-interested persons by fear of punishment or costs; they do resonate with and perhaps perpetuate these characteristics sometime found in philosophically liberal societies as highlighted by Pinckaers.

The western liberal framing also arises in Ackerman's emphasis on consent or choice, and participation versus hierarchy. He explains that the nonviolent paradigm of action is not based on fear or taking lives but on reclaiming power taken away without their consent.[125] However, we ought to ask, what if the people consent to unjust laws or unjust rulers? Are the democratic skills he mentions sufficient to form people and communities that actually perceive the good and have the will to seek it? Becoming what we want our society to become is an insightful

123. Ackerman, *Strategic Nonviolent*, 14.

124. Pinckaers, "Role of Virtue in Moral Theology," 295.

125. Ackerman, *Force More Powerful*, 489.

point, which opens the door to further reflection on the role of virtue. However, again he doesn't enter that terrain other than referring to "skills" which are largely procedural. When Ackerman uses the frame of participation as over against hierarchy in order to uplift the law and end the rule of persons over persons, he exposes his accent on freedom from, i.e. negative freedom. These aspects of choice, procedural skills, and negative freedom all correlate with his social context of western liberal theorizing. Thus, his analysis entails both the strengths and limits of such theorizing. The limits include an emphasis on private autonomy over interdependence and social context, an inadequate assessment of the common good and human excellence, and the risk of an inadequate attention to substantive or positive rights.

In sum, both Sharp and Ackerman offer tremendous benefits to the fields of nonviolence, peacemaking, and to our society in general. Nevertheless, their analysis encounters the following core limits. First, they have an overemphasis on consequences, and utilitarian moral reasoning. This method of moral reasoning yields an inadequate attention to integrating a virtue ethic, which results in a narrow view of prudence; a shift away from personal integration and transformation; maintaining a moral character primarily motivated by fear of punishment; insufficient attention to the formation of kinds of communities needed to envision, strategize, and sustain nonviolent struggle; inadequate assessments of particular nonviolent movements; a disconnect of means and more distant or less visible ends; and easier slippage into practices of injustice and violence. Second, they emphasize wresting power from the other, which entails viewing conflict as adversarial; being highly reliant on the framing found in military language; and de-valuing the nonviolent practice of taking on the suffering in the situation. This limit includes a lack of resistance to using humiliation, which entails an emphasis on aggressiveness rather than assertiveness; ignoring the strengths, truth, or dignity of the opponent; and a de-emphasis on empathy, healing, and reconciliation. Third, they are embedded in western liberalism's narrow framing of moral reasoning options and view of the person, which entails an emphasis on self-interest, choice, procedural skills, and negative freedom.

In the next chapter, I will begin the process of addressing the limits found in the rule-based and strategy-based assessments of nonviolence, which I have indicated in this chapter. I will begin by asking how an appeal to virtue could further illuminate their significance and address some of these limits, particularly in the context of Christian practices of nonviolent peacemaking.

PART TWO

Virtue-Based Assessment
of Nonviolent Peacemaking

2

Virtue Ethics and Scriptural
Models of Jesus

INTRODUCTION

WHAT DOES JESUS OFFER to this discussion on ways of assessing nonviolent peacemaking? In this chapter I begin the process of addressing the limits found in the rule-based and strategy-based assessments of nonviolence discussed previously by exploring virtue ethics and scriptural models of Jesus. First, I explain the basic components of virtue ethics. Second, I explore the models of Jesus' nonviolent peacemaking offered by the scriptural witness. Third, I draw primarily on William Spohn's work on the relationship between scripture and ethics along with attention to core Christian theological themes to illustrate the strong support for a virtue-based approach.

VIRTUE ETHICS

In general, virtue ethics is a teleological approach, which is based on the premise that all human action is directed toward an end. Virtue ethics also implies that the human person is oriented toward a human good, end, or *telos*. In virtue ethics, the human good is both personal and corporate so that moral education requires others, and relationships are central to the human good. Most virtue ethicists offer a broad, complex, comprehensive, and inclusive understanding of the human good. Thus, many forms of life and ways of embodying the virtues are compatible with the human *telos*.[1] Further, our understanding of the human good or *telos* will change and develop during our journey.[2]

In virtue ethics, the human good or *telos* is often described as human flourishing or excellence. Human flourishing entails a life lived in accord with virtue and participation in virtuous relationships.[3] Being virtuous means having a set of related virtues that enable a person to live and act morally well, not simply to do a morally good action, i.e. a proximate good.[4] I understand virtue as a disposition to act, desire, and feel that involves an exercise of judgment and leads to a recognizable human excellence, an instance of human flourishing.[5] Each virtue actualizes and cultivates itself in paradigmatic or core practices.

The virtues and their paradigmatic practices lead us toward and constitute the human *telos*, and thus, differ from a utilitarian understanding of virtue as merely a means to a more external end. Virtue ethics also differs from a deontological understanding of virtue as merely habits to follow the rules. Virtue ethics is focused on the character of persons, which includes a related concern for both acts and consequences.

We learn the virtues through practice, in the company of others, imitating worthy role models, listening to advice of virtuous friends and teachers, hearing stories of virtuous people and following rules of virtuous behavior.[6] Nicholas Gier argues that virtues came before moral rules, which arose from observing such loyal, just, honest, patient, compassionate behavior and their opposing vices.[7] However, learning the virtues also requires continually refining our understanding of the human *telos* through reflection and practice. In turn, we become better equipped at locating the virtues and their content or paradigmatic practices.

In virtue ethics, the primary ethical question asked is "Who are we or am I becoming?" before, "What is the rule?" or "What are the consequences?" James Keenan explains that the real discussion of ethics is not "What should I do?" but more "Whom should I become?" He

1. Kotva, *Christian Case for Virtue Ethics*, 22–23.
2. MacIntyre, *After Virtue*, 2nd ed., 219.
3. Kotva, *Christian Case for Virtue Ethics*, 32.
4. Keenan, "Proposing Cardinal Virtues," 714.
5. Spohn, *Go and Do Likewise*, 28.
6. Kotva, *Christian Case for Virtue Ethics*, 5–6.
7. Gier, "Toward a Hindu Virtue Ethics," 151–62.

expands this latter question into: "Who am I, who ought I to become, and how am I to get there?" The "ought" implies the task of developing a wise vision of human flourishing and an enduring aim to grow.[8] The "how" refers to those habits, capacities, interests, inclinations, precepts, injunctions, and prohibitions that will move us from the answer for question one to the answer for question two. Virtue ethics deals with this transition.[9] For instance, imagine that one desired to grow in courage (who ought I become?) while recognizing that they were afraid of heights (who am I?). Rather than going to the top of a high building, they should regularly practice finding the "appropriate tension," maybe the third or fourth floor initially, to stretch or challenge their self.

Joseph Kotva explains that ethical theory has too often focused on rules, principles, step-by-step decision-making procedures for moral quandaries, and the moral status of particular acts. Virtue ethics is more 'agent' centered and focuses on character traits and development, personal commitments, community traditions, and the conditions necessary for human excellence and flourishing. According to Spohn, "good character produces practical moral judgments that are based on beliefs, experience, and sensitivity more than on [or instead of] moral rules and principles."[10] I will discuss how virtue and rules can work together in my analysis of human rights and virtue in chapters six and seven.

Kotva argues that the rise of historical consciousness in ethics has increased our attention to context. Virtue ethics moves the focus from rules and acts to agents and their contexts.[11] Martha Nussbaum explains that this shift uplifts the significance of the good agent cultivating the perceptive capacity to recognize and describe the morally relevant features of each situation finely and truly, including the features not covered by the existing rule.[12] Further, Kotva claims we need enduring virtues since situations and context change, and thus, virtue ethics takes historical change and human development more seriously.[13]

Kotva argues that modern ethicists' emphasis on rules or consequences has failed to provide a complete picture of human experience.

8. Keenan, "Virtue Ethics," 84–86.

9. Kotva, *Christian Case*, 17.

10. Spohn, *Go and Do Likewise*, 28.

11. Kotva, *Christian Case for Virtue Ethics*, 8–9.

12. Nussbaum, "Non-Relative Virtues," 44.

13. Kotva, *Christian Case for Virtue Ethics*, 10.

For instance, rules or consequences-based approaches give slight attention to friendships and emotions, while virtue ethics more clearly values both. Friendships uplift our discerned commitments and take us beyond treating others as a mere 'duty.'[14] We better develop virtue in the midst of friendships or community. Emotions are sensed as witnesses to our character and as help in directing actions. For instance, empathy helps us to locate those in urgent need and draws us to respond. Alasdair MacIntyre claims that virtues are dispositions to both act and to feel in particular ways.[15] Simon Harak S.J. explains that Thomistic virtue entails expressing the passions in the right way, at the right time, to the right extent, and toward the right person.[16] In turn, the province of virtue includes both acting in the right way and being moved in the right way.[17]

Consequentialism also differs from virtue ethics in four other key ways. First, consequentialism often does not focus on human excellence. Rather, the principle for measuring consequences is often utility, such as in utilitarianism, rather than a vision of the human end. Second, in theory any action is justifiable if it results in the right calculation of consequences. In contrast, virtue ethics prohibits some actions as incompatible with the pursuit of a virtuous life and virtuous relationships.[18] Virtues also consist of paradigmatic practices, which orient the kind of actions we choose. Third, consequentialism often limits virtue to an interior principle of human action so that it becomes a habit of generally good intentions. In contrast, virtue ethics is not a morality of mere intention. Rather, one main task of virtue is to effect coordination between internal and external activity, between our disposition and its realization in actions done and done well.[19] Thus, emotions, needs, habits, commitments, and intentions are focused on as personal sources for moral life.[20] Fourth, consequentialism focuses on the particular acts, such as in act utilitarianism, or rules, such as in rule utilitarianism, rather than

14. Ibid., 10–12.

15. MacIntyre, *After Virtue*, 3rd ed., 149.

16. Harak, *Virtuous Passions*, 90. For Aquinas, different authors interpret the "passions" as fully or in part identical with the emotions. For example, see the Catechism of the Catholic Church, 487–89.

17. Ibid., 96.

18. Kotva, *Christian Case for Virtue Ethics*, 32.

19. Pinckaers, "Role of Virtue," 290, 292–93.

20. Spohn, *Go and Do Likewise*, 30.

focusing on developing character or a course of action beyond a narrow period of time. In contrast to virtue ethics, the ends are generally regarded as extrinsic to the human person or her act.[21]

CHRISTIAN SCRIPTURAL WITNESS

I now turn to explore the Christian scriptural witness to the practices of nonviolent peacemaking, with an eye to assessing the relevance of a Christian virtue-based approach. I begin with the models of Jesus in the Gospels and then broaden the analysis to the early Christians in scripture. I end this section with some brief comments on the Hebrew scripture.

Models of Jesus in the Gospels

A core source for Christian practices of nonviolent peacemaking is the witness of Jesus found in the scriptural text. Some core practices of Jesus illustrated by this text include: becoming vulnerable, proclaiming and inviting participation in the Reign of God, caring for the outcasts and prioritizing those in urgent need, loving and forgiving enemies, challenging the religious, political, economic, and military powers, healing persons and communities, praying, along with risking and offering his life on the cross to expose and transcend both injustice and violence.

Glen Stassen and David Gushee in *Kingdom Ethics* argue that the prophet Isaiah is the place to look for the background of Jesus' teaching on the Reign of God.[22] For instance, in Isaiah they locate key marks of the Reign: God's presence and deliverance from oppression, joy, healing, peacemaking as the instruments of war will be burned, and justice or righteousness. They even find further confirmation of these themes in Paul, specifically in Rom 14:1–16.[23]

In turn, Stassen and Gushee explore connections between Jesus, the Reign of God and the Sermon on the Mount. In this context, they argue that Jesus proclaims that the Reign had come in God's presence through himself, in the justice of feeding the hungry, welcoming the stranger, visiting the sick, and forgiving debts; in the peacemaking of forgiveness and of welcoming the tax collectors, harlots and eunuchs,

---

21. Curran, *Catholic Social Teaching*, 81.
22. Stassen and Gushee, *Kingdom Ethics*, 22.
23. Ibid., 26, 28.

and proclaiming the Gospel throughout the world; in healing the blind, lame, and demon-possessed; and in the joy of the presence of the bridegroom. In general, they argue that each of the main teachings in the Sermon is actually a pointer to the way of deliverance given to us when the Kingdom breaks into our midst. In the first three centuries of Christianity, the Sermon was clearly the charter document for Christian living.[24] Yet today, they admit the Sermon rarely occupies this central role. Stassen and Gushee hope to shift this displacement of the Sermon by arguing that Jesus taught us not hard sayings or high ideals, but concrete practices of how to participate in God's Reign today and prepare for its' full unfolding.[25]

Stassen and Gushee's insight about the Sermon and concrete practices helps us to see how the beatitudes closely relate to virtue. The Sermon begins with the beatitudes (Matt 5:1–8) that make us into blessings and bring blessings during and after our earthly life.[26] The beatitudes relate closely to virtue because they refer to both dispositions and practices that cultivate the kind of persons expressive of God's blessing.[27] For instance, blessed are the poor in spirit, those who mourn, the meek, the merciful, the pure in heart, peacemakers, those who hunger and thirst for justice, and those who are persecuted for justice sake or Jesus' sake. The poor in spirit refers to those who live with a sense of our interdependence with others, especially our dependence on God, and thus, without arrogance. Luke writes blessed are the poor (Luke 6:20), which emphasizes economic justice and the capacity of such poor to acknowledge interdependence.[28] The meek refers to gentleness and humility. Thomas Aquinas amplifies the relation of the beatitudes to virtue

24. Pinckaers supports Stassen and Gushee's attention to the Sermon by arguing that it "must once again become a basic text and primary source of moral theology, ahead of the Decalogue, natural law, or an assemblage of norms or rights established by pure reason." See *Sources of Christian Ethics,* 162.

25. Stassen and Gushee, *Kingdom Ethics,* 29–31. Pinckaers, *Sources* 136–39.

26. Pheme Perkins explains that Matthew "uses the Kingdom beatitudes as paraenesis to indicate the conditions for participating in eschatological happiness." See Perkins "Rejected Jesus and the Kingdom Sayings," 81.

27. Pinckaers, *Sources,* 148, 160. Drawing on Augustine, Pinckaers argues that the relation between the beatitudes and the gifts unites Matthew and Paul closely through Isaiah, 152–53, which supports Stassen's point about the significant role of Isaiah for Jesus' ethics.

28. *New Revised Standard Version.* All biblical notes not from another author come from the NRSV.

when he describes meekness as a virtue, which moderates the passion of anger and calms the desire for revenge.[29] It restrains one from wanting to inflict injury for injury. It enables one to remain tranquil in the face of wrongs done to oneself.[30] Paul offers corroborating evidence by stressing the need of this virtue when he says, "See that none of you repays evil for evil, but always seeks to do good to one another and to all" (1 Thess 5:15).

As the Sermon continues, the practices get more specified in what Stassen and Gushee call transforming initiatives. They see a threefold structure rather than a twofold antithesis. The three components are traditional righteousness, vicious cycle we often get trapped in, and transforming initiative.[31] Stassen and Gushee discover fourteen triads.[32] For instance, Matt 5:21–26 includes the three components in this way: you shall not kill, cycle of being angry or insulting, and go, be reconciled, and make friends with the accuser or enemy. In this case, the "transforming" initiative means the practice transforms the person into an active peacemaker, the relationship into a peacemaking process, and hopes to transform the enemy into a friend.[33]

Stassen and Gushee argue that Matt 5:38–42 offers the following triadic pattern: you have heard an eye for an eye, cycle of retaliating revengefully or resisting violently, i.e., with evil means, and turn the other cheek, give your cloak as well, go the second mile, and give to one who begs.[34] Walter Wink's scholarly work offers some credible reasons for translating the verse as "do not resist violently," rather than nonresistance or passivity.[35] Further, the context of Matthew entailed an oppressive occupation by the Romans, particularly oppressive acts by the Roman military, and an audience of the oppressed and apparently powerless. In turn, Stassen explains how turning the other cheek was taught in order to surprise the oppressor or insulter by taking the initiative, communicating nonviolently that one has equal dignity rather than being hit with a backhand like a slave, and thus, discovering one's power.

---

29. Aquinas, *Summa*, II.II, q. 157, a. 1, 2.

30. Ibid., I.II, q. 69, a.3.

31. Stassen and Gushee, *Kingdom Ethics*, 133–35.

32. Ibid., *Kingdom Ethics*, 142.

33. Ibid., 135.

34. Ibid., *Kingdom Ethics*, 137.

35. Wink, "Beyond Just War," 199. Also see Pope Benedict XVI, Midday Angelus.

This practice of "turning the other cheek" exposes and then refuses to maintain the communication or logic of humiliation, i.e., psychological violence. Those engaging this practice opt out of the cycle of retaliation and violence, and they "transform" the situation by offering humanity a "third way" of nonviolent love that justly restores a sense of shared human dignity. Thus, this practice confronts injustice and initiates the possibility of reconciliation.[36] Often, the first step of social and political nonviolent revolution is the oppressed asserting their dignity and refusing to be humiliated. Isaiah speaks of this in reference to God's Servant who senses God's presence, and thus, "no insult can wound" him (Isa 50:6–7). Contemporary research on the roots of violence suggests that humiliation is the most powerful stimulus for violence.[37]

Stassen and Gushee argue that Matt 5:43–48 reveals the following triad: you have heard to love your neighbor and hate your enemy, do not tax collectors and Gentiles do that, and so, love your enemies, pray for those that persecute you in order to be children of God. In turn, we approximate completion, "perfection" according to Matthew, and becoming "merciful" as God is merciful according to Luke.[38]

The Gospel of Matthew also includes other important peacemaking practices. For instance, when a person sins or ruptures a relationship we ought to speak with that person directly (Matt 18:15). If this falls short of healing, then we gradually enlarge the dialogue with others in the community. Another set of practices is illustrated in the judgment criteria, which are whether we provide food and drink for the hungry and thirsty, welcome the stranger, clothe the naked, care for the ill, and visit the prisoners (Matt 25:31–46).

In the Gospel of Mark, we also find nonviolent peacemaking practices, which amplify the insights articulated by Stassen and Gushee. Examples of nonviolent peacemaking practices found in Mark include healing and restoration, cultivating courage, and offering our life. For instance, Jesus heals the demonic, paralytic, woman with hemorrhage, leper, and Simon's mother-in-law. Jesus not only heals the leper but also insists he show himself to the priest, in order to officially reverse the unclean status and restore him to the community (Mark 1:40–45).[39]

36. Stassen and Gushee, *Kingdom Ethics*, 138–39.

37. Gilligan, *Violence: Reflections on a National Epidemic*, 223.

38. Stassen and Gushee, *Kingdom Ethics*, 140–41.

39. Harrington, "Gospel According to Mark," 601.

Jesus speaks often about courage, "take courage" as he walks on water (Mark 6:47–52), "why are you afraid" after he calms the storm (Mark 4:35–41), "do not fear, have faith" (Mark 5:35–43), and teaches the parable of the lamp (Mark 4:21–25). By cultivating courage, Jesus explains how we can arise with God's grace to the conditions of discipleship. Jesus says we must take up our cross and follow. Those who wish to save their life will lose it, and those who are willing to lose it for Jesus' sake will ultimately save it (Mark 8:34–38). In other words, if we live in a way of possessiveness, particularly of our present lives; then we will end up self-destructing. But if we live in a way of being created or offered as a gift, particularly by offering our present life to expose and transcend both injustice and violence, and to co-create Jesus' peace; then we will end up living with integrity, illuminating human dignity, healing our communities and our relationship with God, and flourishing beyond death. Bernard Haring finds an example of this healing power present in the offering of nonviolent peacemaking: referring to God's suffering Servant, Isaiah (53:5) says, "by his scourging we are healed."[40]

In the Gospel of Luke, we find other nonviolent peacemaking practices emphasized, which adds further support to Stassen and Gushee's work. For Luke, Jesus is the prince of peace and the way of peace (Luke 1:78–79; 2:14). John Donahue argues that Luke "sets the life of a Christian within the framework of proclaiming peace and doing the things which make for peace."[41] This Christian way of peace entails the practices of including outsiders and prioritizing the poor, which challenged the economic and political powers, showing mercy by healing the enemy's wounds (Luke 22:51), and being lambs in the midst of wolves (Luke 10:1–6). These practices are illustrated in stories and teachings such as Mary praising God for lifting up the poor and lowly, the parable of the rich man and Lazarus, the parable of the Pharisee and tax collector, the poor widow's contribution, Zaccheus, the calling of Levi the tax collector to be a disciple, the parable of the lost son, inviting those who can not repay you, "blessed are the poor," the Good Samaritan, telling the soldier to stop extorting money, and the instruction to be merciful as God is merciful. More poignantly, he announces his role and ministry of proclaiming the Reign of God by reading and claiming to fulfill Isaiah's prophecy: "the Spirit of the Lord is upon me, because he has anointed

40. Haring, *Healing Power*, 43.
41. Donahue, "Good News of Peace," 98.

me to bring good news to the poor. He has sent me to proclaim release to the captives and recovery of sight to the blind, to let the oppressed go free, to proclaim the year of the Lord's favor" (Luke 4).

In the Johannine corpus, God is love. Laying down one's life for another is the ultimate expression of love of neighbor and discipleship. In the foot washing (John 13:1–17), "Jesus is presented as servant and symbolically characterizes his impending suffering and death as a work of service."[42] Jesus' self-gift was an act of friendship[43] that transcended notions of superiority and inferiority.[44] Jesus indicates the key practice of transforming relationships into friendships, in this case making slaves or servants into friends saying that he "no longer calls them slaves but friends" (John 15:9–17).

Another key nonviolent peacemaking story in John's Gospel is the woman caught in adultery. The people were taught by Moses to stone such a woman, but Jesus calms the situation by kneeling and drawing in the dirt, and then says, "Whoever is without sin throw the first stone" (John 8:1–11). Thus, he shifts the people's frame from blame and punishment to self-examination and character assessment, as well as from radical "othering" of the target to identification with her. Since they all recognize their share in sin and walk away, Jesus implies that everyone is caught up in and perhaps deeply interconnected in the atmosphere of sin. He then tells the woman to go and sin no more. Therefore, personal and communal healing goes hand in hand. It is inadequate to simply privatize responsibility for sin. Thus, this practice of peacemaking invites each person away from a perception of justice that seeks to inflict further wounds, and toward a more true justice that prioritizes acknowledging the multiple wounds and seeking healing through accountability, repentance and character growth, i.e. restorative justice.

Jesus' nonviolent peacemaking practices pose challenges to military powers, violent revolts, and holy war. For instance, the teachings of Jesus to love our enemies, assert our equal dignity in a transforming nonviolent way, prioritize the poor and outcasts, seek service rather than domination, and aim for reconciliation raise difficult questions for and even suggest a challenge to military powers' dependence on domination, violence, and often on economic injustice. These broad challenges

42. Schneiders, "Foot Washing," 138.

43. Ibid., 142.

44. Ibid., 143.

in Jesus' teaching to military power arise even more clearly when Stassen and Gushee explain more specifically how Jesus' way of peacemaking fulfills Isaiah's prophecy that the Reign of God ushers in a justpeace. Isaiah 2:4–5 describes this justpeace with the words: "Nation shall not lift sword against nation nor ever again be trained for war." Later in Isaiah, the author judges Israel for trusting in military strength for security rather than in the Holy Spirit (Isa 31:1–5 and 32:15). Shifting to trust in God's Spirit yields a delivering justice for the downtrodden and outcasts. Such deliverance arises through God's suffering servant who does no violence (Isa 42:2 and 53:7–9).[45] The servant shall "not call out . . . in the open street" (Isa 42:1), which refers to the tradition of calling out the army for Yahweh war.[46]

During Jesus' time, most Jews hated Rome as their enemy for religious, political, and economic reasons. In turn, Jesus weeps over Jerusalem for not knowing the things that make for peace (Luke 19:42). Thus, Christian Jews refused to participate in the violent revolt in the year 70, but rather spread the Gospel to the Romans, i.e., their enemies. They rejected the circulating ideas of eschatological holy war. Stassen and Gushee explain how in the Revelation to John the followers of the Beast, i.e., emperor, do violence, while those of the Lamb use the Word of God, prophetic witness and martyrdom to conquer the Beast and to cultivate the transformation of the nations. Although the Hebrew Scriptures suggest alternative views of war, Jesus shows us how to interpret them. He never quotes the passages that favor killing, war or national supremacy, but rather those that favor peacemaking.[47]

Stassan and Gushee explain that Jesus directly challenged the resentful teaching of major political movements, including the Pharisees. Most of these movements taught that Israel should be separated from the impure, such as the lepers, sinners, "children, women, and the poor who could not pay the costly temple taxes and fees."[48] In contrast, Jesus fulfills Isaiah's prophecies that holiness meant redemptive compassion and inclusion of the outsider. He ate with sinners, healed lepers, welcomed children, dialoged with and increased the role of women, and prioritized the poor. While most major political movements taught a

---

45. Stassen and Gushee, *Kingdom Ethics*, 150–51.

46. Haring, *Healing Power*, 41.

47. Stassen and Gushee, *Kingdom Ethics*, 152–54.

48. Ibid., 155.

strategy of armed resistance, Jesus enacted a politics of initiative toward the enemy and of repentance for one's own enmity.

Although Jesus also welcomed the emerging belief of a Roman soldier (Luke 7:1–10) and is portrayed as not telling him directly to put up his sword, Stassen and Gushee argue that it is anachronistic to think he must be blessing war-making. They argue that the question for Jews at that time was not about whether or not to join the Roman army since they would not have been invited to join. Rather, the question for them was whether to make war on the Romans.[49] Further, Luke emphasized the inclusion of outsiders (Luke 3:10–14), such as tax collectors and in this case soldiers. In the story above, Luke was not focused on the legitimacy of soldiering. Similarly, Paul says nothing to Onesius or his owner about stopping slavery, because the institution of slavery was not at issue or at least not the first step in promoting Gospel healing. However, perhaps significant for contemporary reflection on war, most Christians now understand the inconsistency of slavery with Jesus' way of love. Similarly, most Christians may come to understand both soldiering and the military institution, in so far as they rely on violence, as inconsistent with Jesus' way of love.

Jesus' saying, "I have not come to bring peace, but a sword" (Matt 10:34, Luke 22:36), indicated warnings to the disciples to expect opposition, arrest, flogging, and slander rather than advocating war-making. Thus, his way of peacemaking involves rather than avoids conflict. When a disciple took his 'sword' comment literally, Jesus responds with impatient dismissal, saying "Enough, already!" In turn, he rejects a disciple's use of the sword in the Garden, because it draws one into the vicious cycle of killing and retaliation.[50]

Univocal Testimony on Nonviolent Peacemaking

Stassen and Gushee support Richard Hays' argument that this trend of nonviolence represents a univocal testimony about Jesus in the New Testament.[51] Further, they agree with William Swartley's argument that this univocal testimony also advocates proactive peacemaking, consisting of positive initiatives to overcome evil by employing peaceable

---

49. Ibid.

50. Ibid., 156.

51. Hays, *Moral Vision*.

means to make peace.[52] The evangelists unanimously portray Jesus as encouraging us to seek the life of vulnerability and service rather than domination over others. Extending this insight, they unanimously portray Jesus in the posture of exposing injustice and violence through humble suffering even to the cross, rather than affirming the prevalent expectations of armed victory over Israel's enemies.[53] For instance, all the Gospels report that Jesus entered Jerusalem on a donkey at the time of Passover, which fulfills Zechariah's prophecy (Zech 9:9–10) of a Messiah of peace who stops war and commands peace to the nations. N. T. Wright argues Jesus' reference to Pilate that Jesus' Kingdom was not of this world meant that he would not lead "an armed resistance movement like worldly kingdom-prophets."[54] Walter Wink argues that Jesus denounces the domination system with its redeemer myth that lives by violence. The domination system includes structures and institutions of violence,[55] as well as the personal desire to dominate others.

All the Gospels also report the story of Jesus clearing the temple of sellers and buyers. Stassen and Gushee argue that this act represented a practice of inclusion toward Gentiles, and thus, a practice of love of enemies. They point out how the story in Matthew cites Isaiah 56, which describes the house of prayer Jesus calls for as being one "for all nations."[56] However, the story of clearing the temple also involved direct challenge to a systemic economic injustice and the religious sacrificial system of violence. The selling of sacrificial animals presented a disproportional hardship and at times even excluded the poor from participating in the rituals. Jesus' general prioritizing of the poor and outcasts presented a pattern of challenging systemic economic injustice, which generates and maintains such poverty. Further, Jesus calls people to exercise "mercy not sacrifice" (Matt 9:9). Rene Girard supports the connection between the temple clearing and nonviolence when he suggests that this story is paradigmatic of Jesus revealing the God of nonviolence and breaking the myth of redemptive violence. Stassen and Gushee point out that Jesus'

---

52. Swartley, *Covenant of Peace*, 46.

53. Hays, *Moral Vision*, 329.

54. Wright, "Kingdom Come."

55. Wink, *Engaging the Powers*, 13–104.

56. Stassen and Gushee, *Kingdom Ethics*, 157.

assertiveness did not injure any people, thus it can hardly be extended to imply support of violence or lethal force.[57]

The Lord's Supper made clear that Jesus' way entailed offering one's body without taking the lives of others, forgiveness, and healing rather than domination and violence. In turn, the practice of the Eucharist cultivates this awareness, appropriate dispositions, and these paradigmatic practices indicated by the Lord's Supper.

In the Garden, he rejects the disciple's use of the sword to protect or defend the innocent, i.e., himself. In his last free act before being arrested, Jesus healed the ear of his enemy, who was struck by the violence of Jesus' disciple trying to defend the innocent (Luke 22:51). He also rejects using legions of angels to fight a war for his sake (Matt 26:51–54), which arguably would have been a "just war."

The pervasive political implications of his way arose early on when Herod wanted to kill him (Luke 13:31).[58] However, they arise even more clearly while under arrest, when he challenges the ultimate authority of Pilate's political power (John 19:9–11) and defines his Reign in terms of truth (John 18:36–38) rather than domination or violence.

At the cross, Jesus forgives those who crucify him rather than calling for retaliation or a type of retributive justice that would perpetuate the myth of redemptive violence. In contrast to Daniel Bell's portrayal of the cross in his claims about virtue ethics and "just" warriors, I would argue that Jesus' cross and our subsequent call as disciples to carry our cross is not analogous to enduring any kind of discomfort or suffering in our lives, such as suffering in a "just" war.[59] Instead, carrying the cross is about voluntarily risking suffering in order to expose and transcend both injustice *and* violence.[60] The disciple's experience of the resurrection and Pentecost—along with the spread of the Gospel to all the nations, indicates the ultimate power of his nonviolent love of friends and enemies. For instance, they experienced an unimaginable conversion from fear to the courage of mission, and often of martyrdom.

Thus, Stassen and Gushee argue for the consistency and thoroughness of Jesus' witness: he fulfilled Isaiah's prophesy that peacemaking

---

57. Ibid.

58. Wright, "Paul and Caesar," 173–93.

59. Pope John Paul II explains that, "violence is the enemy of justice. Only peace can lead the way to true justice." Homily at Drogheda, 19–20.

60. Bell, *Just War*, 99.

would be a key mark of the reign of God.[61] Jesus illustrates the particular peacemaking practices. "For to this you have been called, because Christ also suffered for you, leaving you an example, so that you should follow in his steps" (1 Pet 2:21). Jesus sums up this kind of peacemaking in the new commandment to love as I have loved you (John 15:11–13), i.e., with nonviolent love of friends and enemies.

Early Christians in the New Testament

The New Testament witness includes the peacemaking of early Christians living after Jesus. In Acts, the community lived cooperatively by sharing all resources so that no human needs went unmet. The rich sold what they had to care for the poor (Acts 2, 4) and deacons were ordained to oversee just distribution of material aid to those in need (Acts 6). Thus, community and mutual aid represented twin pillars of early Christian life. Paul's initiative for the churches to collect money for the poor in Jerusalem encountered opposition and led to his arrest and eventual imprisonment in Rome.[62] In turn, the early Christians subtly and increasingly challenged the Roman economic system that profited the privileged at the expense of the poor and marginalized. Further, confrontations with the magic of the day (Acts 8:9–24, 13:6–12, 16:16–18) and idolatrous practices (Acts 17:16–31, 19:23–41) challenged the economic system that depended on them.[63]

Acts also offers the witness of the deacon and first martyr Stephen, who forgives his enemies as they take his life (Acts 6:8—8:1). Other Christian leaders, like Peter and John, clashed with political leaders in Jerusalem and went to prison. Politically, the apostles obeyed God rather than any human, whether Jewish or Roman authority (Acts 2:36, 4:19–20, 5:29).[64] The existence of the church as a group within the empire giving their allegiance to another lord offended the powers and particularly Caesar.[65] Another indication of the political challenge is Luke mentioning that one of the disciples was Simon, the Zealot, which in that context referred to a political movement aiming to incite violent

61. Stassen and Gushee, *Kingdom Ethics*, 158.

62. Swartley, *Covenant of Peace*, 174.

63. Ibid., 172.

64. Ibid., 158, 166.

65. Wright, "Paul and Caesar."

rebellion against Rome (Acts. 1:13). A Zealot in today's terms resonates with "terrorist." Thus, Simon's discipleship suggests the peacemaking practice of engaging and possibly converting people tempted to use or having already used terrorism.

Saul, who practiced violence, persecution, and killing of Jesus' followers, experienced a radical conversion. In turn, he became a peacemaker who united formerly alienated peoples and exhorted reconciliation of those caught in divisive rivalry in the newfound congregations. Saul, who becomes Paul, is also imprisoned. When released, Paul calls the magistrates to offer a personal apology, which would restore the relationship. Thus, he goes beyond the "security of the law of the Pax Romana," which did not emphasize restorative justice.[66] Further, the conversion of Cornelius the centurion primarily exemplifies the uniting of alienated peoples, in this case Gentiles with Jews. But Cornelius also symbolizes Rome, and the Pax Romana it sought through violence, now kneeling before the lordship of Jesus and his way of nonviolent peacemaking.[67]

In the letters of Paul, his distinctive title for God is "God of Peace." Swartley argues that peacemaking is integral to his thought. For instance, Paul portrays all humanity as sinning and in need of God's righteousness and justification. Swartley draws on Christopher Marshall's work to show how Paul's justification by faith indicates a restorative justice practice that is socially and politically relevant.[68] This restorative practice arises from God's model of justification of sinners, i.e., even while we were enemies of God, Jesus' life, death, and resurrection reconciles us to God. In Galatians, Paul's social dimension arises in the union of Jews and Gentiles, rich and poor, free and slave (Gal 3:14). Colossians suggests all creation is recipient of this reconciling peace (Col 1:20). Thus, humans are called to live toward the goal of becoming more and more conformed to the image of Jesus (2 Cor 3:17–18).[69]

Jesus is head over the principalities, powers, rulers and authorities (Col 2:10). He disarmed or de-potentiated them by making a public exposure of them in their violence, particularly at the cross, and thus

---

66. Swartley, *Covenant of Peace*, 168–69.

67. Ibid., 161–62.

68. Marshall, *Beyond Retribution*.

69. Swartley, *Covenant of Peace*, 190–94, 216.

triumphed over them (1 Cor 2:6–8, Col 2:13–15).[70] The powers can be used for good, if in accord with God's way illuminated by Jesus, or for evil.[71] Thus, humans participate in Jesus' way by exposing the violence of such powers and transforming them towards his practices.

For instance, in Romans 12–13, Paul discusses how to not conform to this world, such as how to respond to evil, and our conduct toward rulers. Responses to evil include blessing those that persecute you, never avenging yourselves, leaving room for God's power of accountability, making peace with all, conquering evil with good, and feeding your enemy if they are hungry in part to evoke their repentance.[72] Chapter 13 is primarily about how a minority and oppressed group ought to relate toward rulers, particularly in the political context of Jews and Jewish Christians being expelled from Rome. Wright argues that Paul's underlying point is that social-political transformation is not won by the presumed means of violence. By claiming that Caesar was answerable to God, Paul undermines pagan totalitarianism rather than reinforces it.[73] Paul "does not endow the political order with any inherent divinity."[74] This section is not a doctrine of the state, good for all occasions, nor is it a political theory of the nature of the state, particularly in light of John's critique of this state in Revelations 13.[75] Further, it may be more descriptive of the prevalent ruling authority then prescriptive of government practices, particularly since Christians did not yet hold official government positions. Paul does not directly address the question of unjust governments here, although he clearly claims that our true citizenship belongs in the Kingdom of God (Phil 3:20). However, Paul's central message of Christ crucified would readily bring to mind the injustice of Roman authority.[76] Luise Schottroff argues that the resistance called for in Romans 12 primarily refers to Satan, but since Satan often works in state powers, then Christians must resist unjust state practices and structures.[77] Romans 13:8 immediately follows this section on ruling au-

---

70. Wright, "Paul and Caesar."

71. Swartley, *Covenant of Peace*, 228–30.

72. Ibid., 214, 238.

73. Wright, "Paul and Caesar."

74. Perkins, "Paul and Ethics," 273.

75. Brown, *Introduction to the New Testament*, 572; Pilgrim, *Uneasy Neighbors*.

76. Pilgrim, *Uneasy Neighbors*, 7–36.

77. Schottroff, "Give to Caesar What Belongs," 242–43.

thority and indicates that the new form of life is based on love, and thus, a resistance of embodied love consistent with Jesus rather than through violence.[78]

Paul's use of warfare imagery offers witness against violence and for peacemaking. For instance, "we do not wage war according to the flesh" (2 Cor 10:3–4), nor do we war against human adversaries. Rather, we struggle against spiritual forces of darkness and structures of injustice,[79] with armor and weapons of truth, righteousness, peace, faith, the cross, and the word of God (Eph 6:10–18).[80] According to Haring, the basic truth taught by Jesus was "God is Love." Jeremiah connects violence with untruth (Jer 5:27; 6:7; 9:2–6),), as does Pope Benedict XVI more recently.[81] Haring argues that the fundamental option for the truth of nonviolent love enables us to discover the good or truth in our opponents and a common basis for solving conflicts.[82] Further, the author of Ephesians indicates that Paul was in prison, and thus, this kind of participation in struggle entails a willingness to risk imprisonment, torture and even being killed as both Jesus and Paul experienced.

In turn, Paul describes how the peace of Jesus confronts the peace of the Roman Empire, which was dependent on oppression through economic and military violence. For instance, he opposes Christ crucified to the rulers of this age (1 Cor 2:6–8; 15:24); indicates the folly of trusting in Roman imperial peace and security (1 Thessalonians); and struggles with the Philippians against official persecution (Philippians 1–3). Paul called God King of kings and Lord of lords (1 Tim 6:15) as Jesus is called (Rev 17:14). While many emperors of the time were considered the "Savior of the world," Jesus and God are given this title in the scriptures (1 Timothy, 2 Timothy, and Titus).[83]

The author of 2 Peter explains that practicing particular virtues contributes to experiencing the grace and peace of Jesus in abundance (2 Pet 1:2) as well as to maturity in Christian formation. More specifically, they help us to escape corruption or evil and to participate in the divine nature (2 Pet 1:3–4). Other letters offer sets of virtues to cultivate

---

78. Swartley, *Covenant of Peace*, 240.

79. Wink, *Engaging the Powers*, 3, 49.

80. Hays, *Moral Vision*, 331.

81. Vatican Today, "Christians Need."

82. Haring, *Healing Power*, 51–53.

83. Swartley, *Covenant of Peace*, 252.

and vices to avoid for Christian formation (Rom 1:29–31; 13:13; Col 3:18, Eph 5:22, 1 Cor 5:10–11; 6:9–10; Gal 5:19–23; Phil 4:8).[84]

Hebrew Scriptures

Stassen and Gushee argued that Jesus' teaching on the Reign of God and peacemaking drew primarily on the prophetic works of Isaiah in the Hebrew Scriptures. Most Christians understand Jesus as more adequately or even fully revealing the God who was encountered by the Jewish communities that wrote the Hebrew Scriptures. However, these earlier stories, which are also part of the Christian biblical canon, indicate both a violent and at times nonviolent God. If Jesus reveals the character of God in the above practices of nonviolent peacemaking found in the New Testament, then what do we make of the peacemaking practices and the character of God implied by the Hebrew Scriptures? And how does this earlier witness impact the way we understand the practices indicated by the New Testament?

Reuven Kimelman and Maurice Friedman, both Jewish scholars, argue for the strong presence of nonviolence and love of enemies in the Hebrew Scriptures and Talmud. Kimelman argues that the sign "that Israel is righteous and worships God is that it rejects violence."[85] He describes the notion of reconciliation as controlling the urge to hate and acting so the enemy becomes a friend. Further, he acknowledges the repeating pattern of not trusting in military weapons but in God (Ps 44:7, 20:8; 1 Sam 17:45; Zech 4:6).[86] Friedman points out how the "eye for an eye" thinking functioned to equalize the value of persons and challenge surrounding vengeful cultures.[87]

Norman Lofink, Walter Wink, and Rene Girard argue that the Hebrew Scriptures represent a tradition of communal wrestling with who God is, and a gradual turning away from the image of a God of violence and the myth of redemptive violence is the prevailing myth or dominant religion.[88] Wink coined the phrase myth of redemptive violence, which means the myth of the victory of order not won by the presumed means

---

84. Ibid., 274.

85. Kimelman, "Nonviolence in the Talmud," 38.

86. Ibid., 28, 31.

87. Friedman, "Hasidism," 119.

88. Lofink quoted in Haring, *Healing Power*, 20–23. Wink, *Engaging the Powers*, chapters 1, 2, 6. Girard, "Bible's Distinctiveness," 145–76.

of violence, i.e. violence saves and brings peace.[89] One of the earliest versions of this myth is the Babylonian creation myth. In contrast, Wink argues that the creation myth in Genesis where humans were made from God out of love, in God's image, and for covenant friendship with God challenged the dominating Babylonian creation myth where humans were made out of violence and for a slave-like relationship with god.[90] Wink explains that the Babylonian myth supported the extermination of enemies, male supremacy, human sacrifice to gods, and peace through war.[91] For modern culture, Wink argues that the myth of redemptive violence is the real myth or dominant religion.[92]

In Genesis, the authors portray God as challenging the violent revenge-system in the Cain and Abel story by marking Cain for protection. However, the transformation of the culture and the formation of God's covenant people entailed a gradual process. On the one hand, they portray God as committing mass killing with the flood, of Egypt's first born, and as directing military victories. On the other hand, they portray God as challenging the religious sacrificial system by sparing Isaac, as liberating the oppressed, as inspiring Joseph to reconciliation rather than retaliation, as being credited with victory rather than human military might (Books of Joshua and Judges), and as warning the people of the military and economic violence of kings (1 Samuel). The prophetic witness of Isaiah, Micah, Amos (3:6), Hosea, Zechariah (4, 9), and the Book of Job when taken together suggest strong challenges to trusting in military power, the collusion of military and economic power which oppress the poor, and the cycle of violence, such as the scapegoat mechanism illuminated by Girard.[93]

Lofink, Wink and Girard's argument suggests that the portraits of Jesus in the New Testament reveal a God of nonviolent peacemaking. In turn, Jesus invites humans to cultivate a nonviolent character and nonviolent revolution across society. Therefore, the general direction of the scriptures as a whole seems to reveal God as a God of nonviolence. However, Swartley suggests that we are not in position to call God violent or nonviolent. Yet, God calls us as humans to reflect the non-

---

89. Wink, "Facing the Myth of Redemptive Violence."

90. Wink, *Engaging the Powers*, 15.

91. Ibid., 13–17.

92. Wink, "Facing the Myth of Redemptive Violence."

93. Girard, "Mimesis and Violence," and "Surrogate Victim," 9–32.

violent peacemaking practices of God illustrated by Jesus.[94] The Gospel of Matthew teaches Christians that Jesus is the key interpreter of the Hebrew Scriptures, and thus, Jesus' overwhelming emphasis on nonviolent peacemaking practices indicates the kind of love we are called to embody.

Although I could discuss much more regarding the witness of the Hebrew Scriptures to peacemaking practices, an important point for this project is the notion of a covenant of formation and transformation of God's people.[95] A virtue ethic approach more adequately envisions and assesses this core aspect of the scriptural witness. Swartley suggests that the Torah was not a graceless law code but a way of life with a *telos* of Shalom.[96] Benjamin Farley surveyed the whole scripture for virtues, including the Hebrew Scriptures, and found the following clusters: humbly expecting God's deliverance, virtues of mourning unto repentance, virtues of justice, compassion, and mercy for the powerless and outcast, courage in suffering and willingness to resist the ethos of one's time, and the joy of being blessed by God's presence.[97]

SCRIPTURE, THEOLOGY, AND ETHICS

In order to determine what primary ethical model makes the most sense for assessing Jesus' approach to nonviolent peacemaking, I now turn to the significance of virtue ethics for Christian ethics. I begin with an analysis of the relationship between scripture and ethics, primarily drawing on Spohn's work. Then I examine how some core theological themes resonate with a virtue ethic approach.

Scripture and Ethics

In assessing the relationship of scripture and ethics, Spohn argues that virtue ethics is the best way to appropriate the moral vision and practices of Jesus.[98] He offers three primary reasons. First, it fits the narrative form

94. Swartley, *Covenant of Peace*, 395.

95. Kimelman, "Nonviolence in the Talmud," 24–49.

96. Swartley, *Covenant of Peace*, 378.

97. Discussed in Stassen and Gushee, *Kingdom Ethics*, 49, 51.

98. Spohn is following a tradition grounding moral theology in the person of Jesus, which in recent Catholic thinking was initiated by Fritz Tillmann, *The Master Calls*, 1960 (originally in German, 1937), and extended by Bernard Haring, *The Law of Christ*, 1961. Tillmann pointed to the pursuit of spiritual perfection through the virtues, and that this was the task for every Christian.

of the New Testament and explains how the story of Jesus shapes the moral character of individuals and communities. Second, it attends to the deeper levels of moral living that Jesus addresses, such as the heart, personal center of convictions, emotions, and commitments. Third, it fits the dominant mode of moral discourse in the New Testament, namely, paradigms that establish certain patterns of disposition and action that guide future action.[99] Thus, Spohn would argue that neither an obligation-based set of rules, nor a consequences-based utilitarianism is an adequate way of appropriating the moral vision and practices of Jesus.

The first reason responds to the significance of character and narrative. Spohn suggests that scripture discloses the character of God, which determines the appropriate ways for us to be faithful. For instance, the Good Samaritan story (Luke 10:25–37) shifts the Law teacher's focus from the minimum action required to get eternal life, a kind of mere duty approach or self-preoccupied consequentialism, to the deeper challenge of human excellence in terms of becoming a neighbor or a certain kind of person. Meanwhile, the broader narrative, i.e., the story of the life, death, and resurrection of Jesus, sets the framework for New Testament ethics. In turn, the entire life of Jesus forms the basic norm of Christian ethics. Jesus comes proclaiming the resurgent Reign of God more than moral principles. However, Jesus calls humans not only to formation as most philosophical virtue ethics emphasizes, but also to transformation.[100]

Spohn's second reason responds to the scriptural emphasis on the heart, which infuses behavior with meaning. Dispositions, motivations, intentions, and the basic orientation of life become the focus. Thus, biblical ethics moves beyond rules and principles to the level of transformation of character. For instance, Paul urges putting on the mind of Christ (Phil 2:5), and points to love as the greatest of what lasts (1 Corinthians 13). He also indicates a number of "virtues" and "vice" lists, but refers to them as "fruits" of the Spirit and "works" of the flesh (Gal 5:19–23).[101] Spohn argues that the Sermon on the Mount calls for a radical righteousness of the heart, such as nonviolence, forgiveness, simplicity, and hospitality, more than a detailed code of conduct. Changing the fruits

99. Spohn, *Go and Do Likewise*, 28.

100. Ibid., 28–30.

101. Kotva, *Christian Case*, 120–21.

requires changing the roots (Matt 7:16–20).[102] Kotva suggests that the blessings in the Beatitudes presuppose action, but also commend a posture reflecting certain attitudes and feelings (Matt 5:3, 6, 8). He points out how Matthew's Gospel presumes a connection between the internal and external, as one's conduct flows from, reflects, and shapes one's inner character.[103]

Further, the biblical practice of moral discernment, which sorts out the movements of the Spirit in our hearts, resonates better with virtue ethics' attention to moral maturation and psychology. For instance, Spohn argues that the question is not, what should I do, but what is God enabling and requiring me to do and to be.[104]

Spohn's third reason responds to the scriptural emphasis on paradigmatic stories or practices, which nurture particular dispositions and shape the virtues. Hence, the virtues also entail paradigmatic practices. Spohn suggests that the basic Christian paradigm is found in the shape of the life of Jesus, which arises in Philippians 2. This pattern illustrates self-offering love in radical trust of God. The Good Samaritan parable and the passion narratives give practical content to the command to love the neighbor. The story of Jesus shapes the virtue of justice toward generosity, the virtue of compassion toward surprising recipients, and the virtue of mercy toward forgiveness.[105]

Kotva elaborates on this point about a Christian paradigm by arguing that a clear master/disciple relationship exists, especially in Matthew's Gospel. Virtue ethics likewise suggests that being guided by and following masters or worthy examples is how we learn to recognize and embody the virtues. For example, the disciples follow and share in Jesus' mission (Matt 4:19–20; 8:19–23), while Matthew views Jesus' teaching as a central component of his ministry.[106] Paul also speaks often of "imitating" Christ as Paul imitates him (1 Cor 4:16; 11:1; Phil 3:17).

Both virtue ethics and the scriptures are also attuned to the personal and the corporate. Virtue ethics draws persons toward their *telos*, but the good is not conceived solely in personal terms. Virtuous relationships are constitutive of the *telos* and journey toward the *telos*. Likewise,

---

102. Spohn, *Go and Do Likewise*, 30–31.

103. Kotva, *Christian Case*, 104–5.

104. Spohn, *Go and Do Likewise*, 30–31.

105. Ibid., 31–33.

106. Kotva, *Christian Case*, 107.

Jesus calls specific persons (Matt 4:18–22), speaks about attitudes and feelings (Matt 5:21–24), and suggests rejoicing over the one lost sheep (Matt 18:12–14). But also, Jesus calls the disciples friends (John 15:9–17), and Matthew indicates the importance of Christian community and dealing with sins in a restorative way (Matthew 16–18). Paul speaks of the church as a human body with personally gifted members relating to the various parts of the body (1 Cor 12:12–31), which assumes our interdependence.[107]

However, the scriptures also speak of commandments, rules, and laws. In accord with Thomas Aquinas' general approach, Kotva supports other contemporary thinkers like Wayne Meeks, Thomas Ogletree, and Pinckaers in suggesting that these rules serve the virtues and character development rather than vice versa.[108] In other words, they serve an educative function as summaries of previous wise decisions and for shaping the character of those who have yet to develop practical wisdom.

For instance, in Matthew's Gospel the rules point at or portray the Reign of God or faithful discipleship, and thus, depict or call one to become a certain sort of person. Further, the law language requires a perceptive discernment or prudence not just as a habit for obeying the law but for becoming a person with a particular set of moral virtues. For instance, Jesus suggests some commands are "greater" or "weightier" than others (Matt 22:37–40; 23:23), and some are limited by love and mercy (Matt 12:10–13). Therefore, Kotva argues that Matthew's use of law language, as representative of the Gospels, corresponds well with a virtue ethic approach to scripture. Paul also uplifts the role of such discernment by challenging communities to test everything (1 Thess 5:21), in his treatment of meat sacrificed to idols (1 Corinthians 8, 10), and in the conflict between the "weak" and "strong" (Rom 14:1—15:13).[109]

Paul also provides images of moral progress, which correlate well with virtue ethics' emphasis on moral development. For instance, the image of "walking" (Rom 8:4, 1 Cor 3:3, etc.) envisions continuity and patterns of behavior. Thus, morality is not engaged primarily as discrete acts, judgments, and dilemmas as more rule-based or consequences-based approaches tend toward. Another image Paul offers is the "race" (1 Cor 9:24–27; Phil 3:11–17), which aims toward a goal and requires

---

107. Ibid., 108–9, 121–22.

108. Pinckaers, *Sources of Christian Ethics*, 162.

109. Kotva, *Christian Case*, 116–18, 123.

training. The image of "transformation" arises when he speaks of salvation as a process (2 Cor 3:18), and God working in our growing conformity to Christ (Rom 8:29). Paul challenged the Corinthian community to become more mature (1 Cor 3:1–2; 2 Cor 6:13) and to excel. Thus, both Paul's vision of the Christian life and virtue ethics involve a *telos*-oriented moral growth and the transformation of the person.[110]

Kotva argues that Paul's movement between the indicative and imperative moods suggests another reason for a virtue-based approach to scripture. Kotva explains that the indicative entails Paul recounting what God has done for us, is doing, and will complete, as well as who Christians are and will become. The imperative entails Paul assuming that certain kinds of actions and attitudes, and not others, flow from the kinds of actors he describes in the indicative. This indicative and imperative relationship corresponds to a virtue-like presumption that a certain kind of people will act in a certain kind of way. Kotva also finds resonance between virtue ethic's tripartite structure: what-we-happen-to-be, what-we-could-be, what moves us from the first to the second part; and Paul's indicative and imperative structure. The imperative comes from the incongruity between our goal and our actual state.[111]

Therefore, Kotva argues that rules or duty-based ethics fail to account for Paul's infrequent appeal to rules, his insistence on discernment or testing, and his images of moral progress. Consequences-based ethics fail to account for Matthew's respect for the law or the centrality of Christ's life and teaching.[112] Further, taking a virtue approach to scripture would enable us to appropriate how the scripture provides images of the human *telos*, such as the Reign of God or Shalom, informs our understanding of particular virtues, and shapes our identities and characters through its use in weekly ritual.[113] Keenan supports Spohn and Kotva's analysis by arguing that a virtue approach provides a method for building bridges between scripture and moral theology.[114]

---

110. Ibid., 124–25.

111. Ibid., 126–28. The "what-we-could-be" differs from the tripartite structure Keenan offers, which uses "what-we-ought-to-be" instead.

112. Ibid., 156.

113. Keenan and Harrington, *Jesus and Virtue Ethics*, 40; Kotva, *Christian Case*, 173.

114. Keenan, *Jesus and Virtue Ethics*, 24–30. He also argues that virtue ethics builds bridges between moral theology and other fields such as spirituality, liturgy, and church life.

Theology and Ethics

Several core theological themes also indicate the value and priority of virtue ethics. In Christology, the theme of incarnation implies that Jesus reveals God to us and shows us a life that is fully human. Thus, Jesus gives us a taste of our *telos*. This theme arises from encounter with the life, death, and resurrection of Jesus. In turn, Jesus represents the paradigm for our lives and growth in virtue. Jesus exemplifies not only acts to perform or rules to follow, but the kind of people humans are to become. Any rules and principles arise, point to, and get their meaning from Jesus' life. A virtue ethic is more adequate in affirming these insights about the incarnation and Jesus manifesting our true *telos*.[115]

Sanctification is widely accepted as a teleological concept, which involves the growth and transformation of the person and character toward a "partially determinate picture of the human good or end."[116] Theologians often portray the end as "Christ-likeness" or friendship with God, which entails the development of a specific set of virtues. Sanctification consists of a life-long process where one moves from the kind of person one is to the kind of person God calls us toward.[117]

However, unlike most philosophical virtue ethics, in Christian ethics the theme of grace plays a significant role. The initiation and continuing process of sanctification depends on God's prior initiative beginning with our creation, and God's loving forgiveness. But our participation remains active in the relationship or growing friendship with God, and in sanctification. Thus, moral formation and transformation involves not only interdependence with other humans as most virtue ethics' acknowledge, but also a relationship with God. As we become aware of God's love for us, our human dignity as gifts or children of God, and our struggle with sin, then we live with a conscious sense of God's grace. In turn, our long journey of graced sanctification can generally overcome despair or a grim determination and self-righteousness. Also unlike most philosophical virtue ethics, Christian theology suggests that the *telos* is beyond death. The process begins during our life but we are never

---

115. Kotva, *Christian Case*, 86–89.

116. Ibid., 72.

117. Ibid., 74.

fully conformed to Christ's image or reach the beatific vision entailed in friendship with God in this life.[118]

The themes of human freedom and communal nature in Christian anthropology resonate with the approach of virtue ethics. God's grace does not only help free us from being dominated by our sins, but also frees us to participate in becoming a certain kind of person, i.e., a disciple.[119] Further, our communal nature arises from being born of another, being interdependent in needing each other, and in being interconnected in affecting each other. The goal involves fellowship and service to each other. Hence, both the journey and goal involve shared activity and intimate relationships. Our potential cannot be realized without community.[120]

Terrence Rynne argues that the theme of salvation has often been limited to a satisfaction theory interpreted as Jesus simply paying for our sins by his death, and thus, the life of concrete humans in history contains little salvific relevance. This view of salvation led to forms of passivity or simple support for any appeals to law, which often entails rule-based moral reasoning, and to order, which often entails consequences-based moral reasoning. In contrast, he argues with Yoder for a view of salvation as God suffering, accepting, enabling, and healing human history as a more adequate account of the scriptural witness. Rynne claims that salvation only has meaning if it leads to changed behavior in this world by enlisting humans in the way of the cross, which entails identifying with the poor and oppressed, exposing violence and injustice, and building a more human world.[121] Drawing on Bernard Lonergan's corpus of work, Mark Miller explains that Jesus' work on the cross invites a human response to participate in this work of reconciliation.[122] Virtue ethics more adequately accounts for God's ever-present grace and this view of salvation, which entails the risk of conflict for continual personal conversion and transformation of society.

---

118. Ibid., 74–76.

119. Liberation theology emphasizes a similar point about being freed from sin, and for a life of love. Notably, liberation theologies and virtue ethics have been arising in prominence recently.

120. Kotva, *Christian Case*, 90–92.

121. Rynne, *Gandhi and Jesus*, 155–56, 161.

122. Miller, "Why the Passion," abstract iii.

One of the most prominent Christian systematic theologians is Aquinas. His ethical method arises out of his theological project to explain our procession from and movement of return to God. God is the exemplar and we are God's image. We are hard wired to get back to where we came from, i.e. to live in accord with being God's image. Thus, he also prioritizes virtue ethics, specifically rooting his ethics in the theological virtues.[123]

Therefore, several core Christian theological themes indicate the value and priority of virtue ethics, and thus, provide strong support for considering a virtue-based assessment of nonviolent peacemaking.

SUMMARY

I described some of the basic components of virtue ethics and some general differences with rules-based or consequences-based approaches. I also assessed the Christian scriptural models of Jesus and found an overwhelming and consistent example of nonviolent peacemaking practices. Drawing on Spohn and Kotva along with key theological themes, I illustrated the strong support for the priority of virtue ethics in Christian moral theology. This priority has particular contemporary relevance for assessing the prominence of nonviolent peacemaking as found in Jesus' way.

---

123. Pope, "Overview of the Ethics," 30, 48.

3

A Christian Perspective

The Virtue of Nonviolent Peacemaking

INTRODUCTION

IN THIS CHAPTER I consider the contemporary implications of a virtue-based assessment of nonviolent peacemaking from a Christian perspective. First, I argue that nonviolent peacemaking itself is a distinct and central virtue, especially for Christians. Second, I analyze Christian virtue ethics and contemporary Christian practices of nonviolent peacemaking. I offer examples of three Christian theorists' virtue-based assessments of nonviolent peacemaking. Third, I consider how assessing nonviolent peacemaking as a virtue impacts other Christian virtues and their paradigmatic practices. Fourth, I assess how the particular limits noted in chapter one are addressed by a Christian virtue ethic of nonviolent peacemaking. However, I end by raising some questions about the limits of a virtue-based assessment of nonviolent peacemaking from a Christian perspective.

THE VIRTUE OF NONVIOLENT PEACEMAKING

I now want to draw out some implications, particularly of Spohn and Kotva's arguments for the priority of virtue in a biblically informed Christian ethics. I want to argue not only that the practices of nonviolent peacemaking found in the models of Jesus and the broader scriptural witness ought to be assessed in a virtue-based ethic as Spohn and Kotva's work suggests, but also that nonviolent peacemaking ought to be assessed as a distinct and central virtue.[1]

Strong support exists for recognizing that virtue ethics more adequately appropriates Jesus' moral vision. Thus, the consequences-based argument that Jesus' prevailing practice of nonviolence was a mere strategy or technique for a particular historical context, i.e., before Christians came to political power, encounters a serious challenge. Further, Aquinas and Jean Porter argue that it is impossible to describe a virtue without saying what sorts of actions are typical of that virtue, i.e., paradigmatic actions.[2] The scriptural evidence makes it difficult to argue that the pattern of nonviolent peacemaking or love of friends and enemies would not be *at least* one of those paradigmatic actions that correspond to one of the key Christian virtues; and thus, not a mere utilitarian strategy.

However, a Christian virtue entails key features that are satisfied by the portrayal of nonviolent peacemaking in the scriptural witness. First, a virtue is a habit, disposition, or "practice" that realizes a specific good or instance of human flourishing. Drawing on Haring's work, we may say that the Christian virtue of nonviolent peacemaking realizes the good of conciliatory love that draws the enemy toward friendship.[3] Second, Kotva explains that virtues are a means to and constituent elements of the human *telos*.[4] For Christians, Jesus is the way, i.e., the means, and the one who ushers in the present and coming-to-completion Reign of God, i.e., the *telos*. Thus, Jesus' pervasive and consistent practices of nonviolent peacemaking support the characterization of nonviolent peacemaking as a virtue.

Third, Spohn argues that "each virtue of the Christian moral life is shaped by the story of Jesus and preeminently by its conclusion, the cross and resurrection."[5] The instances of nonviolent peacemaking arise centrally in the models of Jesus, and the power of nonviolent peacemaking to realize conciliatory love is ultimately conveyed in the reconciling cross and resurrection. Fourth, a virtue entails the formation and transformation of character, rather than being primarily an external law

---

1. Parts of this section were previously published in McCarthy, "Catholic Social Teaching," 136–50.

2. Aquinas, *Summa*, IIa IIae, q.58, a.1; Porter, *Recovery of Virtue*, 98–99.

3. Haring, *Virtues of an Authentic Life*, 129–31.

4. Kotva, *Christian Case*, 22.

5. Spohn, *Go and Do Likewise*, 32.

or rule for us to obey by rote. Jesus' practice of nonviolent peacemaking aimed to disclose the conciliatory character of God, and to transform the character of his disciples toward a conciliatory love, especially regarding the outcasts, poor, and enemies. The parable of the Good Samaritan illustrated this purpose well, along with Stassen and Gushee's insights about the transforming initiatives.

Fifth, a virtue consists in being a "practice" rather than being a mere technique or instrument that produces goods tangential to the activity. Spohn explains that "practices" are primarily "worthwhile and meaningful in themselves; the enhancement and satisfaction they bring comes from doing them well." The primary intent of Christian nonviolent peacemaking entails a *satisfaction* found in expressing our love and gratitude for God's love, rather than primarily as an instrument to gain political power or receive the reward of heaven. As far as Jesus' style of nonviolent peacemaking cultivates the transformation of our character, it also entails an *enhancement* deriving from the activity itself, which is a constitutive element of a practice. Further, Spohn argues that practices are activities that make up a way of life. Jesus, often called the "way," offered us a way of life, which entailed central practices such as nonviolent peacemaking that ought to make up a human, especially a Christian way of life, rather than function as a mere technique.

Because the portrayal of nonviolent peacemaking in the scriptural witness satisfies these five key features of a Christian virtue, we ought to consider nonviolent peacemaking a distinct virtue rather than merely subsuming it in the paradigmatic actions of other virtues.

CONTEMPORARY CHRISTIAN VIRTUE ETHICS AND NONVIOLENT PEACEMAKING PRACTICES

Contemporary Christian virtue ethicists Kotva and Spohn find most contemporary virtue ethics insufficient. Kotva argues that most accounts leave out themes of forgiveness and reconciliation.[6] Spohn suggests that moral philosophers tend to shy away from describing the content of the good life. When they do suggest content, they often leave out how we can develop the prescribed virtues. Thus, Spohn argues that the New Testament provides definite content to the moral life, and spirituality offers the practices, which foster the virtuous habits that gradually

6. Kotva, *Christian Case*, 61.

transform our character.[7] For instance, perception, dispositions, and identity are all core components of our character. He argues that the spiritual practice of intercessory prayer sharpens our moral perception. The practices of meditation on scripture and discernment would evoke and direct our moral dispositions. The practices of the Lord's Supper and solidarity with the poor would form our identity.

Although techniques differ from practices, an activity may begin as a technique and evolve into a practice, such as a relationship blossoming into a friendship.[8] In chapter 1, Sharp suggested something similar about the technique(s) of nonviolent struggle as a first step, although he does not articulate the possible evolving practices or nonviolence as a virtue with a related set of virtues.

Spohn argues that the main bridge between the biblical text and contemporary ethical practice is the analogical imagination. Jesus' life story in the text sets patterns that lead us to envision analogous ways of acting that are partly the same and partly different. As disciples grow into the life of Christ, "their imagination spots these patterns and carries them creatively into new realizations."[9]

Stassen coordinated the development of a just peacemaking theory, which consists of a set of practices arising into view by using the analogical imagination. Stassen wants to go beyond the question of permissibility for war that pacifists and just war advocates debate, and attends to the question of practices that prevent war and make us into peacemakers. These practices arise in part from Stassen's insight about the triadic structure found in the Sermon on the Mount described above. For instance, Matt 5:21–26 calls us to go make peace with our adversary, so Stassen finds an analogy with the contemporary practice of cooperative conflict resolution or transformation. Matthew 5:38–43 calls us to delivering love that confronts and hopes for transformation in our enemy, self, and the relationship. Thus, Stassen finds contemporary analogies with nonviolent resistance and independent initiatives. As Matt 6:19–34 calls us to economic justice and making God's just Reign a priority, Stassen finds contemporary analogies with fostering just and sustainable economic development, and with advancing democracy, human rights, and religious liberty. Matthew 7:1–5 calls us to acknowledge responsibil-

7. Spohn, *Go and Do Likewise*, 13.

8. Ibid., 42–45.

9. Ibid., 49.

ity for conflict and injustice, repent and seek forgiveness. Stassen finds a contemporary analogy with practices of national forgiveness and leaders apologizing, which corresponds with the virtue of empathy. Matthew 26:51–52 calls us to recognize that those who take up the sword will perish by the sword. Stassen finds a contemporary analogy with reducing offensive weapons and the arms trade.[10]

Haring is often regarded as one of the most prominent scripture scholars in the 20th Century, and was instrumental in the transformation of ethics toward scripture and more gradually toward virtue in official Roman Catholic teaching. Like Spohn and Stassen, Haring uses the analogical imagination by drawing on Jesus as a healer, the Sermon on the Mount, and the new weapons of peace or "transarmament" from Eph 6:10–18. In turn, he suggests the practice of civilian-based defense (CBD) as a way of cultivating the "transarmament," which aims at healing both public and personal life from the contagion of violence. CBD entails using nonviolent resistance to defend against military invasion, occupation or coups. He argues that the Church is called to be a model of healing as a nonviolent community.[11] Eventually, the U.S. Catholic Bishops officially supported serious research into the possibility of civilian-based defense in 1983; however, such efforts remain quite minimal.[12]

Responding to the Gospel models of Jesus' nonviolent peacemaking and the call to sanctification, Rev. McCarthy suggests refining the practice of the Lord's Supper or Eucharist. He argues for the Eucharistic prayers to include an option which articulates the memory of Jesus' New Commandment to love as he has loved us, love of enemies, his rejection of violence, prayer for his persecutors, and his return of good for evil.[13] Fr. Cantalamessa, the Preacher to the Papal Household, also affirms this growing attention to the Eucharist as the sacrament of nonviolence and God's absolute no to violence.[14]

Some of the other key contemporary uses of the analogical imagination for Christian practices of nonviolent peacemaking include: nonviolent resistance and non-cooperation with injustice illustrated by Martin Luther King; living in relationship with and caring for those in

10. Stassen, "Transforming Initiatives."

11. Haring, *Healing Power*, 46, 51, 96, 98, 126, 129.

12. U.S. Bishops, "Challenge of Peace."

13. Rev. McCarthy, "Nonviolent Eucharistic," 5.

14. Zenit News, "Eucharist is 'God's.'"

urgent need illustrated by Dorothy Day; contemplation and inter-religious dialogue illustrated by Thomas Merton; Truth and Reconciliation Commissions illustrated by Desmond Tutu; cultivating friendship and conflict mediation illustrated by the Community of Sant' Egidio; third party nonviolent intervention illustrated by Christian Peacemaker Teams; and the formation of nonviolent communities illustrated by the Catholic Worker communities.[15]

Christian Theorists: Virtue-Based Assessments

I have argued that a virtue ethic more adequately appropriates Jesus' moral vision and practices for us today, particularly regarding nonviolent peacemaking. I have indicated a number of nonviolent peacemaking practices that arise in the Christian tradition, both during biblical times and more contemporary times.

In Catholic tradition, Aquinas' schema of the virtues has been the predominant virtue framework; however, contemporary thinkers have noticed some key limits of his theological ethics. In the early 1960s, Vatican II addressed two of the main limits by re-appropriating the scriptural witness and Jesus for ethics, and expanding the call to holiness beyond the religious to include the laity.[16] In turn, the key set of virtues and paradigmatic actions have been getting refined.

As mentioned earlier, Jesus' life and teaching, especially the beatitudes, suggests an emphasis on character transformation. Pauline texts even offer a number of virtue type lists. Enhancing the role of scripture for ethics emphasizes some key virtues related to nonviolent peacemaking, which are not adequately emphasized by Thomas. For instance, these include meekness, mercy, peacemaking, gentleness, compassion, gratitude, and forgiveness.[17]

Contemporary Catholic Social Teaching has recently suggested a list of "peaceable virtues" in their 1993 document "The Harvest of Justice is Sown in Peace." They offer this list because they argue "true peacemaking can be a matter of policy only if it is first a matter of the heart." The list includes: "*faith and hope* to strengthen our spirits by placing our trust in God, rather than in ourselves; *courage and compassion* that move

---

15. Online: www.catholicworker.org.

16 Second Vatican Council, *Dogmatic Constitution*, par. 39–41.

17. Stassen and Gushee, *Kingdom Ethics*, 48, 50.

us to action; *humility and kindness* so that we can put the needs and interests of others ahead of our own; *patience and perseverance* to endure the long struggle for justice; and *civility and charity* so that we can treat others with respect and love."[18] We should note in this document the correlation between the arising attention to virtue ethics in the Bishops' thinking, and their strongest argument so far for nonviolent peacemaking as a matter of public policy.

In the midst of this transitioning toward virtue and in the emphasis of certain virtues, three key contemporary theorists argue for a virtue-based approach to nonviolent peacemaking: Bernard Haring, Stanley Hauerwas, and Lisa Sowle Cahill.

Haring defines virtue as a form of competence "that enables us to grasp the melody of life as a whole and to arrive at that basic option for good that brings all of our thoughts, desires, and actions to maturity."[19] Haring argues that character formation is the greatest task in life, since Jesus demands a total change of heart and thus a change in our entire lives. The Sermon on the Mount indicates that Jesus shifts ethics from avoiding, to aiming for the heights.[20] Thus, every Christian is obliged to strive with God's grace for perfection. The cultivation of virtue is immeasurably above the mere observance of law through fear of punishment or hope of reward.[21] The central command to love is less a restraining, and more a personal offer to become a person who loves like Jesus.[22] Haring describes Jesus as the prototype of nonviolent action against injustice and heartlessness.[23]

Haring offers a unique contribution by describing nonviolence as a virtue. He suggests that Gandhi was correct to see nonviolence as a central if not the central all-embracing virtue. The object of Jesus' nonviolence is conciliatory love that turns enemies into friends and sinners into saints. Nonviolence arises in us from the amazement that God believes in our capability for such great things. In turn, nonviolence becomes the ultimate proof of our trust and love.[24] It expresses the praxis of the Reign

18. U.S. Bishops, "Harvest of Justice is Sown in Peace."
19. Haring, *Virtues*, 3.
20. Ibid., 17; and *What Does Christ Want*, 22, 27.
21. Haring, *Law of Christ*, 306, 493.
22. Haring, *What Does Christ Want*, 43–44.
23. Haring, *Theology of Protest*, 16.
24. Haring, *Virtues of an Authentic Life*, 129–31.

of God and the core of the proclamation and attitude of Jesus.[25] Haring attends to the importance of formation by arguing that the Eucharist is vital for cultivating the virtue of nonviolence.[26] The Eucharist understood as a corresponding practice of this virtue raises the significance of Fr. McCarthy's argument for refining the Eucharistic Prayer to explicitly include attention to Jesus' nonviolent peacemaking.

For Haring, nonviolence fosters present opportunities and creates new opportunities for life. As a virtue it functions as a directive to a goal, which forbids concern with the casuistry of just wars, death penalty, and violent revolution without making nonviolence our fundamental concern and attempting to first mobilize all nonviolent methods for the conquest of injustice.[27] Haring argues that it is: "absurd to speak of a 'just war' or absolute [rule-based] pacifism when the furthering of social peace, of justice, and friendship among nations is not given due attention."[28]

Nonviolence involves the energies gathered by love and nourished by faith, hope, and charity, which enable us to love our enemies.[29] In thanksgiving for God's love, humans creatively discover and promote the good in ourselves and in our enemies. We acknowledge that we need them, their experience, and their vision to probe together for a fuller truth, and to even die for those who have offended God.[30] Nonviolence entails an active commitment to freedom and arises from a deep conviction of human solidarity, which enables us to show concern for the liberation of oppressors and the oppressed.

Haring argues that nonviolence consists of a disciplined force for the protection of others, such as in the practice of civilian-based defense. However, true victory is not the same as immediate success as illustrated by the deaths of Jesus and Stephen.[31] In accord with these witnesses, the whole Church is called to be a model of healing, nonviolent community, which cultivates all the virtues characterizing peacefulness and nonviolence. Haring suggests the model of the "wounded healer," with

25. Haring, *Healing Power*, 40.

26. Ibid., 126.

27. Ibid., 12.

28. Haring, *What Does Christ Want?* 202.

29. Haring, *Theology of Protest*, 27–28.

30. Haring, *Healing Power*, 30, 86.

31. Haring, *Theology of Protest*, 28, 33, 35, 53.

its key characteristic of vulnerability, to most adequately understand this mission and ongoing conversion.[32] In contrast, Sharp and Ackerman de-emphasize empathy, healing, and reconciliation. For Haring, the key challenge entails how much of our energies of nonviolent love humans set free and coordinate with a view to the gradual liberation of all, i.e., the full realization of every person and their capacities.[33]

From my reading of Haring, although he recognizes nonviolence itself as a virtue, his description of the distinct good it realizes lacks the element of truth, which Gandhi emphasizes. In my upcoming discussion on Gandhi, I elaborate on what Gandhi means by "truth" and the implications for related practices. Also, Haring does not offer a set of core practices that correspond to the virtue of nonviolence, particularly third-party nonviolent intervention and Truth and Reconciliation Commissions. Finally, Haring discusses other virtues but fails to develop clearly how the virtue of nonviolence qualifies or uplifts other key virtues.

Stanley Hauerwas argues that the centrality of nonviolence is the hallmark of the Christian moral life.[34] Christian pacifism corresponds to the virtue of fidelity to God's will and witnessing to God's kingdom.[35] He also uplifts the virtues of patience, hope and justice. Patience entails not trying to make the world the Kingdom but being faithful to the Kingdom by showing to the world what it means to be a community of peace. Christians cultivate hope in the God who promises that faithfulness to the Kingdom will be of use in God's care for the world. Justice arises from people who know their possessions always have an aspect of gift. In turn, justice derives neither from envy or fear nor through the barrel of a gun.[36]

Hauerwas emphasizes the narrative quality of virtue. Sharing in the story of the life of Jesus forms our character and re-engenders the discipleship community.[37] We need to hone the descriptive skills provided by a truthful narrative in order to see situations more fully and in a light that enables us to live in accord with our moral commitments. In

---

32. Haring, *Healing Power*, 129.

33. Haring, *Theology of Protest*, 54.

34. Hauerwas, *Peaceable Kingdom*, xvi.

35. Cahill on Hauerwas, *Love Your Enemies*, 226.

36. Hauerwas, *Peaceable Kingdom*, 103–4.

37. Cahill on Hauerwas, *Love Your Enemies*, 226.

turn, such an ethic of virtue intends to free us from the assumption of felt "necessities" and "givens" we often accept as part of our descriptions and decisions, especially when choosing violence.[38]

The politics of the Kingdom reveals the insufficiency of all politics based on coercion and falsehood, and thus, Hauerwas finds the true source of power in servant-hood rather than dominion.[39] He argues that war functions as the means a people use to protect not only their own existence but also their interpretation of their existence. Hence, in a sense it often does not need "justification."[40] Yet, a community that witnesses to God's refusal to give up on God's creation, i.e., the history of God's peaceable kingdom, reveals the world's true history. The Christians' moral equivalent to war entails first offering themselves without taking another's life. Yet, Hauewas argues that the essential problem for the elimination of war lies in our imagination. The alternative history of God's peaceable kingdom provides the context for such moral imagination.[41]

In turn, he argues that war has been eliminated as a practice for those that participate in God's history, and the Christian task is to witness to this fact with an enthusiasm that cannot be defeated. Thus, one step at a time Christians must work to make the world less war-determined, while believing that a community nurtured on the habits and relations of peace may see new opportunities not otherwise present. Being a kind of people freed from the assumption that war is our fate creates such opportunities.[42]

Within this peaceable kingdom, his attention to the virtue of peacemaking would shift the discussion from what criteria or rules must be met to justify war, to what practices might serve to guide our peacemaking initiatives and to indicate a genuine commitment to peace. For Hauerwas, peace or peacemaking is not the avoidance of conflict, as many rule-based assessments often imply.[43] Thus, he argues that virtues make it possible to sustain a society committed to risking conflict

---

38. Hauerwas, *Peaceable Kingdom*, 123–24.

39. Cahill on Hauerwas, *Love Your Enemies*, 226–28.

40. Hauerwas, *Should War*, 38.

41. Hauerwas, "Should War Be Eliminated?" 422–23.

42. Ibid., 424.

43. Hauerwas, "Peacemaking," 318.

and working out differences short of violence.[44] Hauerwas explains that peacemaking is often seen as a political strategy, rather than a disposition forming the self. Further, "peacemaking is that quality of life and practices engendered by a community that knows it lives as a forgiven people," and thus, lives in truth.[45] In turn, cultivating this virtue requires communities of forgiveness and reconciliation.

The virtue of peacemaking implies imaginative creativity built on habits of peace. But, the absences of these habits make violence seem like the only alternative. Our imagination has been stilled by not practicing confronting wrongs in order to avoid violence. Hence, Hauerwas argues that peacemakers must also require the development of political processes and institutions that engage such conflict transformation.[46]

Hauerwas offers a lot of insight for this book; however, he stops short of a clear set of core practices for the virtue of peacemaking. He particularly leaves out civilian-based defense and the "nonviolent Eucharist" as described by Fr. McCarthy. Because of the popular tendency to describe war as a way of "making peace," the virtue of nonviolent peacemaking provides added precision.

In her book *Love Your Enemies*, Cahill argues that a rule-governed ethic fails to account sufficiently for pacifism, and that a virtue ethic is more conducive to such nonviolent peacemaking. Pacifism is best understood neither as a development out of the "war-justifying problematic" of rule and exception, nor a development of its criteria-oriented pattern of investigation, such as the criterion of the absolute value of human life. Nor is it based on the theory that the violence of modern war will always be disproportionate.[47] As I explained in chapter one, she argues that just war theorists often "grapple with pacifism by posing it as an absolute rule against violence."[48] This way of assessing nonviolent peacemaking is congenial to the rule-exception premises of just war theory. Further, it still assumes that "moral obligations can and should be best articulated in rules about permitted and excluded varieties of specific conduct."[49]

---

44. Hauerwas, "Christian Critique," 479.

45. Hauerwas, "Peacemaking," 319, 321.

46. Ibid., 325–26.

47. Cahill, *Love Your Enemies*, 232.

48. Ibid., 210.

49. Ibid., 212.

In contrast, she begins with the "radical community of disciple-ship that Gospel preaching of the kingdom creates" and seeks a way of life consistent with incorporation into Christ. Rather than focusing on action-guiding norms, she suggests a focus on the formation of communities analogous to biblical communities in terms of their challenge to standard patterns of social living.[50] The virtue question, "what kind of community are we becoming," takes priority over what are the rules or consequences of a particular act.

With this approach, she argues that compassionate pacifism lives out of an inner transformation of one's life in Jesus Christ rather than being born in rules from without. Thus, pacifism represents a *conversion*-governed activity. One experiences being loved and forgiven by God, which evokes faith and commitment as a disciple. It is a commitment to embody the Reign of God "so fully that mercy, forgiveness, and compassion precludes the very contemplation" of doing violence to another person.[51] With virtue ethics, Cahill affirms that love in Matthew's Sermon is more a way of acting than merely an emotion; and thus, it consists of paradigmatic practices such as identifying the concrete needs of victims and perpetrators. Thus, she challenges the claim we can love our enemies while we kill them, as some Christians suggest.[52] As a disciple the pacifist sees the presence of God in all persons and prepares to bear the cross as a member of the body of Christ. Thus, a discipleship character born of love orients the pacifist to act in nonviolent ways.[53] In contrast, Sharp and Ackerman's emphasis on nonviolent sanctions tends to maintain a moral character too often motivated by fear of punishment.

Cahill suggests that pacifism has historically had two different basic orientations: obediential or fiduciary, and empathetic or compassionate. The obediential type imitates the qualities of God disclosed in Jesus because the sovereign Lord requires this. Love of enemies is understood as a witness that transcends and even contradicts human moral sensibilities. Cahill argues that the representatives of this type are Tertullian, H. R. Niebuhr, Yoder, and Hauerwas. The empathetic type roots the nonviolent response in a sense of compassion for fellow humanity and solidarity with all persons for whom Christ died. The representatives of

---

50. Ibid., 13–14.

51. Ibid., 2.

52. Augustine, Ramsey, and Daniel Bell would be examples of this thinking.

53. Cahill, *Love Your Enemies*, 31, 175–77, 233.

this type are Erasmus, George Fox, Dorothy Day, and Merton. The empathetic type resonates more fully with a virtue ethic assessment, with its emphasis on being compassionate, living in solidarity, and being moved or attracted by the good or value in other persons. The obediential type resonates with a virtue ethic assessment to the extent it seeks to imitate the character of God, but less so to the extent it emphasizes obeying a rule that the sovereign Lord requires.

For Cahill, Christian discipleship is integral and distinctive though not necessarily separatist; and it is geared toward cultural transformation more than adaptation. She senses that change according to the Christian Scriptures never arises through "intentional adherence to a superior moral system," but through conversion to compassion. For instance, the Christian scriptures illustrate a "preference for parable, story, image, and exhortation over moral argument, and ambivalence toward law." Cahill claims that "just" war theory differs from pacifism both by being normally construed as a rule-based moral system and *more significantly* by not addressing the Christian pacifist's question about what the Kingdom is or entails. Further, she argues that the essential ingredients of moral discipleship are "inclusive forgiveness and compassionate service," which are grounded in converted community life. From this life "nonviolence flowers," and thus, she argues that nonviolence and the unwillingness to harm seem virtually required by the essential Christian virtues, such as forgiveness and compassion.[54]

She even wonders if the virtues of compassion and mercy survive the limited or just war project. For instance, she argues that beginning with the "right of self-defense, even when exercised on behalf of an innocent victim," shifts the foundation of moral reflection away from the Gospel and its emphasis on virtue.[55] Rather than a discipleship of love, the cross, and the call to holiness, moral reflection arises out of self-assertion and/or the limitation of the obligations to include, love, forgive, and serve.[56] In an analogous attempted shift, the Good Samaritan story illustrates the lawyer's attempt to inquire about the limit or minimum he must do for eternal life, which Jesus challenges by calling us to become perfect or merciful like God.

54. Ibid., 238–39.
55. Example: Jesus rebukes Peter for violently defending Jesus' innocence.
56. Cahill, *Love Your Enemies*, 239.

The teleological aspect of virtue arises with her pointing to the pacifist's sense for the presence of God's Kingdom found in the concrete reality of forgiveness and neighbor love. She claims the immediacy and accessibility of the presence of God's Kingdom combined with its "out of reach" dependence on God's sovereign and gracious acts function as the eschatological tension. This 'future' power in the present sustains compassion, forgiveness, and nonviolence as the edge of God's healing action in history.[57]

Cahill offers many key contributions, particularly regarding Catholic Social Teaching. Yet, she stops short of arguing for a distinct virtue of nonviolent peacemaking. Thus, she doesn't develop a core set of corresponding practices.

Instructively for my argument, another contemporary Christian theorist attempts a virtue-based approach to "just" war theory. Daniel Bell offers some important contributions to engaging acute conflict, especially in the U.S. context. However, crucial limits remain which illuminate the significance of a virtue-based approach to nonviolent peacemaking and to specifically acknowledging the virtue of nonviolent peacemaking. Bell seeks to re-center the just war tradition in the Christian church rather than the state. He focuses on the importance of cultivating virtues, particularly justice in one's daily life as necessary to exercise a "just" war. I agree with his strong critique of the "public-policy checklist" approach to the "just" war criteria that often functions in the state, particularly the U.S.[58] I applaud his mentioning of "developing alternatives" to war as key to the "last resort" criteria.[59]

Bell's approach *may* not theoretically negate the virtue of nonviolent peacemaking. But his failure to acknowledge the specific virtue does have some significant implications, especially for Christians. First, his approach calls us "as Christ's body" to "become just war people" rather than a nonviolent peacemaking people.[60] This vision of human excellence undercuts our call to holiness as followers of Jesus. Recognizing the virtue of nonviolent peacemaking more adequately expresses Jesus' vision of the Reign of God and more adequately allows us to participate in our call to holiness. For instance, he argues that "disciples who are just

57. Cahill, *Love Your Enemies*, 246.

58. Bell, *Just War*, 245.

59. Ibid., 193.

60. Ibid., 66, 101.

warriors will devote *as much* [my italics] time and energy to establishing and improving means other than war . . . as they do to sharpening the instruments of war."[61] If it is Christ we follow, shouldn't it be at least *more time* if not *far more* time? Second, by describing "just" war as a form of "taking up the cross," Bell distorts the purpose of Jesus' cross and his call for us to carry our cross as mentioned above in the discussion on the scriptures.[62]

Third, his approach fails to mention or account for the implications of human dignity. For instance, the potential for the enemy to transform has nothing to do with the "goodness" they have due to their human dignity as creatures of God. This appears to limit his moral imagination for "alternatives to war," particularly some of the core practices of a virtue of nonviolent peacemaking as this book illuminates. Further, this inattention to human dignity fails to uplift the significance and practices of the virtue of humility, which the virtue of nonviolent peacemaking uplifts as described below.[63] Cahill and some others who clearly acknowledge our human dignity, recognize that loving in accord with our dignity, specifically as disciples called to "love our enemies," is not consistent with killing them. However, Bell maintains that such killing in a "just" war is a positive act of loving them.[64] He assumes war can be humanized and does not appear to adequately wrestle with whether the activity of war itself corrupts humans. Thus, he rejects Catholic Social Teaching's recognition of war as a "lesser evil," a tragedy, and in Pope John Paul's words a "defeat for humanity."

Fourth, without the virtue of nonviolent peacemaking he fails to adequately consider the qualifications to the virtue of justice as centered on restorative justice oriented toward friendship and particularly the practice of Truth and Reconciliation Commissions. In the next section, I discuss these qualifications in more depth. Fifth, Bell still tends to describe nonviolence primarily as a strategy with the usage of "toolboxes" to refer to pursuing means other than war.[65]

It remains unconvincing or at least unclear if Bell's project to ground just war in Christian discipleship is successful. However, for the purpose

61. Ibid., 205.

62. See 58.

63. See 89.

64. Ibid., 88.

65. Ibid., 205.

of this book it does appear clear that missing the virtue of nonviolent peacemaking has significant implications for engaging acute conflict, for other virtues, and for living out Christian discipleship. Hence, the work of Haring, Hauerwas, and Cahill offer valuable contributions toward recognizing the virtue of nonviolent peacemaking and the potential implications for Christian discipleship.

IMPACT ON CHRISTIAN VIRTUES
AND PARADIGMATIC PRACTICES

I now consider the impact of a virtue-based assessment of Christian nonviolent peacemaking on key Christian virtues and their corresponding paradigmatic practices. On the one hand, assessing nonviolent peacemaking as a virtue qualifies key Christian virtues, such as justice and courage, along with their paradigmatic practices. On the other hand, it also uplifts a set of particular virtues, which often get less attention when nonviolent peacemaking is assessed as primarily a rule or a strategy. For instance, these uplifted and sometimes even qualified virtues include prudence, humility, solidarity, hospitality, and mercy.

In virtue ethics, the moral life anticipates growth opportunities more than reacts to dilemmas by merely applying rules or techniques.[66] Therefore, prudence is not simply understood as a habit for carefully obeying the law as in a rules-based approach, nor is it a mere technique for choosing the action with the better consequences as in a consequences-based or utilitarian approach. Rather, prudence understood as a virtue entails a practice of directing the moral agent(s) to transform their deeper desires into habits of virtue. Further, prudence regulates the moral virtues, such as justice and courage, by directing them toward their end.[67] Prudence does this by helping us determine the mean between too much and too little, or what exactly we need to grow in virtue by locating the appropriate tension, i.e., the objectively right.[68] Prudence perceives and determines which courses of activity and specific actions would instantiate the virtues in the specific situation of our lives, i.e., what concretely is the end of a particular virtue relative to the person, and relative to the demands of equality and the common good. However,

---

66. Keenan, "Ten Reasons Why," 361.

67. Keenan, "Virtue of Prudence," 260.

68. Keenan, "Ten Reasons," 360–61.

the specific actions are not the means toward an external goal of virtuous behavior, but rather they are the virtuous behavior.[69] Prudence reflects not only on a specific act or its end, as in a rules or consequences-based assessment, but also on how all of one's acts as a whole fit into the end of human life.[70] In turn, self-understanding is central to prudence, which sets short and long-term goals for growing in virtue.[71] Political prudence directs us toward the common good on which our personal good depends, and significantly assists the formation of a just society.[72]

The virtue of humility suggested to Thomas Aquinas the practice of honoring others, due to what they have of God. Keenan describes humility as knowing the truth of one's place, going against the extremes of pride or domination and self-deprecation.[73] Haring suggests humility arises first from our creature-status or our being given into the world, including our dependence and limits. It also entails the grateful acknowledgement of our own dignity granted by God, including our gifts and possibilities. Humility prepares persons to accept and offer forgiveness. Haring calls humility a cardinal virtue as it "serves as the foundation for the whole edifice of Christian virtue."[74] In turn, corresponding practices today would include being much more committed to human dignity, the universal common good, and international consensus and international modes of action, rather than unilateral or small-scale, interest-based group action. Other practices include contemplation and inter-religious dialogue illustrated by Merton, and conflict mediation illustrated by the Community of Sant' Egidio.

Thomas did not directly address the virtue of solidarity, but recent Catholic Social Thought and liberation theology has highlighted it. For Pope John Paul II, the virtue of solidarity is "a firm and persevering determination to commit oneself to the common good; that is to say to the good of all and each individual." Further, he argues that communion is the perfection of the virtue of solidarity with the poor and oppressed.[75] This virtue arises from Jesus' practice of prioritizing the poor and out-

---

69. Porter, *Recovery of Virtue*, 158–60.

70. Pope, *Ethics of Aquinas*, 40.

71. Keenan, "Ten Reasons," 361.

72. Aquinas, *Summa*, II.II, q.47, a.11; a.10, ad 2.

73. Keenan and Harrington, *Jesus and Virtue Ethics*, 191.

74. Haring, *Law of Christ*, 546–47, 551.

75. John Paul II, "On Social Concern," sections 38, 40.

cast, as well as from acknowledging our social nature, interdependence, and interconnectedness.[76] Solidarity entails taking the victim's side *as* our own. By sustained concrete commitment and affection the victim's side becomes our own. In discerning the 'victim,' the priority for the poor and vulnerable suggests asking, whose equal dignity is unequally threatened, or whose basic rights are most imperiled?[77] Developing the virtue of solidarity entails "cultivating an awareness of the need to forge new ties with the oppressed and to nurture a dialogical, mutually benefi-cial, relationship with them," with the aim of transforming the structures of society.[78] The practice of living with and caring for those in urgent need illustrated by Dorothy Day corresponds to this virtue, as well as the practice of simplicity illustrated by the Bruderhof and Catholic Worker communities.

In acute conflict situations, we would offer solidarity not only with those who are attacked or with those whose basic human rights are violated, but also with those poor and vulnerable who will suffer the most if we choose to engage in the preparation for war as well as in its enactment. For instance, in the recent U.S. wars this would include those without homes, health care or jobs in the U.S. and the civilians in Iraq or Afghanistan, especially those described as "collateral damage." Further, solidarity involves concern for the dignity of those who exercise lethal force, and closely examining if they are acting in accord with their dignity, what kind of people are they generally becoming, and what kind of society are we becoming. For instance, our soldiers' high suicide rates, increasing levels of Post Traumatic Stress Disorder and mental illness, disproportionate rates of homelessness, incidents of murder, child ne-glect and sexism would have heightened relevance.[79] Finally, solidarity includes care for ecology, not merely due to our interconnectedness, but also since ecological damage from war activities most pervasively affects the poor.

76. Sobrino, *Principle of Mercy*, 90–91; Hollenbach, *Common Good*, 189.

77. O'Neill, "Visions and Revisions," 34; "No Amnesty," 638–56.

78. Vogt, "Common Good," 403, 405. Vogt argues that the virtue of compassion focuses on the suffering of specific individuals and emphasizes the affective dimension. Thus, it is a prerequisite for the ability to develop solidarity. I would add that the virtue of empathy, i.e., a capacity to feel and imagine what others are going through, whether suffering or joy, is also central for developing the fullness of solidarity.

79. See 134–35 for more details.

Thomas also did not directly address the virtue of hospitality. This virtue aims at welcoming and often restoring to the community family and friends, the stranger or outcast, those difficult to love, the enemy, new developing life, other animals, and the gift of creation as a whole.[80] Corresponding practices would include: creating houses of hospitality illustrated by the Catholic Worker movement; providing water and ensuring basic human rights for the undocumented; creating the conditions for significantly decreasing, and perhaps ending, abortions and providing basic needs for all children; and creating space for all creation to thrive.

Thomas understood the virtue of mercy as the greatest of the virtues that unites a person with a neighbor. Pope John Paul describes mercy as "promoting and drawing the good from all the forms of evil existing in the world" and in persons.[81] Keenan describes mercy as the willingness to enter into the chaos of another so as to answer them in their need.[82] Thus, mercy entails the practices of listening, being present, and considering the human needs such as meaning, bonding, autonomy, and subsistence. Mercy disposes one to release the tension and possessiveness of situations by instilling a sense of gift and even a wider window for grace. Mercy involves that risk of discomfort, suffering, and even death with an orientation toward perfecting justice. Corresponding practices would include unarmed civilian peacekeeping or third party nonviolent intervention illustrated by Christian Peacemaker Teams, living with and caring for those in urgent need, and even Truth and Reconciliation Commissions illustrated by Tutu.

Key virtues qualified by the virtue of nonviolent peacemaking include charity, justice and courage, as well as Keenan's cardinal virtues of fidelity and self-care, if one were to take his approach. The virtue of nonviolent peacemaking, distinct from the Thomistic virtue of charity, entails particularly drawing enemies toward friendship, and deals with conflict or acute conflict, which call forth a unique set of paradigmatic practices. The Thomistic virtue of charity particularly cultivates friendship with God, which does include loving what God loves, such as strangers and enemies. Thus, the virtue of nonviolent peacemaking

80. Ibid., 412.
81. Pope John Paul II, "Rich in Mercy."
82. Keenan, *Moral Wisdom*, 124.

more appropriately fits as a sub-virtue that arises most fully from charity, as does the virtue of mercy in a Thomistic framework.

Thomas described justice as the main moral virtue directed at right relations with others by rendering what is due. He points to the practices of nonmaleficence and praying for our enemies. He also argues that human law should ultimately intend human friendship.[83] The virtue of nonviolent peacemaking, along with Christopher Marshall's recent work on the scriptural witness of justice, would qualify the virtue of justice to focus more clearly on restorative justice with the *ultimate* intention toward friendship.[84] Yet, restorative justice would primarily aim at healing wounds such that persons are restored to participation in the community with a commitment to basic human rights. The virtue of nonviolent peacemaking would include this, but primarily entail drawing the enemy into friendship, which is a deeper more lasting transformation or good.

Pinackers argues that key differences exist between some western liberal versions of justice and the Christian virtue of justice. For instance, Sharp and Ackerman tend toward the liberal version, which conceives the person as self-centered; and thus, justice aims at a balance of power for the well-being of the majority. Christian tradition primarily conceives of the person as more mutually oriented; and thus, aims not merely at respecting rights but at a certain kind of honor and love for all people. The virtue of justice with the particular aid of the virtues of charity, mercy, and nonviolent peacemaking finds its perfection in friendship.[85]

In turn, the corresponding practices for the virtue of justice would include non-cooperation with injustice illustrated by King, Truth and Reconciliation Commissions, and cultivating friendship, especially with the outcasts, illustrated by the Community of Sant' Egidio. Further, those who aim for justice with the death penalty, and even some who advocate "just" wars will likely become less and less able to maintain such strategies while sincerely trying to cultivate this transformed virtue of justice, particularly if done in connection with the other virtues mentioned.

For Thomas, the virtue of courage most characteristically arises in endurance rather than attack, because it is more difficult to control

---

83. Aquinas, *Summa*, I-II, q.57, a.1–2; II-II, q.83, a.8; I-II, q. 99, a. 2. For Thomas, "right" exists when our relations allow for the satisfaction of our natural needs.

84. Marshall, *Beyond Retribution*.

85. Pinckaers, "Role of Virtue," 295–96.

fear rather than act aggressively. Thus, martyrdom represents its principal act and exhibits most completely the perfection of charity.[86] For Thomas, courage involves strenuous effort to overcome obstacles to the good.[87] Hauerwas explains that courage entails the confidence that God will complete God's work in us even if our enemies take our lives.[88] The virtue of nonviolent peacemaking clarifies or expands the paradigmatic practices of the virtue of courage to the practice of suffering out of reverence for the dignity of others (and self) by risking, perhaps even giving one's life without the distortion of our dignity created by relying on lethal force or by taking another's life. In the early 1980's some Filipinos of the People Power movement often used the word *alaydangal* for nonviolence, which translates as "offer dignity to." Like Pope John Paul II and Pope Benedict XVI, these Filipinos sensed that violence in itself obscures the dignity of both victim and perpetrator, and thus, cultivated this virtue of courage.[89] Corresponding practices would include nonviolent resistance illustrated by King, unarmed civilian peacekeeping or third party nonviolent intervention illustrated by Christian Peacemaker Teams, and civilian based defense.

Keenan has proposed a new set of cardinal virtues based on our types of relationships: prudence, justice for general relations, fidelity for our special relations, and self-care for our unique relation to self.[90] The virtue of nonviolent peacemaking would qualify the virtue of fidelity by accenting a willingness to risk conflict within our special relations of blood, marriage, friendship, sacrament, etc., with the aim to deepen these relations. With the virtue of nonviolent peacemaking, conflict functions to expose the deeper wounds and needs in our relations, with the aim of conciliatory love. This qualification protects against special relations becoming a kind of blind support, a mere source of comfort, or a structure to maintain the status quo under almost any circumstances. For instance, friendship in U.S. culture can often mean to merely support the other's actions regardless of what choices or habits they engage. Corresponding practices for the virtue of fidelity would now include

86. Aquinas, *Summa*, I-II q.123, a.6 and I-II q.124, a.3.

87. Pope, "Overview," 44.

88. Hauerwas, *Christians Among*, 161.

89. John Paul II, Homily at Drogheda, 19–20. Sacred Congregation, "Instruction on," sect. xi, par. 7.

90. Keenan, "Proposing Cardinal Virtues," 723–28.

nonviolent communication illustrated by Marshall Rosenberg or the CARA process illustrated by Pace Bene, mediation or counseling, shared prayer, and the sacrament of reconciliation.[91]

The virtue of nonviolent peacemaking would also qualify the virtue of self-care as our unique relation to our self. With nonviolent peacemaking, we would attend more closely to the types of violence we often inflict on ourselves and to the practices, which bring balance and a transformative healing to our person. For instance, the virtue of nonviolent peacemaking would indicate practices for self-care such as meditation or centering prayer to re-orient a fragmented way of life, the sacrament of reconciliation, counseling, retreats, and various artistic endeavors, such as journaling, dance, or playing an instrument. The virtue of nonviolent peacemaking also provides an emphasis on the source and value of our dignity, our deeper connection with others, and thus, allows us to understand self-care in a way that more easily transcends self-preoccupation and the unwillingness to lay down our lives for others.

ASSESSMENT OF CHRISTIAN APPROACH

In chapters two and three I have initiated the process of addressing the limits found in the rule-based and strategy-based assessments of nonviolence described in chapter one. I argued that Christian practices of nonviolent peacemaking are most adequately assessed through a virtue-based ethic and that nonviolent peacemaking itself represents a distinct and central virtue, especially for Christians. Then I offered examples of three contemporary Christian theorists' virtue-based assessments of nonviolent peacemaking. In turn, I considered how the virtue of nonviolent peacemaking uplifts other virtues and qualifies key virtues.

I have noticed a number of ways a virtue-based assessment arising from the Christian tradition addresses some of the limits suggested from chapter one. Key limits addressed of the rule-based assessments include the following. They tend to focus on whether to use violence or not, and thus to neglect practices to guide our peacemaking initiatives. They tend to blur nonviolent peacemaking with either nonresistance or just war theory, with the associated narrow view of nonviolence as a mere abstaining from violence or conflict. They give inadequate attention to virtue, which often results in a narrow view of prudence as a mere habit

91. Pace Bene, "Four Steps."

to obey the rule(s), and in neglecting the kinds of persons or groups who do the interpreting and weighing of rules.

Key limits addressed of the strategy-based assessments include the following. They overemphasize utilitarian reasoning, which often leads to conceiving the practices of nonviolent peacemaking as mere techniques; to a shift away from personal integration and transformation; to maintaining a moral character primarily motivated by fear of punishment; and to an insufficient attention to the formation of kinds of communities needed to envision, strategize, and sustain nonviolent struggle. They emphasize wresting power from the other, which often leads to a willingness to use humiliation and ignoring the dignity of the opponent, and to de-emphasizing empathy, healing, and reconciliation. They perpetuate western liberalism's tendency to narrowly frame the moral reasoning options, which too often leaves out a virtue ethic.

However, limits also remain of this virtue-based appeal arising from Christian tradition. First, to what extent can we translate various Christian arguments about virtue into other religious traditions or more public traditions of discourse and policy? Second, even if such arguments about virtue can be translated into other religious traditions, do such traditions indicate a similar priority toward a virtue ethic, especially regarding their nonviolent peacemaking practices? Third, even if such arguments about virtue can be translated into more public traditions of discourse and policy, to what extent will they be persuasive enough amongst competing arguments to form such policy?

In the next chapter, I continue to address some of the limits that arose in the rule-based and strategy-based assessments. But I also engage the above questions about virtue as I explore Gandhi and Khan's contributions to a virtue of nonviolent peacemaking.

4

Hindu and Muslim Contributions

Gandhi and Abdul Ghaffar Khan

INTRODUCTION

IN THIS CHAPTER, I continue to address the limits of the rule-based and strategy-based assessments elaborated on in chapter one. However, I also move toward addressing some of the questions noted at the end of chapter three concerning the translatability of a Christian virtue-based assessment of nonviolent peacemaking practices within other religious frameworks, and the persuasiveness of a virtue-based approach in public discourse and policy. I approach these questions by first exploring Gandhi's theory of nonviolence and corresponding practices, as a representative figure of Hinduism. Next, I explore Abdul Ghaffar Khan's theory of nonviolence and corresponding practices, as a representative figure of Islam. Although these figures draw closely on their religious traditions, I am not suggesting they function to embody the whole religious traditions of Hinduism and Islam. Finally, I summarize their contributions to a virtue-based assessment of nonviolent peacemaking.

GANDHI

Gandhi has been the most prominent modern nonviolent leader. He offers invaluable insight into a virtue-based assessment of nonviolent peacemaking, and into the questions about the limits of a Christian virtue-based assessment for public policy.

Historical and Social Context

Gandhi was born on October 2, 1869, in India during the British colonial rule. His father died when Gandhi was sixteen. In 1891, he traveled to England to study law. Two years later, he journeyed to South Africa for work but encountered severe color discrimination. In response to this, he committed himself to transforming racial injustice. In 1894, he organized the Natal Indian Congress to promote political participation of Indians living in South Africa. Ten years later he established a weekly journal called *Indian Opinion* and organized Phoenix Settlement as a place to live in community, simplicity, as vegetarians and to train for campaigns. Gandhi's first *Satyagraha* (most basically "clinging to truth,") campaign began on September 11th, 1906 regarding a proposed law discriminatory to Indians. The British first imprisoned him in 1908 but he continued negotiating with British leaders, initiated a second *Satyagraha* campaign, and eventually wrote *Hind Swaraj*, i.e., self-rule, in 1909. From 1910 to 1914 he established Tolstoy Farm focused on training people in *Satyagraha*, initiated a third *Satyagraha* campaign, underwent public fasts, and spent more time in prison, but eventually he negotiated the Indian Relief Act, which removed some of the burdens for Indians. Then he left South Africa for good and sailed to India.[1]

In 1915, Gandhi established the Sabarmati Ashram in India to train *Satyagrahis*. Two years later he began leading *Satyagraha* campaigns for rights of peasants in the British colony. From 1919 to 1929 he led two all-India *Satyagraha* campaigns, fasted multiple times as penance for violence committed by his own people, was imprisoned multiple times, and became leader of the Indian National Congress. The third all-India *Satyagraha* began in late 1929 and involved the historic Salt March of 1930, which challenged the British Empire for making poor Indians pay for Indian salt as a way to promote the sales of British salt in India. Rows of nonviolent Indians continued to approach the armed guards as they continually struck the Indians. This event succinctly exposed the brutal violence of British colonialism in contrast to the nonviolent quest for independence of the Indian people. In 1932 and onward, Gandhi shifted his emphasis to removing "untouchability" within the Indian people in part to strengthen their collective commitment to nonviolence. Untouchability referred to those considered unclean and even below the

---

1. Gandhi, *Gandhi Reader*, 511–13.

lowest caste. Gandhi's new emphasis included numerous fasts, even risking death, and a new publication called *Harijan*, a term Gandhi coined for the untouchables and which meant "children of God." Many people attempted to take his life. In 1942, the Indian Congress passed the final all-India campaign with Gandhi as the leader. More fasts followed to spur negotiations and to end communal violence. As negotiations for independence intensified, Gandhi tried to ensure Hindu-Muslim unity but ultimately India split with the formation of Pakistan. At times, the British sought to divide and disrupt Hindu-Muslim relations before the official split. Yet, India gained its independence in 1947. Six months later Gandhi was assassinated.[2]

Theory of Nonviolence

Gandhi's theory of nonviolence arises out of his sense of God, as being in all of us, so that all humans exist in unity as one. Thus, he argues that the sin of one affects us all and in a sense arises from us all. Hence, Gandhi says that because the "sin of one is the sin of all," humans shall not "destroy the evildoer but to suffer for" them.[3] Further, because humans exist in unity, Gandhi claims that human nature unfailingly responds to the advances of love sooner or later.[4]

The ultimate aim for human life is the vision of God, and the most apt way Gandhi found to describe God is Truth.[5] In turn, truth functions as the goal for humanity.[6] However, humans reach truth only by means of nonviolence, i.e., *ahimsa*.[7] For Gandhi, nonviolence is love in essence, but also includes non-injury, sympathy and compassion.[8] Since means and ends are one and the same in his worldview, Gandhi argues also that God is love, or nonviolence.[9] Further, Gandhi claims that when the

---

2. Ibid., 513–17.

3. Gandhi, *Collected Works*, vol. 43, March 16, 1930. See also *Essential Writings*, 77.

4. Gandhi, *Collected Works*, vol. 68, December 24, 1938; *Essential Writings*, 122.

5. Gandhi, *Collected Works*, vol. 63, August 29, 1936; *Essential Writings*, 75.

6. Gandhi, *Collected Works*, vol. 31, July 15, 1926; *Essential Writings*, 100.

7. Gandhi, *Collected Works*, vol. 87, April 18, 1947; *Essential Writings*, 125.

8. Gandhi, *Collected Works*, vol. 68, December 29, 1938; *Essential Writings*, 112. Gier, *Virtue of Nonviolence*, 31.

9. Gandhi, *All Men*, 63–64; *Essential Writings*, 73.

"practice of nonviolence becomes universal then God will reign on earth as God reigns in heaven."[10]

The method Gandhi coins for this human adventure toward God is *Satyagraha*, which means firmly holding to truth. In Indian languages, truth also means "the real" and "the good." *Satyagraha* is the power or force, which arises from a relentless search for truth and living in accord with truth.[11] Key aspects of this truth include the ultimate unity of all being, and human equality.[12] Michael Nagler explains this truth according to Gandhi as: "there is no such thing as a 'win/lose' confrontation because all our important interests are really the same, that consciously or not every single person wants unity and peace with every other."[13] However, each of us perceives truth partially, and thus, Gandhi argues that no violence is permitted to impose one's partial sense of the truth as if it were the complete truth.[14] Humans lack the capacity to know the absolute truth, and even if we could, Gandhi says persons cannot be coerced to truth.[15] In order to be open to the fuller truth, humans ought to recognize our own partial perspective and be open to the truth from others. Further, in conflict situations the method of *Satyagraha*, which lights up the unity of truth and nonviolence, ought to be relied on to bring out the latent truth under or beyond the partial truths present in conflict.[16]

The basic principles of *Satyagraha* include the following. First, the means more fully determine the ends, so that destructive means like violence will never bring constructive ends such as a functioning democracy and a justpeace. Violence destroys not only because it kills but also since it promotes disunity, distrust, denial of our dignity, and often hatred, along with habits of violence. In the short-term, we may not notice this, but a larger view shows how we end up "lurching from crisis to crisis when we try to 'solve' our problems with violence." Second, humans should fight against the evil intentions, acts, and systems—not

10. Gandhi, *Essential Writings*, 95.

11. Gandhi, *Selected Works*, 185; *Essential Writings*, 87.

12. Gier, *Virtue of Nonviolence*, 148.

13. Nagler, "Hope or Terror," 7.

14. Rynne, *Gandhi and Jesus*, 48.

15. Gandhi, *Collected Works*, vol. 19, March 23, 1921; *Essential Writings*, 87. Gier, *Virtue of Nonviolence*, 148.

16. Rynne, *Gandhi and Jesus*, 48.

the person doing evil acts. In other words, the human dignity and life of the opponent or so-called enemy remains in the front of one's consciousness and orients how we engage them. Third, actions have more consequences than the immediate, visible results we aim at. For instance, often the longer-term positive effects of constructive means such as nonviolence ripple out farther than persons ever imagine. Nagler explains that nonviolence sometimes works in the immediate, visible way, but always works in the more lasting, long-term, both in regards to character development and structural transformation. Nagler argues that destructive means such as violence sometimes works in the immediate, visible way, i.e., "stability," but never works in the long-term way.[17]

For instance, the Salt March of 1930 did not fully change the immediate law it aimed at, but it transformed the character of large numbers of Indian people toward a firmer courage and wider imagination about their potential. Further, the violence of the British in this incident seen in stark contrast to the nonviolent actors of India, worked in the immediate way by generally maintaining the salt law, but it also deflated Britain's standing in the international community, which significantly contributed in the long-term to Indian independence.

The method of *Satyagraha* focuses on cultivating the "willingness to take on suffering in order to win someone over who is acting wrongly,"[18] and as a way to fight injustice.[19] Gandhi did not have a low value for life, rather he realized that in the long-term this method results in the least loss of life, ennobles those who lose their lives, and enriches the world for their sacrifice.[20]

Satyagraha activates a kind of force or power that changes people for the better, whether in the short-term or the long-term. Kenneth Boulding calls this "integrative power," which entails acting in accord with our human dignity and drawing the dissident back into the community sooner or later. Boulding says, "sanctions alone, threat alone, will not do this. If we think of power merely in terms of threat power, we will get nowhere." Threat or destructive power means, "If you don't give me what I want, I'll give you something you don't want." Political institutions and the military too often rely on this type of power. Economic or

17. Nagler, "Hope or Terror," 19–21. See Mirror Neurons in bibliography.

18. Ibid., 18.

19. Gandhi, *Collected Works*, vol. 14, January 24, 1918; *Essential Writings*, 91.

20. Gandhi, *Collected Works*, vol. 28, October 8, 1925; *Essential Writings*, 93.

productive power represents another key type of power, which means "I'll give you something you want if you give me something I want." Economic and some government institutions often rely on this type, which can be exploitive at times.[21] In contrast, Gandhi explains that nonviolent noncooperation aims not to punish or inflict injury on the opponent, but rather to make them feel that in us they have a friend, and thus, to reach their heart.[22] This represents a stark contrast to both Sharp and Ackerman who emphasize nonviolent sanctions, which impose punishment, costs, and suffering on the opponent, and generally are less willing for the nonviolent actors to take on the suffering.

As an example of integrative power, Gandhi's practice of *Satyagraha* aimed at and led to friendship with his British opponents, and led India and Britain into an era of cooperation and mutual benefit. In contrast, Algeria used violent means to gain their independence against French colonialism. Not only did they lose nearly 900,000 lives and India lost only a few thousand, but also this method strained the relations between Algiers and France almost to the present day.[23]

Gandhi says, "Nonviolence is the greatest virtue, cowardice the greatest vice." While this virtue springs from love and always offers to suffer this vice springs from hate and always willingly inflicts or permits suffering. He continues, "Perfect nonviolence is the highest bravery," i.e., expression of courage.[24] Further, for Gandhi, nonviolence is not merely a private virtue but a social or public virtue, which ought to be extended to the national and international scale. Gandhi points to the example of Jesus' suffering, and says, "Jesus lived and died in vain if he did not teach us to regulate the whole of life by the eternal Law of Love."[25]

The virtue of nonviolence expresses the distinct good of truth understood as the ultimate unity of all being and human equality. This also includes drawing enemies toward friendship. Further, this virtue uplifts the significance of other virtues. Gandhi said, "*Ahimsa* (nonviolence)

21. Nagler, "Hope or Terror," 23. Boulding, *Three Faces of Power*. See Mirror Neurons in bibliography.

22. Gandhi, *Collected Works*, vol. 68, October-November 1938. Cited in *Essential Writings*, 98.

23. Nagler, "Hope or Terror," 22.

24. Gandhi, *Collected Works*, vol. 42, October 31, 1929. Cited in *Essential Writings*, 107.

25. Gandhi, *Collected Works*, vol. 68, January 2, 1939; *Essential Writings*, 107.

does not displace the practice of other virtues, but renders their practice imperatively necessary before it can be practiced even in its rudiments."[26] For instance, Gandhi indicated the virtues of humility, patience, self-control, self-suffering, power, and courage are essential to nonviolence and to defeat the temptation to retaliate and respond with violence.[27] The attention to the poor and marginalized, which characterizes the virtue of solidarity, also became especially significant for Gandhi's practice of *Satyagraha*.

Describing nonviolence as the greatest virtue along with a corresponding set of virtues suggests that Gandhi did not view nonviolence as rule-based, i.e., as primarily a rule against violence. Nonviolence primarily entails character transformation and developing a corresponding imagination, which moves the person or a society along the spectrum from cowardice, to the capacity for violence, and ultimately to living nonviolence, i.e., Satyagraha. Gandhi said it was "personal to everyone," and thus, based on the present development of the character and perception, i.e., the virtues, formed within the context of the person's life story.[28] In other words, nonviolence is not primarily a "mechanical matter" either as an absolute rule against violence, or as a rule with a set of exception-making criteria like the "just" war theory.[29]

However, like Aquinas' virtue-based ethic he does associate other rules as pointers to developing virtue. For instance, he says in general it is better to fight the aggressor, even with violence, than to resort to the passive form of being a coward.[30] In the face of injustice, if a person sincerely only sees two choices, violence or passivity, then Gandhi suggested to choose violence. However, if a person chooses violence, then after the incident the person is not triumphal, but rather the person ought to commit herself to addressing the root causes of violence in the society, which led to such an incident.[31]

26. Cited in Gier, *Virtue of Nonviolence*, 136.

27. Gandhi, *Collected Works*, vol. 68, January 28, 1939; *Essential Writings*, 123. Gier, *Virtue of Nonviolence*, 121.

28. Gier, *Virtue of Nonviolence*, 54.

29. Gandhi, *Collected Works*, vol. 28, 3.

30. Gandhi, *Collected Works*, vol. 13, 232; *Harijan 4* (March 28, 1936), 49; Gier, *Virtue of Nonviolence*, 53–54.

31. Gandhian Institute Bombay and Nagler, class notes.

Further, Gandhi did not view nonviolence primarily as a strategy based on utilitarian reasoning as found in Ackerman and Sharpe. He says that nonviolence primarily entails a life force or way of life, which implies as complete self-purification as is humanly possible.[32] Gandhi said, "Utilitarianism is a heartless doctrine and has done harm to humanity. The only real, dignified, human doctrine is the greatest good of all (*sarvodaya*), and this can only be achieved by uttermost self-sacrifice."[33] In utilitarianism, the means are more independent, external, or lacking inherent connection to the ends. Gandhi explains the difference between utilitarianism and his understanding of nonviolence, "one rupee can buy us poison or nectar, but knowledge and devotion (or nonviolence) cannot buy us salvation or bondage."[34] The latter represent not media of exchange but the things we actually and ultimately desire. While utilitarianism often requires the most efficient or painless means to maximize pleasure, attain one's political objectives, or serve the greatest good for the greatest number, virtue ethics often entails difficulty, challenge, struggle, and at times intense suffering.[35] Resonating more with virtue, Gandhi focuses his method of *Satyagraha* on the willingness to take on suffering in order to transform injustice and relations of hostility.

In Gandhi's *Sataygraha*, the means more fully determine the ends than in utilitarianism. Maganbhai Desi, who worked with Gandhi in India, specifies the following as Gandhian means: virtues of honesty, sincerity, love, charity, integrity, and rectitude. The utilitarian approach, which separates more the means from ends, can more easily slip into justifying violent means to an apparent peaceful end, such as the atomic bombing of Japan to end World War II.[36] In the context of a virtue-based approach, the focus on human character and the virtues as constituting the human good would less likely resort to such a means. Further, Gandhi claims that since we inadequately know the consequences in advance, the means which we have control over must be kept as "pure," holy or as similar to our envisioned ends as possible.[37]

32. Gandhi, *Collected Works*, vol. 62, February, 1936; *Essential Writings*, 110.

33. Cited in Gier, *Virtue of Nonviolence*, 136.

34. Gandhi, *Hindu Dharma*, 161; Gier, *Virtue of Nonviolence*, 142.

35. Gier, *Virtue of Nonviolence*, 142.

36. Ibid., 143.

37. Weber, "Nonviolence Is Who," 256.

By comparing Gandhi's non-utilitarian view to Sharp and Acker-man, the implications arise more clearly. Their utilitarian approaches view conflict as adversarial and the primary purpose as defeating the opponent by wresting power away from them. In contrast, Gandhi shows primary concern with re-establishing communication rather than defeating the adversary. He views the opponent as a partner in the struggle to satisfy the needs of all.[38] In turn, the primary adversary is the unjust or violent qualities of persons or groups rather than the persons or groups themselves. Thus, rather than accepting the tactic of humiliat-ing the opponent, a Gandhian approach emphasizes non-humiliation of the opponent, since nonviolence includes care for the fuller psychologi-cal and spiritual aspects of all persons, i.e., their truth or human dignity.

Sharp and Ackerman's vision of a better society emphasizes growth in freedom from oppression and for control of one's own life. In contrast, Gandhi's vision of a better society primarily requires approximation of truth, to which the opponent offers a contribution. Both Sharp and Ackerman suffer from the limits of western liberal theorizing, such as the view of morality as either rules-based or consequences-based, and the view of the person as primarily a self-interested calculator. Gandhi transcends these limits with his virtue-based assessment and view of the person as oriented to truth.[39]

Finally, Sharp implies that virtue is a mere inner attitude or inten-tion, which fails to establish a practical course of action or capacity to influence political events.[40] In contrast, Gandhi argues that nonviolence is itself a virtue ordered to specific paradigmatic practices and their ex-cellence. For instance, Gandhian nonviolence meant both the practices of a constructive program and obstructive program. Therefore, I now turn to the paradigmatic practices of Gandhian nonviolence.

Paradigmatic Practices

In order to become a *Satyagrahi* and to cultivate the virtue of nonvio-lence, Gandhi encouraged and organized thorough training methods,

38. Ibid., 258.

39. These differences resonate somewhat with the two notions of freedom, freedom of indifference and freedom of excellence, explicated by Pinckaers, *Sources of Christian Ethics*, 329–77, and his two concepts of justice in "Role of Virtue in Moral Theology," 294–97.

40. Sharp, *Gandhi as Political Strategist*, 303–4.

which uplifted paradigmatic practices. Gandhi argues that the training for nonviolence is much harder than the training for violence.[41] One of the key ways to organize such training entailed creating small communities, which soon developed into ashrams later in his life. The term ashram indicates the presence of an explicit spiritual center to the community and Gandhi's evolving self-understanding as a spiritual leader.

According to Gandhi, the first essential of this training consists in a living faith in God. Hence, this enables one to rely on God rather than the sword. Further, although a person may become capable of using the sword one refuses such use because one more clearly knows *every* person represents the image of God. As a result of this knowledge, practitioners of nonviolence must cultivate the art of dying rather than killing. This requires developing a capacity for sacrifice of the highest type in order to be free from fear. As the Christian scriptures proclaim that love casts out fear, Gandhi argues that the practitioner of perfect nonviolence must overcome all kinds of fear, except the awe of God. Not only does nonviolence protect the soul but also one's honor, because being nonviolent is living in accord with being an image of God or our human dignity.[42]

The use of vows or commitments to certain goods functioned as one of the key ways Gandhi used to train *Satyagrahis* to develop the virtue of nonviolence and the related set of virtues.[43] Besides the vows to truth and nonviolence, Gandhi also encouraged the following vows for his *Satyagraha Ashram*: control of the palate, nonstealing, nonpossession, *swadeshi*, tolerance, and the removal of untouchability. For instance, nonstealing required using only the food and clothing one needs. Nonpossession requires continuously simplifying one's life by generally keeping what is basically necessary for the nourishment and protection of one's body. *Swadeshi* requires that one never use articles or products, which conceivably involve "violation of truth in their manufacture or on the part of their manufacturers." In Gandhi's context, this meant not using clothing made from England, Germany, or some companies in India because of the exploitation of workers and harm to the poor. In fact, he created a Village Industries Association to advocate buying not only Indian by especially from the poorer villages of India. Tolerance requires

41. Gandhi, *Collected Works*, vol. 67, May 4 and 14, 1938; *Essential Writings*, 107.

42. Gandhi, *Collected Works*, vol. 67, May 4 and 14, 1938, and vol. 72, August 27, 1940; *Essential Writings*, 107–9.

43. Gier, *Virtue of Nonviolence*, 126.

equal respect for the other principal religious faiths of the world as one's own. This entails the prayer that the defects of each faith, which have arisen due to human imperfection, may be overcome, and that one does not try to convert others to one's own faith. The removal of untouchability required a rejection of "caste," with its "implications of superior and inferior status" or "pollution by contact."[44]

Heartfelt prayer served as the most powerful practice or weapon for Gandhi in overcoming cowardice and other bad habits.[45] He explains that only prayer offers inner peace, and allows us to properly serve our fellow humans. Prayer cultivates a wide-awake consciousness of reality and of God. It also purifies the heart and cultivates humility.[46]

For Gandhi, the practice of fasting frees the soul for efficacious prayer. Thus, he suggested regular fasting as a way to repent of one's own sins and also for sins of others.[47] Gandhi's conviction of the ultimate unity of all being implied that the sins of others could to some degree be set on the path of healing, if he were to take on or enter into the suffering by fasting. For instance, he fasted against the violence committed by his people at Chauri Chaura in 1922. Gandhi believed that he could not demand deep commitment to truth and nonviolence by his people while he found wavering or sin in himself.[48] In all, he entered into eleven public fasts to end violence and injustice, at times even to the point of nearing death. Gandhi provided some guidelines for fasting, especially for political issues that included:

1. being the right person for the job, i.e., known and cared for by many;

2. having the right audience, i.e., only offer toward a lover or one who cares for you;

3. for a reasonable/doable request;

4. as last resort; and

5. if consistent with methods of the campaign and the person's life.

44. Gandhi, *Collected Works*, vol. 13, May 20, 1915; *Essential Writings*, 156–58.

45. Dear, *Essential Writings*, 129.

46. Gandhi, *Collected Works*, vol. 42, January 23, 1930, vol. 28, September 24, 1925 and vol. 61, June 8, 1935; *Essential Writings*, 130–34.

47. Dear, *Essential Writings*, 43.

48. Gier, *Virtue of Nonviolence*, 58.

The significance of prayer and fasting led Gandhi to support a national day for these two practices, which would include the suspension of all unnecessary business.[49]

Living in *ashrams* with these vows, prayers, and fasting, Gandhi came to express two main arms of nonviolence: constructive program and obstructive program.[50] The former meant cooperation with good, while the latter meant non-cooperation with evil. The constructive program entails social uplift of the community, such as empowering the poor and vulnerable through education, job training, political participation, experiments in community living, farming, simplicity, the creation of parallel institutions such as national schools and local courts, the removal of untouchability, and the promotion of Hindu-Muslim unity.[51] Along with fasting, Gandhi notably responded to violence in his movement by shifting the focus to constructive program, e.g. Chauri Chaura in 1922. When his co-leaders got upset with this, he explained that the people have awakened to their own power, without yet controlling this power. Further, the principle of *swadeshi* or localism, which suggested that work on the local scene would have ripple effects on the wider world; functioned as a key ingredient to the constructive program. For example, *swadeshi* included the use of homemade goods such as hand-spun and hand-woven cloth. The Indian practice of spinning your own cloth was a form of empowering the indigenous poor and creating an alternative economic structure to challenge the injustice of the British economic system. Another example of *swadeshi* was his discerned commitment to stay in India rather than going to practice *Satyagraha* in the U.S. with the civil rights movement. Instead, Martin Luther King came to India to learn about Gandhi and then returned to his local scene in the U.S. King began to live out the practice of constructive program later with his Poor People's Campaign.

The obstructive program entails withdrawing support from unjust practices or systems. For instance, practices of this arm would include strikes, boycotts, tax resistance, civil disobedience, becoming a conscientious objector to war, etc. Gandhi valued both arms as important for

49. Gandhi, *Collected Works*, vol. 16, October 4, 1919; *Essential Writings*, 138.

50. Nagler coined the term "obstructive program" which directly confronts systems of power with strikes, boycotts, civil disobedience, etc. *Is There No Other Way?* 177.

51. Nagler, "Hope or Terror," 32; Nanda, *Mahatma Gandhi: A Biography*, 121–22; Singh, *Constructive Programmes*, xiv.

nonviolent social movements. However, he found that prioritizing the constructive program provided the more effective arm for long-term social transformation. In fact, he thought doing the constructive work well, would result in rarely if ever needing to resort to the obstructive program.[52]

As Gandhi grew wiser and more experienced, he began to center his activity on serving and uplifting the poor, i.e., the *Harijan*. This practice directly grew out of his understanding of God, illustrated by his claim that the only way to serve God was to serve the poor.[53] Similar to Latin American liberation theology, Gandhi maintained that God assumed a priority for the poor and oppressed.[54] Further, Gandhi explained that life aims at unity with God and all being. To accomplish such unity requires deliberate sharing of the suffering of others and the eradication of this suffering, e.g., nursing the sick.[55] The practice of fasting intimately connects to serving the poor for Gandhi. For instance, he claimed that identification with the starving poor lacks much meaning without the partial experience of such poverty through the practice of fasting.[56] Gandhi argued that without a belief in the constructive program persons could not develop a concrete feeling for the starved millions, and without such a feeling one could not fight nonviolently.[57] This value for feelings and emotions contrasts with Sharp's de-valuing of them in his strategic-based approach. Further, Gandhi offers this piece of advice for discernment and following God's will: "Whenever you are in doubt, or when the self becomes too much with you, apply the following test. Recall the face of the poorest and weakest person whom you have seen, and ask yourself if the next step you contemplate is going to be of any use to that person. Will that person gain anything by it? Will it restore that person to a control over her or his own life and destiny? In other words, will it lead to freedom for the hungry and spiritually starving millions? Then you will find your doubts and your self, melting away."[58]

---

52. Nagler, "Hope or Terror," 32–33.

53. Gandhi, *Collected Works*, vol. 28, October 25, 1925; *Essential Writings*, 81.

54. Gier, *Virtue of Nonviolence*, 60.

55. Gandhi, *Collected Works*, vol. 28, October 25, 1925 and vol. 73, February, 15, 1941; *Essential Writings*, 81, 114.

56. Gandhi, *Selected Works*, vol. 5, August 29, 1926, 402–3; *Essential Writings*, 139.

57. Gandhi, *Collected Works*, vol. 76, April 12, 1942; *Essential Writings*, 124.

58. Gandhi, *Collected Works*, vol. 89, August, 1947; *Essential Writings*, 190–91.

Contributions to a Christian Approach

Gandhi offers significant contributions to Christian virtue-based assessments of nonviolent peacemaking. First, Gandhi offers a clear interpretation of Jesus as a nonviolent peacemaker, whose law of love calls all Christians to an analogous path. In turn, Gandhi gives even stronger credence to those Christians who offer a similar interpretation of Jesus, such as Haring, Hauerwas, and Cahill. For instance, Gandhi describes Jesus' practices of nonviolence as "par excellence," and argues that orthodox, especially Western Christianity has distorted or even negated the message of Jesus.[59] Gandhi said, "Living Christ means a living Cross," which meant to Gandhi a willingness to suffer as Jesus did, i.e., with nonviolent love.[60] He invites Christians to cling to the Sermon on the Mount, and argues that humanity can be saved only through nonviolence, which represents the central teaching of the Bible.[61] Andre Trocme argues that Gandhi showed the political effectiveness of the Sermon on the Mount.[62]

Gandhi's assessment of nonviolence as the greatest virtue offers a second key contribution. He further clarifies the object or distinct good this virtue expresses as the truth of human equality and the ultimate unity of all being. Further, it also includes drawing enemies toward friendship, as did Haring in his description of the object of the virtue of nonviolence. In turn, Gandhi offers evidence that the virtue of nonviolence translates across some religious traditions. He also heightens the significance of this virtue, by calling it the greatest. Gandhi sheds light on how this virtue raises the significance of other connected virtues, such as humility, solidarity and patience; and how this virtue qualifies other key virtues, such as courage, power, and fidelity.

For instance, the perfection of the virtue of nonviolence is considered the highest form of courage. Gandhi explains that aggressive and retaliatory courage illustrates a complete lack of self-control and a kind of impotence.[63] With the courage of the violent, their shield consists in their weapon, such as a spear, sword, or rifle, while God functions as the

---

59. Gandhi, *Collected Works*, vol. 62, May 20, 1936 and vol. 21, 1921; *Essential Writings*, 79.

60. Gandi, *Young India*, Dec. 31, 1931. Rynne, *Gandhi and Jesus*, 27.

61. Gandhi, *Collected Works*, vol. 21, 1921, vol. 68, December 24, 1938; *Essential Writings*, 79, 123.

62. Rynne, *Gandhi and Jesus*, 1

63. Gier, *Virtue of Nonviolence*, 121.

shield of the nonviolent. The "courage of the violent" is more limited than the courage of the nonviolent.[64] The virtue of power entails practices that actualize a kind of integrative, shared or non-zero-sum power called *sakti* power. By our very existence in unity with all being we have the capacity for this power, which aims to disarm and reconcile warring peoples.[65] By revealing truth, the virtue of nonviolence qualifies Keenan's virtue of fidelity so that our special relations become geared toward realizing the deeper truth about each person and about the relationship, even if conflict ensues. Gandhi also qualifies the virtue of fidelity with a corresponding practice of fasting with or to transform the heart of the other in the special relationship. Gandhi's principle of *swadeshi*, which emphasizes working on the local scene and allowing the fruits to ripple out into the wider world or more general relations, reinforces the virtue of fidelity in its relation to the virtue of nonviolent peacemaking.

Gandhi's practices of nonviolent peacemaking offer a third key contribution. He both reinforces some key Christian practices, but also introduces some unique practices. For instance, Gandhi reinforces the Christian practices of cultivating a living faith in God, prayer, fasting, creating nonviolent communities, and serving the poor and outcast. However, Gandhi accents the practice of fasting in a unique and intense way, particularly with his specific guidelines mentioned above. With his attentiveness to the ultimate unity of all being, fasting aims to highlight this unity and to share more deeply in the suffering that the violence of others creates in the human family, such as the riots of his people. He also underwent fasts in order to enter into deeper solidarity with the poor. Even more, at times he offered to fast unto death, unless violence stopped or an unjust law was ended.

The practice of the constructive program as one of the two main branches of nonviolence represents another Gandhian accent. The obstructive program tends to be the more popular notion of nonviolence in mainstream society. However, Gandhi argues that nonviolence not only includes the constructive program but should also prioritize it. The practices of ashrams to train satyagrahis and the development of local peace teams to restrain violence also provide key contributions.

The ways Gandhi's assessment addresses key limits of the rule-based and strategy-based assessments of nonviolence offers a fourth

64. Gandhi, *Collected Works*, vol. 72, August 27, 1940; *Essential Writings*, 109.

65. Gier, *Virtue of Nonviolence*, 121–22.

contribution. Key limits of the rule-based assessments that Gandhi addresses include the following. First, they tend to associate nonviolence with lacking a practical ethic. Gandhi, perhaps more clearly than any nonviolent actor, illuminates the practical ethic and potential of nonviolent peacemaking. Second, Gandhi's Satyagraha campaign's offer evidence that nonviolent peacemaking protects and promotes human rights more effectively than rule-based approaches often suggest. Third, Gandhi's emphasis on nonviolent training, particularly in *ashrams*, addresses the rule-based limitation that often yields a truncated character and neglects the importance of community formation.

Key limits of the strategy-based, primarily utilitarian assessments that Gandhi addresses and corrects include the following. First, they emphasize wresting power from the other, and thus, understand conflict as adversarial. Gandhi emphasized integrative power that draws people together and aims for friendship. Second, they lack resistance to using humiliation and ignoring the strengths, truth, or dignity of the opponent. Third, they de-value the role of feelings and empathy in the formation of strategy, while Gandhi particularly emphasizes feeling for the extreme poor. Fourth, they give insufficient attention to community formation. Fifth, they de-value the nonviolent practice of taking on the suffering in the situation. Sixth, they suffer the limits of the western liberal framing of morality and view of the person, as disconnected and self-centered. Gandhi offers a virtue-based frame that emphasizes the intimate relation between means and ends, and more adequately senses persons as interdependent and interconnected, i.e., the ultimate unity of all being.

Gandhi's direct participation in political discourse and public policy offers a fifth key contribution. Gandhi experimented with a language and practices that could speak to and enrich all humans. For instance, Gandhi attempted to speak of God in a more accessible fashion with the language of truth. For instance, truth entailed the recognition of human equality and ultimate unity. Further, truth language meant to recognize the truth in each person and to confess the untruth, evasion, and hypocrisy in oneself.[66]

Gandhi's practice of negotiation with British leaders included an appreciation for the truth in his opponent along with the principles of "no fresh issue" and "non-embarrassment." No fresh issue meant that

---

66. Douglas, *Non-Violent Cross*, 35, 38.

if he found himself in a position of advantage politically, he would not push beyond the specific issue for whatever he could get.[67] Such pushing would redefine the struggle as a power struggle rather than a conversation. Gandhi aimed less for the wresting away of power and more for friendship with his opponent.

The Indian National Congress supported his education policy that aimed to increase character building and practical skills rather than overemphasizing academic knowledge. Similar support arose for his economic policy, which focused on the principle of *swadeshi*. For instance, this included an orientation to homemade goods. However, his defense policy calling for a peace army to use nonviolent resistance against a potential Japanese invasion during World War II faced too much opposition in the Indian Congress. Most congresspersons accepted *Satyagraha* as a strategy toward political freedom, but not as a creed or way of life.[68] Nevertheless, the policy of creating peace teams or armies did have success on more local issues, such as confronting riots.[69]

Gandhi also made political claims about democracy and nonviolence. He argued that to become truly democratic a society must become courageously nonviolent.[70] True democracy depends not on the military and police.[71] Gandhi explained that as persons have the capacity to practice nonviolence, so do nations who are made up of persons.[72] In western democracy, Gandhi saw a flawed system that uses the name democracy to exploit others. He claimed that when violence primarily sustains a democracy then that society cannot adequately care for the weak.[73] Gandhi rooted democracy in the worth of the person, and in the decisions of the majority and the rights of the minority. Further, he suggested that ideal democracy would aim for more direct democracy rather than settle for representative democracy.[74]

---

67. Metta, "Glossary."

68. Nanda, *Mahatma Gandhi*, 206, 215–17.

69. Shepard, "Soldiers of Peace."

70. Gandhi, *Collected Works*, vol. 68, November 5, 1938; *Essential Writings*, 119.

71. Epigrams of Gandhiji, Democracy section.

72. Gandhi, *Collected Works*, vol. 68, November 5, 1938. Cited in *Essential Writings*, 119.

73. Gandhi, *Collected Works*, vol. 68, November 5 and Dec. 29, 1938; *Essential Writings*, 119, 112.

74. Bhattacharyya, *Evolution of the Political Philosophy*, 479.

ABDUL GHAFFAR KHAN

I now turn to examine the nonviolent peacemaking of Abdul Ghaffar Khan, whose practices arose within the Islamic tradition. I continue the broadening of the virtue-based assessment to nonviolent peacemaking as I move further into public discourse and I discover unique practices Khan offers as I move toward public policy.

Historical and Social Context

Khan lived in the North-West Frontier Province of India during British rule in the 1900s. He was born in 1890 and died in Pakistan in 1988. He became a friend and companion of Gandhi, and earned the nickname "Frontier Gandhi" for best mirroring Gandhi's way. Khan organized over a hundred thousand people in the practice of nonviolence.[75]

The British and the Pathan tribes of India struggled in violent guerrilla warfare since the mid-1800s. Raised a Muslim, Khan also attended a Christian mission school where he learned a generosity and love that became key factors in cultivating a desire to serve his suffering and impoverished people. In turn, he began schools for his people against the wishes of the British and the Islamic Mullahs, whom the British often upheld in power.[76] Khan intended the schools to educate the villagers of the reforms he planned to introduce. For example, the Province's budget mostly centered on the military and police while social assistance, education and sanitation received inadequate attention. Because of these schools, the British authorities warned Khan to cease his work.[77] In spite of danger, he toured many villages, led teach-ins in restricted areas, and depended on fasting for insight about how to serve. Since the people in power felt threatened, he spent many years in and out of prison. However, the cult of revenge and violence entrenched in Pathan society functioned as one of his major obstacles. Beneath this Pathan violence and ignorance, Khan saw extraordinary endurance and courage, which he committed to lifting up and inspiring. As he began to hear about Gandhi's nonviolent campaign and serving God by serving the poorest of God's creation, he realized that his work with the Pathans entailed not only social uplift, but also the path to freedom.[78]

75. Easwaran, *Nonviolent Soldier*, 16, 88.

76. Ibid., 64.

77. Sharp, *Waging Nonviolent Struggle*, 115.

78. Easwaran, *Nonviolent Soldier*, 69–71, 78, 95–101.

After his wife died in 1926, Khan intensified his work by publishing a journal and encouraging women to participate more fully in society. Khan argued that we men have made a grave mistake following custom and degrading women. He also traveled around India encountering the spirit of revolution, and returned with a challenge to the pride of his people. They responded with an army of nonviolent soldiers, trained and professional. This transformation from intense violence to nonviolent resistance illuminated Gandhi's claim that especially those seriously willing to fight for a cause could prove the virtue of an engaging that transcends violence, i.e., a "nonviolence of the strong."

The *Khudai Khidmatgar* or "Servants of God" became history's first mass professional nonviolent army. They promised to serve humanity in the name of God, to refrain from violence, to forgive, to not create enmity, and to live a simple and active life.[79] Their training camps emphasized volunteer work, such as cleaning houses, spinning cloth, opening schools, and setting up village councils. The unity or solidarity of Pathans took center stage.[80]

In 1930, cries of independence arose throughout India. The Servants of God began educating and organizing. The British arrested Khan and others. As nonviolent protests erupted, troops fired on this disciplined peace army. Without panic the next line stepped forward and received bullets. This continued off and on for the next three to six hours and became known as the Kissa Khani Bazaar massacre with an estimated 200 killed. Finally, troops refused to fire but the repression continued the next few days. By the end of that month the Servants of God had over eight thousand volunteers. Soon a temporary truce was signed with the Frontier receiving significant concessions, although increased suppression followed later.[81] Nevertheless, by 1938 the "Servants of God" grew to more than 100,000.[82]

After Khan got out of prison, he toured the villages visiting the poor and uplifting the women. He also affirmed the value of Hindus as well as Christians and Jews as traditional "Men of the Book." In the spirit of the constructive program of nonviolence, Gandhi came with him and

---

79. Ibid., 104–13.

80. Sharp, *Waging Nonviolent Struggle*, 199–20.

81. Easwaran, *Nonviolent Soldier*, 117–29.

82. Sharp, *Waging Nonviolent Struggle*, 124.

spoke to the Pathans about removing anger and fear in their heart and challenged them to live nonviolence between each other.[83]

As the work for independence continued, WWII began, so the British clamped down on the leaders with many arrests. Hindus and Muslims began to riot, as the political leaders of each group struggled against eachother. However, no riots occurred in the Frontier. Gandhi and Khan tried to travel and calm the violence elsewhere. After the war, the British granted independence but the country split into a Muslim based Pakistan and a Hindu based India. Nevertheless, the transfer of power from the British reflected a deep mutual regard unique in colonial history. Other colonial transitions in the near future failed to approach such fellowship. Eknath Easwaran attributes this to the good will of the nonviolent resistance that "fought" without retaliation and with suffering.[84] Notably, since many leaders of Pakistan resisted the power of nonviolence and Hindu-Muslim unity, Khan spent more time in jail and detention in Pakistan than during British rule.[85]

Theory of Nonviolence

Khan's theory of nonviolence arises out of discernment of his Islamic tradition and his encounter with Gandhi. Like Gandhi, Khan believed all religions were "based on the same Truth." Khan describes nonviolence as love, which stirs courage in people.[86] Nonviolence coincides with Islam, which he describes as selfless service, faith, and love. By faith he means recognition of the spiritual laws that underlie all life, of the nobility of human nature, which implies the ability of people to respond to the spiritual laws, and the power of love to transform human affairs.[87] This recognition of the power of love to transform resonates with the *Qur'an*, when it says, "requite evil with good, and he who is your enemy (or hated) will become your dearest friend (or intimate). But none will attain this save those who exercise patience and self-restraint and are greatly favored by Allah."[88] Khan said, "if you plant a slap after having

83. Easwaran, *Nonviolent Soldier*, 133–57.

84. Ibid., 165–79, 182–83.

85. Wali Khan, "Life and Thought," 21. For further analysis of Khan after the independence from Britain see R. Gandhi, *Ghaffar Khan*, 200–265.

86. A. Khan, *My Life and Struggle*, 143–44, 194.

87. Easwaran, *Nonviolent Soldier*, 13.

88. Brendt, *Non-Violence*, 54–57. *Qur'an*, trans. A. Yusuf, Surah 41:34–36, 319.

been provoked by a slap, then what is the difference between the follow-ers of the *Qur'an* and the evildoer?"[89] Mercifulness is one of the most cited and revered attributes of Allah and is expected of Muslims.[90]

Like Khan's context in the Pathan culture, the social context of the *Qur'an* included a vengeful spirit of many Arabs transformed by the pos-itive quality of *hilm*. This virtue means to channel feelings and passions, by remaining calm and undisturbed even when provoked by others. Muslims so highly regarded *hilm* that it should determine all human re-lations. Key scholars refer to *Hilm* as the "dominant virtue in the *Qur'an*" and the spirit which "dominates the ethos of the *Qur'an*."[91] In the *Qur'an*, the virtue of *hilm* resonates with the virtue of humility, which was also uplifted by the virtue of nonviolent peacemaking in the Christian ap-proach. For instance, the *Qur'an* says "the true servants of the Beneficent God are they who walk on the earth in humility, and when the ignorant address them (insolently) they say, Peace."[92]

To strengthen his sense of Islam and nonviolence, Khan points to the Prophet following the creed of nonviolence in Mecca. Khan said to his Servants of God, "I am going to give you such a weapon that the police and the army will not be able to stand against it. It is the weapon of the Prophet, but you are not aware of it. That weapon is patience and righteousness. No power on earth can stand against it. Endure all hard-ships. Victory will be yours."[93] The Prophet also said, "God fills with peace and faith the heart of one who swallows his anger, even though he is in a position to give vent to it."[94] In Mecca, the Prophet declared sanctuaries and was known for saying, as Jesus said on the cross accord-ing to Christians, "Forgive them Lord, for they know not what they do."[95] The *Qur'an* lifts forgiveness over strict retributive justice by saying "the recompense for an injury is an injury equal thereto (in degree): but if a person forgives and makes reconciliation, his reward is due from Allah."[96]

---

89. A. Khan, "Address to Muslims," quoted in Ramu, *Badshah Khan*, 93.

90. Abu-Nimer, *Nonviolence and Peace Building in Islam*, 68; *The Qur'an*, trans. A. Yusuf, Surah 7:151, 6:165.

91. Mohamed, "Evolution," 90–92.

92. *Qur'an*, trans. A. Yusuf, Surah 25:63.

93. Easwaran, *Nonviolent Soldier*, 103, 117.

94. Abu-Nimer, *Nonviolence and Peace Building in Islam*, 67.

95. Ibid.

96. *Qur'an*, trans. A. Yusuf, Surah 42:40.

Khan's understanding of nonviolence resonates more with a virtue-based assessment. For instance, his servants of God took an oath to practice virtue. Khan elicited obedience by the right of love, i.e., by their attraction to the good and a desire to serve, rather than by fear of punishment or failing to follow the rules.[97] A virtue-based ethic lends one to act primarily out of attraction to the good, rather than a sense of duty or fear of punishment. Further, he says that nonviolence stirs courage in people, i.e., it is a force of character transformation. Comparing the two freedom movements in his province, Khan argued that the "violent movement created fear and cowardice," weakening "people's courage and morale," while the nonviolent movement "made people fearless and brave," inspiring a "high sense of morality."[98] Khan explains that the truly brave or courageous must be right, which resonates with Aquinas' claim that the true virtue of courage requires the virtue of prudence and justice.[99] Further, Khan claimed that love, i.e., nonviolence, creates more than violence. Thus, this creative ability highlights the role of the imagination, which also resonates with a virtue ethic approach. Finally, in his re-education of his people toward nonviolence, he drew on the Pathan tradition wherein each tribe had a shrine of a great saint, i.e., a model of virtue.[100]

In contrast to a strategy-based assessment or a mere policy to be used when it seems expedient, Khan understands nonviolence as an article of faith. Gandhi's insistence on truth and nonviolence in all of life's affairs attracted Khan. Thus, he resigned with Gandhi from the Congress Working Committee, which argued for using lethal force against a potential Japanese attack during World War II.[101]

Khan's theory of nonviolence was deeply immersed in his attention to the poor. For instance, part of his draw to Gandhi's insistence on nonviolence in all of life's affairs involved his experience of Gandhi as a seeker attempting to serve God through serving the poorest of God's creation. Khan thought the freedom, which nonviolence claimed to usher in, ought to be measured by how quickly the lot of the poorest

97. Easwaran, *Nonviolent Soldier*, 112, 155; A. Khan, *My Life and Struggle*, 96.

98. Khan, *My Life and Struggle*, 143.

99. Aquinas, *Summa*, IIa IIae, q.123, a.5; Ia IIae, q.65, a.1.

100. Easwaran, *Nonviolent Soldier*, 101, 131.

101. Ibid., 10, 78.

Pathans would improve.[102] His attention to the poor resonates well with another Muslim peacemaker in Bangladesh, Ahmed Giasuddin, who teaches that we should go and live with the poor. We should know their problems, build them up, and help them know their power.[103]

Paradigmatic Practices

In order to cultivate nonviolence, Khan indicates a set of paradigmatic practices. Similar to Gandhi, he was a vegetarian and often relied on the practice of fasting. However, Khan's accent on this practice involved engaging it primarily for discernment. Through fasting he found a single purpose: to serve God in the spirit of Islam, i.e., to submit. Since God needed no service, Khan decided to serve God's creatures. He gained a conviction about his calling and would not seek rest in this life.[104]

The practice of building schools emerged as a key type of service. Many of his people wrestled with ignorance and illiteracy, which made it difficult for them to organize and resist the British, particularly without a reactive violence. These schools taught agriculture and sanitation, while speaking of the values of sacrifice, work, and forgiveness. The schools challenged both the British, who feared an awakened peasantry, and the Mullahs, who feared the people refusing to give alms.[105]

Like Gandhi and Jesus, Khan's service particularly focused on the poorest of the poor. His schools aimed at these segments of the population. In his speaking, he repeated two main objectives: one to liberate the country and the other to feed the starving and clothe the naked. Part of this attention to the poorest, gave rise to Khan's focus on women. He argued that the traditional system of *purdah* unjustly restricted their participation in society. Again, Khan drew on the core Islamic faith in the *Qur'an*, which he argued taught that women deserved an equal share with men. For instance, "If any do deeds of righteousness—be they male or female—and have faith, they will enter Heaven, and not the least injustice will be done to them."[106] Khan claimed that the oppression of women arose due to men ignoring the ways of God and the Prophet.[107]

---

102. Ibid., 17, 78.

103. Abu-Nimer, *Nonviolence and Peace Building in Islam*, 57.

104. Easwaran, *Nonviolent Soldier*, 71.

105. Ibid., 66, 78–79.

106. Qur'an, Surah 4:124. Also see Surah 16:97, 40:40, 53:45, 92:3, 75:39.

107. Easwaran, *Nonviolent Soldier*, 104, 133.

Perhaps the most distinctive practice Khan offers emerged in the creation of the "Servants of God." They grew into the first mass professionally trained army of nonviolence. They based their way on Islamic principles of universal brotherhood, submission to God, and the service of God through the service of God's creatures. Nonviolence arose in the heart of their oath, which included a promise to practice virtue. They committed to resolving all internal differences and feuds before joining. Other aspects included platoons, officers, army discipline, and marching songs:

> We are the army of God,
> By death or wealth unmoved.
> We march, our leader and we,
> Ready to die.
>
> We serve and we love
> Our people and our cause.
> Freedom is our goal,
> Our lives the price we pay.[108]

They opened schools, did work projects, provided order at public gatherings, and courageously offered their lives in resistance to the British occupation.

Contributions to a Virtue-Based Assessment

Khan makes the following key contributions to a virtue-based assessment of nonviolent peacemaking. First, he broadens the significance of this type of assessment to include the Islamic tradition. As a practicing Muslim, he draws on core teachings about Allah, the Prophet, and the *Qur'an* in his assessment of nonviolent peacemaking. Thus, he exposes a popular myth that Muslims cannot be committed nonviolent peacemakers.[109] He also challenges Muslims to prayerfully search their tradition and attend to the components, which encourage nonviolent peacemaking practices. Like Gandhi, his strong resonance with virtue ethics suggests the virtue of nonviolence translates across some significant religious traditions.

Second, Khan contributes a set of key practices, particularly building a mass professional nonviolent army. This suggests that nonviolence

---

108. Ibid., 13, 112, 113.

109. Nagler, *Is There No Other Way*, 243–47.

entails practices capable of addressing larger-scale conflict rather than only for personal or small-scale conflict. Third, Khan contributes to challenging the myth of nonviolence as a weak force that only works against weak opponents.[110] The British often ruthlessly imposed their colonialism, but especially in their attempts to control the Pathans. Khan offers a number of examples, such as being forced to strip, having a noose tied around their testicles and pulled so that when they fainted the British threw them into a tub of urine and excrement.[111]

Fourth, Khan contributes evidence that extremely violent persons in the midst of a violent culture contain the potential for transforming into disciplined practitioners of nonviolence. This transformation occurs in the context of leadership emphasizing a virtue-based assessment of nonviolence rather than primarily a rule or strategy type assessment. Further, this evidence supports Gandhi's claim that the truly nonviolent have the capacity to use violence and choose to reject it, rather than those who are passive or cowardly. Khan's work challenged the myth that nonviolence offers a way for the nice or soft, rather than the strong and courageous.[112]

Fifth, Khan contributes to addressing the limits of the rule-based and strategy-based assessments of nonviolence. Key limits of the rule-based assessments that Khan especially addresses include the following. First, they truncate the imagination of nonviolent peacemaking practices, such as by associating nonviolence with lacking a practical ethic, especially for large-scale, international conflicts. Second, they associate nonviolence with the passive, cowardly, or weak. Third, they imply a narrow view of prudence as primarily following rules rather than directing the development of key moral virtues, such as courage and patience.

Key limits of the strategy-based assessments that Khan especially addresses include the following. First, they shift away from personal integration and transformation, while Khan emphasized the transformational practice of fasting and integrating truth and nonviolence in all of life's affairs. Second, they maintain a moral character primarily motivated by fear of punishment rather than love or attraction to the good, which Khan highlights in his educational approaches. Third, they

---

110. Ibid.

111. A. Khan, *My Life and Struggle*, 145.

112. Nagler, *Is There No Other Way*, 243–47.

de-value the nonviolent practice of taking on the suffering in the situation, while Khan made this central to the "Servants of God" peace army.

SUMMARY OF CONTRIBUTIONS

In sum, Gandhi and Khan offer key elements to a virtue-based assessment of nonviolent peacemaking.

1) They demonstrate that a virtue-based approach functions within other religious traditions and cultures, and even within a religiously plural society. With their realization of the Truth grounding all major religions, they willingly worked across and learned from various traditions.

2) Their approach certainly resonates with the Christian virtue-based emphasis on conciliatory love and drawing enemies toward friendship, as well as on the priority of the poor and marginalized. Gandhi particularly emphasized Jesus' practices of nonviolence as par excellence. Gandhi also assessed nonviolence as the greatest virtue, but he extends the object or distinct good of this virtue as expressing truth, which entails human equality and the ultimate unity of all being. Gandhi offers a recasting of the priority of the poor and marginalized with language of the constructive program, as the main arm of nonviolence.

3) Both Gandhi and Khan regularly engaged in the practice of fasting.

4) They each promoted the practice of forming peace teams or armies. Khan illustrated that extremely violent persons in the midst of a violent culture contain the potential for transforming into disciplined practitioners of nonviolence.

5) They demonstrated how a virtue-based approach impacts public discourse and policy.

PART THREE

U.S. Public Discourse and Policy

5

Initial Implications of a
Virtue-Based Assessment

INTRODUCTION

To this point I have analyzed religious teachings and figures that support a virtue-based assessment of nonviolent peacemaking. This chapter moves us into the question of whether these three religiously grounded assessments are both translatable and persuasive in U.S. public discourse and policy formation, and if so, to what extent. First, I begin by describing and assessing the predominant methods of moral reasoning in U.S. public discourse and policy, particularly around issues of acute conflict and peace work. I use the U.S. military to exemplify both a key player in forming the culture, from which arises our public discourse and policy, and in illustrating the effects and limits of U.S. public discourse and policy. Second, I argue for a virtue-based method by drawing on the U.S. example of Martin Luther King and reflecting on a contemporary organization called the Nonviolent Peaceforce. Third, I explain how the role of virtue in U.S. public discourse and policy should be enhanced and qualified by the virtue of nonviolent peacemaking. However, I also acknowledge three key limits of a virtue-based assessment for U.S. public discourse and policy.

MORAL REASONING IN U.S. PUBLIC
DISCOURSE AND POLICY

In the U.S., a form of liberal, Western moral theory tends to predominate in public discourse and policy formation. In this framework, the general moral options seem to be between obligation-based approaches, with categories such as principles, rules, duties, law, and human rights, or consequences-based approaches, particularly utilitarian versions that focus on strategy and preference satisfaction. For instance, Rawls affirms this framework of options and argues for a rights-based theory of justice.[1] Philosophically liberal ethical thinkers often see the two general moral approaches described above as the only choice, and thus often exclude the possibility of a virtue-based approach.[2] However, each of these two predominate moral options can also generate a virtue theory about how virtues might function in their respective approach. For instance, virtues and their core practices could primarily function to help us follow the rules, or as a mere means (e.g., tool) to some more external end, rather than being more integrated or more fully determining of the near and distant end(s). In both versions of moral reasoning in this context, the virtue of prudence often gets narrowed to self-interested rationality.

In this context of moral reasoning, Adam Smith is a seminal thinker in the development of the predominant virtues in the U.S., particularly for white, middle-upper class males. Smith's four cardinal virtues include self-command, prudence, benevolence, and justice, but self-command is pervasive through all of these as the virtue that rightly orders, controls, and moderates our sentiments or passions. Rather than adopting a perfectionist approach, Smith understands virtue to function with a kind of ordinary prudence. Thus, one often does his public duty when called upon, but tends to mind to his own business and become an apolitical citizen.[3]

The various virtues that arise within the two predominant methods of moral reasoning in the U.S. closely relate to deep-seated values and commitments. Robert Bellah argues that an elaborate, well-institutionalized civil religion exists in the U.S. alongside the explicitly religious traditions. This civil religion expresses itself in a set of beliefs, symbols, and rituals. For instance, he examines a number of presidential inauguration addresses and founding documents to discover what people say on solemn occasions, because this is often "indicative of deep-seated

---

1. Rawls, *Theory of Justice*. In contrast, MacIntyre argues for a virtue-based ethic, *After Virtue*, 3rd ed. Also see Slote, "Virtue Ethics and Democratic Values," 5–37.

2. Hauerwas, *Peaceable Kingdom*, 20.

3. Berkman, "Recent Theological Developments."

values and commitments that are not made explicit in the course of everyday life."[4]

What are some of these values and commitments, which give form to an implied U.S. *telos*? Bellah argues that the words and acts of many founding fathers were selectively derived from Christianity, but this civil religion is not Christianity itself. Rather, the god of this civil religion is "unitarian," austere, more related to order, law, and right than to salvation and love. Drawing on Washington and Jefferson, Bellah argues that key leaders in the U.S. often consider the U.S. as established by God to be a light to the nations. During the civil war, Bellah argues that the theme of sacrifice was "indelibly written into the civil religion," particularly through the words and death of Lincoln. This theme found physical and ritualistic expression in national cemeteries and holidays, such as Memorial Day.[5]

These values and commitments provide some of the goods from which conceptions of public virtue arise. However, in our moral culture focused on rules or utilitarianism, such people normally make the virtues even less explicit than the deep-seated values and commitments. Nevertheless, Bellah's account suggests that people in the U.S. often translate, knowingly or not, religious themes, values, and virtues into broader public discourse. This translation is not always smooth, such that some of the original or traditional ways of understanding the themes and values often get transformed, sometimes to a great extent. Further, the values and virtues of civil religion also get translated into religious traditions, often challenging and sometimes revising traditional religious understandings of their own values and virtues. For instance, although the Christian scriptures speak quite often about care for the poor and outcast, a number of U.S. Christians and congregations fail to prioritize care for the poor by either simply blaming the poor for their struggle or supporting policies that increase wealth inequity. Another example is U.S. Christians that often support any war the U.S. enters rather than adhering to "just" war theory in Christian tradition, not to mention Jesus' witness of nonviolent peacemaking.

---

4. Bellah, *Beyond Belief*, 170, 175.

5. Ibid., 175–79.

U.S. Military and Moral Reasoning

Within the U.S. context where rules-based and utilitarian-based methods of moral reasoning predominate, our public discourse and policy around issues of acute conflict and peace work take on particular characteristics. The U.S. Military functions as a key player in *forming* the culture, from which arises our public discourse and policy-making. Further, the U.S. Military represents a helpful illustration of the *effects* of such discourse and policy.

Residents in the U.S. often lift up those in the U.S. Military as our "heroes" or models of virtue and excellence. Former member of the U.S. Military Andrew Bacevich explains that soldiers have come to signify "who we are and what we stand for," while being elevated to the "status of national icon." The phrase "support the troops" readily finds expression on bumper stickers, in every-day conversation, in the media, in religious sermons, and on the lips of most politicians. Bacevich argues that the "one unforgivable sin" in our society, particularly for political elites, entails appearing as or actually failing to support the troops.[6]

Our society's language and symbols often consist in framing and metaphors of stark competition, us vs. them, either/or, blame and punishment, threat power, and types of violence, which resonate with a militaristic worldview.[7] Such language and symbols regularly show up in children's cartoons and toys, video games, key sporting events, television and movies, journalism and political discourse, school discipline methods, and our criminal justice system that is largely immersed in a retributive justice model. Wink describes the pervasiveness of this language and symbols as the "myth of redemptive violence," which he argues functions as our society's dominant religion.[8]

Our financial habits and policy also support this high regard, emphasis and apparent dependence on the military, particularly for its high-tech weaponry and for the soldiers who employ it.[9] For instance, in FY 2011 (Oct. 1, 2010 to Sept. 30, 2011) our Congress spent about 58 percent ($700 billion) of its discretionary budget on the military and war supplements, while only about 4 percent went to education and about

6. Bacevich, *New American Militarism*, 1–2, 23–25.

7. Ibid.; Clymer, *America's Culture of Terrorism*; Waldrep, ed. *Documenting American Violence.*

8. Wink, "Myth of Redemptive Violence."

9. Bacevich, *New American Militarism*, 1.

1.5% ($19 billion) went to international poverty-focused development and humanitarian assistance.[10] This $700 billion for the military does not include the cost of nuclear weapons, Veterans affairs, and interest from past Pentagon spending, such as past wars.[11] In 2009, the U.S. spent about *46 percent of all global military expenditure*, with the second highest country at 6 percent.[12] In 2008, despite a global recession the U.S. generated *68 percent ($37.8 billion) of global arms sales*, including 70 percent of arms sales to developing countries.[13] In 2005, the U.S. had 737 military bases around the world.[14]

Global Distribution of Military Expenditure[15]

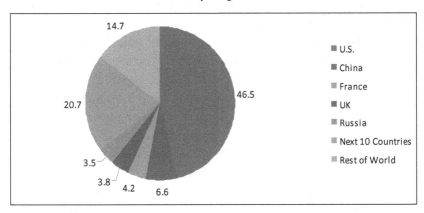

In 1961, President Eisenhower warned us about the potential abuse of the "military-industrial" complex as a key aspect of our financial and political habits. More recently, John Perkins described his life as an "economic hit man" that participated in the coordination of U.S. corporate and national interests, World Bank loans, and CIA or military intervention.[16] Others describe the "Iron Triangle" as the collusion of some con-

10. National Priorities, "Discretionary Budget." OMB, "U.S. Dept. of Defense." U.S. Catholic Bishops, "Hill Notes." The full budget includes mandatory spending programs, such as social security, medicare, and medicaid.

11. Friends Committee, "How Is?"

12. Shah, "World Military Spending."

13. Shanker, "U.S. Increases Its Share;" Shah, "Arms Trade is Big-Business."

14. Johnson, "737 U.S."

15. Shah, "World Military Spending."

16. Larrow-Roberts and Perkins, "Breaking Out," 329.

gresspersons, Department of Defense officials, and military contractors. This triangle includes contractors lobbying and giving campaign contributions, congress providing contracts and weak oversight, and DOD officials asking for more weapons, overlooking contractor cost overruns and later receiving high paying lobby jobs with such contractors. These claims deserve further investigation and ongoing vigilance. Not only does the U.S. military significantly shape our culture and public discourse indirectly through language, symbols, and financial habits, but also Bacevich argues that senior military leaders have directly sought a larger influence in policy formulation, rather than merely executing the policy of civilian leadership.[17] Reports of Lt. General Caldwell's attempt to use "psych ops" on U.S. Senators and other VIPs toward gaining more funds and troops in Afghanistan offer just one example.[18]

The U.S. Military represents a very ordered and rule-based culture, and yet in terms of forming strategy it often relies on utilitarian calculations. In this context of moral reasoning, the U.S. Department of Defense argues that the ultimate function or ends of the U.S. military consists in serving liberty, opportunity and prosperity. This entails being a beacon of light to those in dark places, a commitment to democratic values, and serving our national interests.[19] Our past commander in chief, George Bush, put it this way: "Throughout our history, love of country and the hope of peace on earth have inspired America's armed forces . . . You are helping bring freedom, security and peace to millions in Iraq and Afghanistan and elsewhere, and you are helping to protect the American people here at home."[20]

Toward these ultimate or general ends, the U.S. military usually describes its more proximate function or end as the waging and winning of wars. However, in 2005 a new directive came out to indicate that the "job of planning and training to win the peace after a war is now virtually as important to the military as the conflict itself."[21] In this context, stability represents peace. For instance, in Iraq this includes building a government from scratch, ensuring access to water and power, and

---

17. Bacevich, *New American Militarism*, 30.

18. Hastings, "Another Runaway General."

19. U.S. Dept. of Defense, "National," 7; U.S. Marines, "First to Fight."

20. Bush, "President Extends."

21. Sappenfield, "New Military Goals."

"stamping out insurgents."[22] In the 2008 National Defense Strategy, the key objectives included: defend the homeland, win the long war against violent extremist movements, promote security, deter conflict, and win our nation's wars.[23] The 2010 Quadrennial Defense Review lists the following key objectives: prevail in today's wars, prevent and deter conflict, prepare to defeat adversaries in a wide range of contingencies, and preserve and enhance the force.[24]

In order to attain these ends a core part of the training in the U.S. military entails developing a "warrior ethos,"[25] which consists of some key values and virtues. Generally, these often include integrity, honesty, courage, and loyalty.[26] For instance, the Army focuses on loyalty, duty, respect, selfless service, honor, integrity, and personal courage.[27] The Marines and Navy focus on honor, courage, and commitment.[28] The Air Force emphasizes integrity, service before self, which explicitly prioritizes rule following, and excellence in all they do.[29] Discipline, obedience, and patriotism represented other character traits often associated with military personnel.

Without intending any disrespect to the U.S. Military or individual soldiers, the training methods for inculcating these virtues and some key aspects of the actual military culture have come under scrutiny. For instance, J. Joseph Miller argues that they tend to adopt a "technician's mode" of teaching, which leads to a stifling of discussion and a rigidity of thinking. He explains that the military comfortably adopts the rule-based role-model approach to teaching ethics. But they experience much more discomfort with the process of philosophical reasoning and questioning that functions as a central part of inculcating virtuous behavior, especially prudence.[30] The illegality of selective conscientious objection, i.e., the right of a soldier to refuse to participate in an unjust war, along with policies that refuse to negotiate with our enemies

---

22. Ibid.

23. U.S. Dept. of Defense, "National."

24. U.S. Dept. of Defense, "QDR," slide 3.

25. Sappenfield, "New Military Goals."

26. Wolfendale, "Developing Moral Character."

27. U.S. Army, "Soldier Life."

28. U.S. Marines, "Core Values;" U.S. Navy, "Personal Development."

29. U.S. Air Force, "Core Values."

30. Miller, "Squaring the Circle," 205, 208.

or "terrorists" illustrate this devaluing of deliberative reason.[31] Further, virtuous action requires not merely the performance of good action but the exercise of rational moral agency and deliberation. In some cases, the minimal hours devoted to ethics training as compared to other areas of military training also expresses this devaluing of moral deliberation.[32] For instance, a 2006 US Army Training and Leadership Development report stated "initial and annual ethics training will (each) be one hour in duration."[33] Only these two sessions were required in a year. In other contexts, when training attends to moral reasoning, the purpose clearly states for the discernment of duty, i.e., a rule-based approach. Thus, these characteristics of military training particularly create problems for developing virtue and more generally for taking seriously the role of virtue in our peacemaking practices.

However, Dr. Wolfendale argues that larger issues of military culture itself also function as obstacles to cultivating virtues. For instance, she suggests that these include the way in which unit cohesion develops in the military, and the way in which military personnel learn to kill and to think about killing. In the military world, group bonding entails cultivating the dispositions to work in an authoritarian, hierarchical, order-based, and group-oriented environment. She argues that unit cohesion often arises from unofficial rituals, which include brutal and humiliating bullying or hazing. In turn, new recruits get desensitised not only to their own suffering but also to inflicting suffering on others. Empathy and tolerance of dissent within the group are eroded. Thus, this reinforces a type of obedience *more* mechanical than reflective as central to effective military functioning.

Lt. Grossman, also a psychologist, historian, and professor, explains how the military transformed its training to kill methods after WWII. Studies indicated that only 15–20 percent of soldiers along the line of fire actually fired their weapon in WWII. He argues that military history confirms this pattern of trying to overcome an "innate resistance to killing" in at least 98 percent of persons, if not all. Since WWII, a new level of "psychological warfare" on our own soldiers developed. This

---

31. Foster, *"One War at a Time,"* 18.

32. Wolfendale, "Developing Moral Character."

33. Dept. of Army, Army Training.

included particular attention to recruiting the more malleable brains of teenagers.[34]

Dr. Wolfendale explains that the training of people to kill in the military involves the dehumanisation of the enemy, the use of morally neutral language, and the displacement of responsibility for the violence of war. Soldiers get desensitised to the *idea* of killing by using names like "towel-heads" or "animals," and by painting the enemy as morally, racially, socially, or physically inferior.[35] Lt. Grossman argues that such emotional and intellectual withdrawal often arises from these tactics of cultivating moral, cultural, and social (or class) distance, which helps persons to "think the unthinkable." Grossman also adds "mechanical distance" which refers to the video game-like unreality of killing through screens and thermal or sniper sights.[36]

Soldiers get desensitized to the *act* and *responsibility* of killing by using language like "engaging" the "target" in their training. Lt. Grossman describes the Pavlovian and Skinnerian conditioning processes of training as "doing the unthinkable." For instance, rather than shooting at bull's eye targets, they now shoot at human shaped targets with immediate feedback. Denial defense mechanisms, which he calls "denying the unthinkable" represent another key element of the training. The constant rehearsals of killing often generate a denial that one actually kills another human in actual war. Additionally, an embedded sense of group absolution for killing arises along with encouragement from leaders to presume justification for the killing of enemy combatants.[37] These above training processes and traits typify what psychologists call "moral disengagement," which research indicates to be common in military personnel and linked to problematic forms of obedience and violations of International Humanitarian Law.[38] A soldier who fought in Somalia in 1993 remarked: "And it was so much like basic training, they were just targets out there, and I don't know if it was the training that we had ingrained in us, but it seemed like a moving target range, and you could just hit the target and watch it fall and hit the target and watch it

34. Grossman, *On Killing*, 3–4, 251, 264–65, 332.

35. The language some U.S. Soldiers used at Abu Ghraib for the prisoners they tortured.

36. Grossman, *On Killing*, 160.

37. Ibid., 148–55, 251–56, 323.

38. Muñoz-Rojas and Frésard, *Roots*, 8–10.

fall, and it wasn't real."[39] Another soldier said of his first experience of killing, "When I killed, I did it just like that. Just like I'd been trained. Without even thinking."[40] Wolfendale argues that killing is experienced as a thoughtless action divorced from any moral context. Thus, it often bypasses moral autonomy, which significantly truncates the development of virtue.

Similar troubling elements show up in Spc. Peterson's and Ethan McCord's stories. Peterson interrogated suspects in Iraq, but resisted some of the techniques and soon committed suicide in 2003. The official probe of her death noted "earlier she had been reprimanded for showing *empathy* for the prisoners." They described her as unable to be two people, one in the cage and another outside the wire. They critiqued her for failure to separate personal feelings from professional duties.[41] Soldier Ethan McCord found two children wounded by U.S. helicopter fire. As one boy died in his arms while he tried to save them, and then being told harshly by his superior to leave them go, i.e., "what the f--- are you doing," he found himself struggling and seeking counselling. Yet, his superiors scolded him by saying, "get the sand out of your vagina."[42] Other soldiers report similar scolding and use of this sexist phrase.

Such training, group bonding and absolution, and devaluing of empathy and counselling lends military obedience more readily to become destructive precisely due to the crippling of moral capacities that would normally prevent immoral and destructive obedience. A 2002 study on dysfunctional military decision-making indicated that "groupthink" and ignoring moral principles remains a problem, even among leadership, such as colonels and captains.[43]

Key questions a virtue-based approach would ask about our training and our moral activity is "who are we becoming?" and "who ought we to become?" not only in the moment or short-term but also in the long-term. Jeffery Bordin argues that the present kind of military training often creates greater psychological problems after combat. Some finally begin to reflect on the morality of their actions only after com-

---

39. Moore, "Ambush in Mogadishu."

40. Grossman, *On Killing*, 257.

41. Mitchell, "U.S. Soldier,"

42. McCord, "Eyewitness Story,"

43. Bordin, "On the Psychology," 3, 28.

bat, and struggle with how easily they killed.[44] Others suffer various forms of post-traumatic stress syndrome, with over 60,000 diagnosed by the Veterans Association in 2007.[45] Another study showed one-third (340,000) of vets from Iraq and Afghanistan who received veterans care between 2001–2005, got diagnosed with a psychosocial disorder, while one-quarter (260,000) had a mental illness.[46] However, some reports indicate that the Army pressures doctors not to diagnose post-traumatic stress syndrome and soldiers not to even receive counseling.[47] Research indicates that those with post-traumatic stress syndrome commit acts of violence nearly four times more often (13.3) than other veterans (3.5). Developing research focuses on another form of post-traumatic stress syndrome called perpetration-induced traumatic stress, which raises serious questions about the trauma of *committing* the act of violence itself, not simply being around it.[48]

Since a virtue-based approach emphasizes who our soldiers and their families are becoming as persons, the following issues become key indicators in assessing the morality of U.S. military activity. Soldiers face epidemic suicide rates at 120 veterans per week in 2005 and over twice the rate of other Americans.[49] Suicides of army recruiters through April 2009 reached three times the overall army rate in 2008, and the general army rate of suicides rose higher through May 2009 than in 2005.[50] This approach would also take more seriously the soldiers' levels of drug use and violent crime, such as murder, abuse of children and women.[51] Peterson and McCord offer a striking illustration of the embedded sexism along with the devaluing of counseling and empathy, which represents a central capacity for a healthy person and society. Homelessness represents another key indicator a virtue approach lifts up. Veterans

44. Capt. Kilner, "Military Leaders to Justify Killing," 5.

45. Kay and Estrada, "Female Veterans Report."

46. Reuters, "Mental Illness Common."

47. Yoanna and Benjamin , "Coming Home;" McCord, "Eyewitness Story."

48. MacNair, "Perpetration-Induced Traumatic Stress," 266.

49. ABC News, "US Army;" Keteyian, "Suicide Epidemic."

50. Thompson, "Why Are Army;" DeLuce, "US Army Base Shuts Down."

51 Philips, "Casualties of War;" Fort Carson in Colorado has had 10 soldiers arrested for murder or manslaughter since 2006. The 4th Brigade has a murder rate 20 times that of young males in the U.S. as a whole. Associate Press, "Child Abuse," and Chin, "Child Abuse;" Kay and Estrada, "Female Veterans Report," and CNN, "U.S. Marine Guilty."

make up 25% to 33% (nearly 195,000) of all homeless, while only making up 11% of the population.[52] These statistics and testimony resonate with training in a kind of virtue, which, as one former First Sergeant puts it is "designed to tear apart the civilian"[53] and which embodies chants like:

> Hey, hey, Captain Jack,
> Meet me by the railroad track,
> With your rifle in your hand,
> I want to be a killing man.[54]

Former soldier Kenneth Eastridge, serving ten years for accessory to murder, says, "The Army trains you to be this way. In bayonet training, the sergeant would yell, 'What makes the grass grow?' and we would yell, 'Blood! Blood! Blood!' as we stabbed the dummy. The Army pounds it into your head until it is instinct: Kill everybody, kill everybody. And you do. Then they just think you can just come home and turn it off. . . . If they don't figure out how to take care of the soldiers they trained to kill, this is just going to keep happening."[55] And perhaps, as we have seen above, the training to kill itself is just as much a problem?

Persons and institutions may incorporate virtue in rules-based or utilitarian-based moral reasoning, but this often leads to a limited or distorted conception of virtue and in the kind of virtues emphasized. In key ways, the U.S. Military often exemplifies this limited conception. The role of virtue in the discourse and training of the U.S. military en-counters at least three significant limits, which contribute to forming a culture with significant effects on our public discourse and policy. First, virtue is not adequately taught. Second, the virtues represent less of a virtue-based ethic and more of a theory about how virtue functions in a rules-based or utilitarian-based way of moral reasoning.[56] For instance, prudence tends to be primarily about either a habit for following duty or the rules; or about using whatever means considered "necessary" to attain strategic ends or an immediate goal, such as winning a war, rather than prudence being ordered to human flourishing and the common good for all people. The narrow conception of prudence as self-interested

52. CNN, "Former Addict"; Ponder, "Suicide and Homelessness."

53. Powers, "How to Survive Military Basic Training."

54. Garamone, "March to Marine."

55. Philips, "Casualties of War."

56. Stanford Encyclopedia, "Virtue Ethics."

rationality (often short-term focused) merely gets re-framed as ensuring the national interest. Third, the kinds of people too often being created by inculcating these military virtues raise serious questions about their well-being and subsequent effects on our society.

In the U.S. context, the limits of rules-based or utilitarian-based methods of moral reasoning extend further. Pinckaers argues that western liberal moral theory often envisions the person as self-centered, rather than having a natural inclination to know and love, and as social by nature.[57] In turn, he claims that liberal justice too often aims at the equality between rights of individuals to satisfy their needs, rather than restoring right relationship and aiming for friendship. Society primarily gets viewed as a collection of self-interested persons that justice tries to organize in order to maintain a balance of power and contribute to the well-being of the majority, rather than the common good of all persons. He argues that liberal societies at times view persons as morally either good or evil, rather than acknowledging both the good and evil within each person.[58]

Hauerwas argues that not all societies emphasize rules like U.S. society. Our rules seem to hold the promise of impersonal justification of moral behavior and the appearance of ensuring objectivity. In turn, people in the U.S. often dismiss questions about our ultimate end (*telos*) or "the good life," since they do not seem subject to rational argument. U.S. thinkers tend to assume morality primarily entails quandaries, such as a conflict between rules, and thus, we give little attention to how and why a situation gets described as a moral problem. He argues that the stress on rules fails to develop virtues to sustain us in negotiating irresolvable moral conflicts. Thus, U.S. residents cultivate too little imagination and practices to face moral dangers, especially of violence.[59]

Hauerwas describes peace or peacemaking as reconciliation, truth, or a justpeace rather than reducing it to the avoidance of conflict. In comparison, U.S. public discourse and policy, particularly in the military tends to reduce peace to the notion of stability. Further, Hauerwas argues that virtues make it possible to sustain a society committed to risking conflict and working out differences short of violence. Rather than a positive disposition forming the self, people often view peace-

57. Pinckaers, "Ethics, 134.

58. Pinckaers, "Role of Virtue," 295.

59. Hauerwas, *Peaceable Kingdom*, 19–22.

making as a mere political strategy. In contrast, the virtue of peacemaking implies imaginative creativity built on habits of peace that confront wrongs in part to avoid violence. But especially in a rules-based or utilitarian-based framework of moral reasoning, the absence of these habits and the consequent stilled imagination make violence too often seem like the only alternative.

In sum, the predominance of rule-based and utilitarian-based moral reasoning in U.S. public discourse and policy fails adequately to highlight and develop virtues, and offers inadequate imagination and practices to confront and break the cycle of violence. Core elements of the U.S. military represent one key cause and consequence of these limits on our public discourse and policy, particularly around issues of acute conflict and peace work.

MARTIN LUTHER KING: VIRTUE-BASED MORAL REASONING

Martin Luther King exemplifies how a virtue-based method of moral reasoning, particularly a virtue-based assessment of nonviolence, can both function well in and correct key limits of U.S. public discourse and policy. King illustrates how such an approach protects and promotes human rights as well as offers strategic effectiveness in the U.S.

As a Christian proponent of nonviolence, King thoroughly resonates with a Christian, virtue-based assessment of nonviolent peacemaking and the related set of virtues. He also draws heavily on Gandhi's virtue-based theory and practice of nonviolence. For King, nonviolence evokes the internal transformation, which cultivates the conciliatory love and creation of a beloved community.[60] This corresponds to the virtue of nonviolent peacemaking cultivating conciliatory love that draws the enemy toward friendship. King explained that the aim never entails defeating or humiliating the oppressor(s), but rather winning their friendship and understanding, as Gandhi did with the British leaders in India. Also, as Gandhi understood the virtue of nonviolence as aiming at the truth of our equal dignity and ultimate unity, King affirms the dignity of all persons, as well as all persons being interdependent and all life being interrelated.[61] King realized "that a synthesis of Gandhi's method of

---

60. King, "Pilgrimage to Nonviolence," 39; King, "Stride Toward Freedom," 487.

61. King, "Stride Toward Freedom," 449, 468–69; King, "Where Do We Go From

nonviolence and the Christian ethic of love is the best weapon available to Negroes for this struggle for freedom and human dignity."[62] Gandhi helped King realize how the ethic of love could function in social transformation, rather than merely for individual relationships.[63] Gandhi's work and later emphasis on untouchability in India offered insight to King's work on racial issues in the U.S.[64]

Further, King argues that nonviolence in its truest sense is a way of life rather than a mere technique or strategy. Part of this insight arose when he recognized his need to let go of his gun for protection against potential intruders. As Gandhi taught, King argued that the means people use must be as pure as the ends people seek. For King, violent means never bring permanent solutions, solve no social problem, and merely create new and more complicated problems. As for Gandhi, a nonviolent campaign requires training and preparation, which forms habits and transformation of character. For instance, self-purification is one of the four key steps.[65] The workshops in self-purification infuse our moral deliberation with the disposition for other-regarding love, which grounds the virtue of prudence. Thus, the virtue of prudence is not reduced to self-interested rationality or "national selfishness," but entails the primacy of a disposition for other-regarding love or "international brotherhood," which recognizes and honors the human dignity of the other.[66] Further, the virtue of prudence directs the moral agent(s) to grow rightly into one's orientation to moral virtue, rather than functioning merely as a habit to obey rules or merely as a technique for choosing the action with the better consequences.

King's virtue-based approach critiqued a view of law or policy, which equated positive or written law with justice, and thus dissuades from breaking laws. In contrast, King argued for the distinction between just and unjust laws. A just law "uplifts human personality," humanizes, lights up our dignity, and cultivates a healthy character; while an unjust law "degrades human personality," de-humanizes, clouds our dignity, and entangles our character. "One who breaks an unjust law must do so

---

Here?" 626.

62. King, "Tribute to Gandhi."
63. King, "Pilgrimage to Nonviolence," 38.
64. King, "My Trip to the Land of Gandhi," 27.
65. King, "Stride Toward," 450, 482; King, "Letter From," 290, 301.
66. King, "My Trip," 29.

openly, lovingly, and with a willingness to accept the penalty," even if it's imprisonment. Those who do this in order to arouse the community's conscience over its injustice are expressing the highest respect for law.[67]

King understood the public practice of nonviolent direct action as bringing "to the surface hidden tension that is already alive," rather than creating tension. This practice exposes injustice so that the community can see it clearly and then engage in fruitful public discourse or negotiation. He contrasted this practice with those who are more devoted to order or stability, which prefers a negative peace that entails the absence of tension or conflict.[68] For instance, this emphasis on order is congruent with present U.S. policy that too often simply understands peace as stability.

The public characteristic of King's discourse and campaigns illustrates that the practices corresponding to the virtue of nonviolent peacemaking avail themselves to others beyond religious actors. Some of the particular practices included collecting the facts about possible injustice, negotiation, self-purification, and direct action, which risked suffering to expose injustice and violence. To the extent persons participate regularly in these practices, they are more likely to experience character transformation and cultivate the virtue of nonviolent peacemaking. Rather than conceiving of nonviolence as a mere private or group virtue, King illustrates how the virtue of nonviolent peacemaking actualizes a fundamental capacity of a broader range of, if not all, humans for recognizing our equal dignity and practicing conciliatory love. To the extent this virtue cultivates the recognition of our equal dignity, it satisfies a key requirement of public discourse, i.e., basic respect. Thus, this virtue contains a more humanistic dimension even if we do not all agree on a full conception of human excellence as its ultimate aim or *telos*. Therefore, King's discourse and campaigns illustrate that people ought to conceive this virtue as a publicly accessible and civic virtue rather than as private or merely for religious persons.

King's virtue-based approach also allowed him to see the interrelatedness among racism, poverty, and war along with the need to eradicate them together.[69] He spoke about these on various occasions, particularly toward his final days. In fact, King was assassinated exactly one year

67. King, "Letter From," 293–94.

68. Ibid., 295.

69. King, "Testament of Hope," 315; King "Where Do We Go From Here?" 628.

after his public declaration to end the war in Vietnam. In this speech, King most clearly articulated the interrelationship between "racism, materialism (e.g., poverty) and militarism." King realized how the exorbitant funding for preparing and engaging in war curtailed the poverty programs, which were a key part of ending racial injustice.[70] Noticing the systemic disease, King called for a revolution of values. "A true revolution of values will lay hands on the world order and say of war- 'This way of settling differences is not just.' This way of burning human beings with napalm, of filling our nation's homes with orphans and widows, of injecting poisonous drugs of hate into the veins of peoples normally humane, of sending men home from dark and bloody battlefields physically handicapped, psychologically deranged, cannot be reconciled with wisdom, justice and love. A nation that continues year after year to spend more money on military defense than on programs of social uplift is approaching spiritual death."[71]

King's virtue-based approach to nonviolent peacemaking yielded considerable success in de-legitimizing racism, ensuring some civil rights, arousing the dignity of many oppressed persons, illustrating the public accessibility to the practices and virtue of nonviolent peacemaking, and broadening our view on issues of law, peace, and the systemic connections of racism, poverty, and war. However, with his early death considerable work remains. By re-engaging his virtue-based approach to nonviolent peacemaking, U.S. residents can continue to heal and transform our society, including our public discourse and policy.

Nonviolent Peaceforce: Moving Toward a Virtue-Based Alternative

A contemporary illustration of how U.S. residents could move towards a virtue-based approach is by supporting the Nonviolent Peaceforce. This organization has considerably less traction in U.S. discourse and policy compared to the U.S. military, particularly in regards to cultivating virtue and being responsible to ensure peace and prevent violence. However, in light of the limits about the predominant methods of moral reasoning and the role of virtue in the U.S. military, we ought to consider some alternative approaches.

70. King, "Beyond Vietnam."
71. King, "Where Do We Go," 631.

In 1999 at the Hague Appeal for Peace some participants conceived of the Nonviolent Peaceforce, which they later launched in India in 2002 as an international NGO. They have a representative governing body. Over seventy member organizations from five continents and over forty countries make up the Nonviolent Peaceforce. Participants include religious and non-religious persons. They have regional offices across the globe and local chapters in the U.S. In 2007, the Nonviolent Peaceforce acquired special consultative status with the Economic and Social Council of the UN. They function on a mere budget of five million per year.[72]

The Nonviolent Peaceforce describes itself as a "nonpartisan unarmed peacekeeping force composed of trained civilians from around the world." They aim to develop into a large-scale force in order to protect human rights, deter violence, and help create space for local peacemakers to carry out their work. In order to attain these larger ends, Nonviolent Peaceforce's central practice entails deploying field teams to conflict areas upon invitation most often by local peace and human rights groups. They have deployed field teams to Sri Lanka and presently deploy in the Philippines and South Sudan. In the field they work and live directly in the communities, provide protective accompaniment to human rights workers and at times police engaged in investigations, proactive engagement with armed actors, interactive monitoring and observing, modeling daily nonviolent behavior, serving as a communication link between all key actors, creating space for and facilitating dialogues, verification and rumor control, saving civilians from crossfire, and interposition by putting their bodies in between hostile parties. In the Philippines, they helped recover children abducted for the purpose of becoming soldiers. In South Sudan, they have protected refugees, children and women, as well as engaged genocide prevention work in Jonglei at the request of the UN Refugee Agency. Beyond the field teams the Nonviolent Peaceforce also builds capacity for nonviolent intervention, conducts public awareness campaigns, and does political advocacy to increase support and recognition of the effectiveness of civilian nonviolent intervention.[73]

Nonviolent Peaceforce training attempts to instill a core set of values and virtues. For instance, the Nonviolent Peaceforce welcomes criticism and aims to cultivate a spirit of wonder, flexibility and humility.

72. Nonviolent Peaceforce, "Who We Are," "Convening Event," "Frequently."
73. Nonviolent Peaceforce, "Mission," "Frequently," 5.

They value the primacy of those most directly involved in the conflict, nonpartisanship, human rights and international law. They commit to nonviolence understood as more than not causing direct harm, but also building local capacity and social structures that support development and the well being for all. The training calls for understanding trainers as facilitators and conflicts as opportunities for growth, as well as active participation, embracing diversity, openness and transparency, dialogue, and positive feedback.[74]

In addition, they aim to create the kinds of persons aware of their own competencies and behaviors. They also cultivate people aware of their own identity and both how it may be perceived and affect behavior. Nonviolent Peaceforce enables people to realize their own potential for violence and aggression, to deal with fear, and to defuse anger and aggression.[75]

Although Sharp failed to adequately consider a virtue ethic he does contribute to our understanding of how nonviolent strategies, such as those used by Nonviolent Peaceforce, form persons and a society. For instance, he argues that nonviolent strategies contribute to decentralizing and diffusing effective power, which in turn, empowers the oppressed. For Sharp, those using nonviolence often become more respectful of life, more able to think through problems and to adhere to their decisions in difficult circumstances. Nonviolent strategies tend to promote growth in non-government institutions as a part of the diffusion of effective power. Society becomes more resistant to oppression and more able adequately to meet human needs, which include physical, psychological, social, and political needs.[76]

Significantly, the Nonviolent Peaceforce grows out of a tradition oriented to large-scale peace teams, which Gandhi initiated and Khan enlarged. Gandhi called for the creation of *Shanti Sena*, a peace team or army. Some residents of India established local peace teams to prevent rioting; however, the call for a national peace army to confront a potential Japanese invasion never materialized in part since Japan did not attack. Khan created the first mass professional nonviolent army in the *Khudai Khidmatgar*. Nonviolent Peaceforce's understanding of nonviolence is in many ways consistent with Gandhi, Khan, and King,

---

74. Nonviolent Peaceforce, "Core Training."

75. Ibid.

76. Sharp, *Social Power*, 345, 369.

although some members lean toward a strategic-based approach. The Nonviolent Peaceforce gives significant attention in their training to developing a range of capacities or virtues, such as humility, which relate closely to nonviolence. In contrast to the U.S. military chant to become a "killing man," I recommend considering the kinds of persons cultivated in Nonviolent Peaceforce's tradition, who during Khan's time ritualized this chant:

> We are the army of God,
> By death or wealth unmoved.
> We march, our leader and we,
> Ready to die.
>
> We serve and we love
> Our people and our cause.
> Freedom is our goal,
> Our lives the price we pay.[77]

ENHANCING AND QUALIFYING THE VIRTUES

Building on the insights from MLK and the Nonviolent Peaceforce, I recommend the following ways that the presence of virtue in general should be enhanced in U.S. public discourse and policy, as well as how other virtues and practices should be qualified by the virtue of nonviolent peacemaking.

The first way a stronger presence of virtue ought to be enhanced consists in emphasizing the development of moral agency, responsible choice or rational deliberation, i.e., the virtue of prudence, in all persons. In this chapter, I described the inadequate attention to this in key patterns of the U.S. military, but also in the rule-based or utilitarian-based assessments of nonviolence in chapter one. I recommend teaching prudence as a habit to perfect our human inclinations for the good into moral virtues, not primarily to follow rules, to locate any instrumental means to some more external end, or simply to be cautious. Sawatsky argues that the focus of ethical training ought to be on "creating people with an imagination and a character that has the capacity to respond wisely to the diversity and complexity of life."[78]

---

77. Easwaran, *Nonviolent Soldier*, 113.

78. Sawatsky, *Justpeace Ethics*, 7.

Emphasizing the questions "who are we becoming?" and "who ought we to become?" which entails explicitly engaging our vision of human excellence or our *telos*, offers a second way the presence of virtue in general ought to be enhanced. When people do this, then we will more clearly see some key limits about the kinds of people and society we are becoming with our emphasis on the U.S. military for cultivating virtue and ensuring peace. U.S. residents would also engage more seriously and regularly the adequacy of the various aims and visions of human excellence, rather than limiting ourselves to rules and utilitarian calculations. Thus, a more clear understanding arises regarding how our "ends," such as stability, yield certain habits and practices and how our practices, such as nonviolent peacemaking, perpetuate certain "ends" or answers to the question, "who ought we to become?"

For instance, Maryann Cusimano Love argues that the kind of peace the U.S. Department of Defense emphasizes is stability or order, which draws primarily from the tradition of realism.[79] This type of peace tends to embody a "negative peace," which too often maintains considerable injustice in the form of structural and cultural violence, such as massive income disparities, racism, environmental degradation, etc. This vision of peace yields habits and practices focused on superior military or political force along with state sovereignty and national interests. Meanwhile, she argues that the U.S. Department of State emphasizes democratization, which primarily entails habits and practices ensuring political and civil rights more than social and economic rights. However, this vision of peace offers more adequate attention to development. In contrast, she argues that Catholic Relief Service offers a more healthy vision that emphasizes right relationship, the universal common good, human dignity, a fuller range of human rights, and sustainability. Drew Christianson supports Love's claim about these divergent views of peace and elaborates on the Catholic view. He argues that for John Paul II, the Catholic "convoy concept" of peace found its substance in solidarity, which entails human rights, development, nonviolence, and forgiveness.[80] This Catholic vision of peace yields habits and practices that prioritize nonviolent peacemaking by attending to the healing of human persons, meeting human needs and caring for creation, i.e., eco-human

79. Love, *"Emerging Norms."*

80. Christianson, "Catholic Peacemaking, 22; Pope John Paul, "On Social Concern," no. 39–40; "Hundredth Year," no. 52; "No Peace Without Justice."

development. Therefore, this vision tends to embody a more "positive" or "justpeace," which often transforms unjust structures and cultural legitimizations of violence so as to cultivate flourishing relationships.

Another example of the significance of analyzing our "ends" and the implications for our habits, arises with the various visions of democracy. In contrast to the U.S. Department of State's predominant version of democracy, Gandhi argues that if the nominally democratic are to aim for true democracy, then they must become courageously nonviolent. Otherwise, they will likely become increasingly exploitative, and unable to care for the weak.[81] Further, he says a country committed to nonviolence is not deterred by foreign aggression because sufficient numbers of its citizens would become the kinds of people prepared to non-cooperate and even lay down their life.[82] Gandhi argues that the U.S. has become the richest country in large part by exploiting the so-called weaker nations, and to protect these riches we too often depend on the assistance of direct or structural violence. He explains that to live for the nonviolence of a true democracy entails giving up this unjust distribution of resources and not living by the spoils of violence.[83] Finally, he argues that we should aim for more direct democracy rather than settle for mere representative democracy.[84]

Explicitly naming the virtue(s) which some strategies or policies would likely cultivate in the people represents a third way this presence of virtue ought to be enhanced. This could entail briefly explaining what the policy makers mean by these virtues, including their set of core practices, and the kind of vision(s) of human excellence they might constitute. In turn, our country would enjoy a more transparent and adequate way of assessing our public discourse and policies. Obama's 2010 National Security Strategy moves us in this direction with attention to "living our values" and the "power of our example," but the clarity on virtues remains underdeveloped.[85] For instance, a strategy or policy could say that 'x' element would likely cultivate the virtue of courage understood as realizing the good of endurance rather than aggression in the midst of fear or threat. The core practices of this virtue could

81. Gandhi, *Collected Works*, vol. 68, November 5, 1938; *Essential Writings*, 119.

82. Gandhi, *Collected Works*, vol. 87, April 4, 1947; *Essential Writings*, 118.

83. Gandhi, *Collected Works*, vol. 68, December 29, 1938; *Essential Writings*, 112.

84. Bhattacharyya, *Evolution*, 479.

85. Obama, "U.S. National Security Strategy," 2010, 36.

include suffering out of reverence for the dignity of all people and non-cooperation with injustice, etc. This virtue fits with a vision of human excellence as becoming a global citizen with respect for all people, etc. Then in assessing the strategy, we could ask "does this policy really cultivate this virtue and get us toward this vision" and "is this who we hope to become?"

The virtue of nonviolent peacemaking also ought to qualify the kinds of virtues and practices in public discourse and policy. This virtue entails practices that realize the goods of conciliatory love, and the truth of our equal dignity and ultimate unity. An example of how this could impact U.S. policy arises in the 2006 and 2010 National Security Strategies descriptions of promoting human dignity.[86] Rather than merely focusing on defending liberty, justice, and poverty-focused development this component could now explicitly include the "promotion of nonviolent peacemaking practices," as constitutive to realizing the good of human dignity. This does not imply that nonviolent peacemaking becomes an absolute rule in this context, but it does imply that nonviolent peacemakers represent the kinds of people we sincerely hope to become. Thus, our policy would neither describe military violence as some neutral instrumental means or "tool" to some more external end, as in utilitarian reasoning; nor as an occasional "necessary" act, as in rule-based, "just" war reasoning.[87] Instead, with more emphasis our policy would explicitly describe all violence as tragic, our sincere desire and commitment to diminish it and ultimately our hope to eliminate it as key to persons realizing the fullness of our equal dignity.

A second example of how this virtue could impact U.S. policy and discourse arises in reference to "preventing attacks against us and our friends," and "preventing our enemies from threatening us, our allies, and our friends."[88] A virtue of nonviolent peacemaking approach would not draw stark "us vs. them" interpretations. In recognition of our ultimate unity and equal dignity, the aim becomes to prevent attacks against all people not merely against our friends and us. Policymakers would

86. Bush, "U.S. National Security Strategy," 2006, sect. II; Obama, "U.S. National," 2010, 39.

87. U.S. Dept. of Defense, National Defense Strategy, 6.; U.S. NSS, 2010, 22. It is also notable in these documents how often "violence" is used to describe other people's acts, but "force" is used to describe destructive and lethal activity by the U.S. military.

88. Bush, "U.S. National," 2006; Obama, "U.S. National," 2010, 7.

use alternative language such as "potential partner" rather than the language of "enemy." Their central aim would entail reconciliation and friendship rather than isolation, defeat, and even destruction of such persons.[89] Obama's policy of "engagement" with some "adversaries" in part moves us in this direction.

Uplifting the significance of paradigmatic practices offers a third example of how this virtue would impact U.S. public discourse and policy. For instance, attention to the virtue of nonviolent peacemaking would assist the shift from overemphasized discussions such as those on the criteria or rules to justify war, to discussions on which regular daily practices might guide our peacemaking initiatives and indicate a genuine commitment to peace. The virtue of nonviolent peacemaking and its' related set of virtues make it more possible to sustain a society committed to practices that risk conflict and work out differences short of violence.[90] In collaboration with twenty-three other scholars from various denominations, Stassen developed "just peacemaking theory" to guide our peacemaking initiatives and indicate a genuine commitment to peace by public authorities.[91] These practices are: "support nonviolent direct action; take independent initiatives to reduce threat; use cooperative conflict resolution; acknowledge responsibility for conflict and injustice and seek repentance and forgiveness; advance democracy, human rights, and religious liberty; foster just and sustainable economic development; work with emerging cooperative forces in the international system; strengthen the United Nations and international efforts for cooperation and human rights; reduce offensive weapons and weapons trade; and encourage grassroots peacemaking groups and voluntary associations."[92]

The virtue of nonviolent peacemaking would also qualify important virtues in public discourse and policy. First, the virtue of justice would now entail practices that cultivate the good of right or healthy relationship. Thus, the paradigmatic practices of justice would be primarily oriented to restorative justice rather than retributive justice or a mere "fairness" understood as "those who do similar things get similar

---

89. U.S. DOD, NDS, 9; Obama, "U.S., National," 2010, 19.

90. Hauerwas, "Christian Critique," 479.

91. Stassen, *Just Peacemaking: Transforming Initiatives*, 234.

92. Stassen, *Just Peacemaking: The New Paradigm*.

rewards or punishments," as articulated by the U.S. Air Force.[93] Further, the value of justice in general would hold a much more prominent place in our set of values. For instance, in the U.S. military only the Air Force explicitly includes it in their set of core values, and in public discourse freedom often gets much more attention.

Second, the virtue of courage would entail practices that realize the good of endurance in the midst of fear or threat, since it is more difficult to control fear than to act aggressively. Gandhi called the virtue of non-violence the highest form of courage. A paradigmatic practice of courage would be suffering out of reverence for the dignity of others (and self) by risking, perhaps even giving one's life without the distortion of our dignity created by relying on lethal force or by taking another's life.[94] In turn, this would shift our vision of the kinds of "heroes" upheld in our public discourse around issues of peacemaking or acute conflict. Further, in the tradition of virtue illuminated by the Christian theorists, Gandhi, and Khan, the virtue of courage must involve prudence and justice, when dealing with others. Thus, a mere risking of one's life is insufficient for the virtue of courage.

The virtue of nonviolent peacemaking also uplifts various virtues, which often get ignored or de-valued in public discourse and policy. For instance, these include the virtues of solidarity, mercy, humility, patience, hospitality, and empathy. For social inquiry, Hollenbach accents the virtue of epistemological humility, described as a kind of awe-filled wonder and expectation for growth in knowledge. He also accents the virtue of "intellectual solidarity," described as a "readiness to take others seriously enough to engage them in conversation about their vision of what makes life worth living and how they live out this vision day by day."[95] Catholic Social Teaching contributes to the insight of peaceable virtues by suggesting virtues such as faith, hope, compassion, and civility. Sawatsky proposes a set of virtues that arise in the context of a commitment to a "justpeace ethic" based on restorative justice, which

93. U.S. Air Force, "Core Values."

94. Not only would nonviolent peacemakers, like Jesus, MLK, and Gandhi illustrate this; but it may be instructive to consider the practices of pregnancy and giving birth as paradigmatic for the virtue of courage.

95. Hollenbach, *Global Face*, 44–50.

includes the virtues of transformation, needs-focused, and generations lens, etc.[96]

LIMITS OF VIRTUE IN PUBLIC DISCOURSE AND POLICY

I have argued that a virtue-based assessment of nonviolent peacemaking addresses several key limits of the two common, contemporary ways of assessing nonviolence in public discourse and policy: first, primarily as a rule against violence, which is rules-based, and second, primarily as a strategy or technique, which is consequences-based and often utilitarian in form. I argued that nonviolent peacemaking represents a distinct virtue that functions within various religious traditions and cultures, and even within a religiously plural society. I have also argued that a virtue-based approach can function well in and address key limits of U.S. public discourse and policy, particularly around issues of acute conflict and peace work.

However, a virtue-based approach also faces a few key limits. First, virtue ethics and the thicker vision of human excellence it implies faces difficulty making headway into a public discourse and policy that largely depends on rules or utilitarian forms of moral reasoning. Such a shift requires time and education to transform us into the kinds of people who rely more readily on the insights of virtue ethics.

Second, virtues arise out of and tend to be associated with particular traditions or narratives. Thus, in a heavily pluralist society such as the U.S., a variety of virtues, understandings of the virtues, paradigmatic practices for the virtues, and visions of human excellence exist. This reality makes the dialogue about these issues at times difficult and lengthy. Sometimes these particularities function to ensure an identity, whether grounded in a political party, religion, race, sex, career, etc. Therefore, there can be a strong resistance to risking change in one's identity by potentially transforming one's virtues or even embracing another's virtues.

Third, a virtue-based approach functions well when a significant number of people desire to become virtuous or at least care about whom they are becoming, and that people who do care have developed a minimum level of virtue in order to adequately participate in and organize society. For now there still may be significant numbers of people who do not fall into one or both of these categories. Thus, a virtue-based

---

96. Sawatsky, *Justpeace Ethics*, 18.

approach would benefit from other ethical forms of reasoning and poli-cymaking for U.S. society.

Therefore, in the next chapter I turn to human rights theory as one potential way to address these limits of virtue ethics for public discourse and policy.

6

Contributions of Human Rights Discourse

INTRODUCTION

IN THIS CHAPTER I address some key limits of a virtue-based assessment of nonviolent peacemaking for public discourse and policy. To this end, I explore certain aspects of human rights discourse as a way to supplement a virtue-based assessment. First, I describe some general characteristics of human rights theory. Second, I briefly examine some key limits of human rights theory in order to indicate more clearly why it functions to supplement rather than replace a virtue-based assessment. Third, I analyze the contributions that certain aspects of human rights discourse can offer a virtue-based assessment for public discourse and policy.

HUMAN RIGHTS THEORY: BASIC CHARACTERISTICS

A theory of human rights characteristically addresses the following key questions.

1. Who is the subject or bearer of rights?

2. What is the force or nature of rights?

3. What is the object of rights or what good do we have a right to?

4. Who is the respondent of rights or who has the duty to meet the claim?

5. What grounds are used to justify the rights?[1]

---

1. O'Neill, *Christian Social Ethics*, 66.

A theory of human rights tends to share the following basic responses to the above questions. The subject of human rights refers to the notion that all persons due to their humanity equally possess rights. These rights arise prior to any legislative enactments, constitutional arrangements, or judicial decisions. Rights enjoy a presumptive primacy in moral discourse, such that they typically override mere interests or utilitarian calculations. Rights also have a "graduated urgency corresponding to the varying importance and necessity of the value [or need] that they protect."[2] Rights require the assignment of duties to the pertinent individuals, groups, or institutions and the provision for their enforcement. In human rights theory, the justification offered for attributing rights to persons is the recognition of human dignity, which differs from every kind of merit. The concept of dignity usually refers to a "property possessed by something in virtue of some other property it possesses," such as one's natural capability for rationality.[3] For instance, a human rights theory might argue that our capacity for exercising rational agency (autonomy) requires that recognizing human dignity entails treating persons with equal concern and respect. In this type of theory, particular rights and duties may be derived from the necessary conditions for rational action, such as basic freedoms and minimal welfare.[4]

HUMAN RIGHTS THEORY: TYPES

There are various human rights theories, which extend these basic characteristics in different directions. One key type for this project is philosophical liberalism, which represents the dominant type in U.S public discourse and policy. Some of the main representatives of this type include Milton Friedman, Robert Nozick, John Rawls, Maurice Cranston, and Joel Feinberg. Although important differences exist between them, they do tend to offer a similar view of the person. Society tends to be viewed as a collection of largely disconnected self-interested autonomous and sovereign selves that justice tries to organize in order to maintain a balance of power and contribute to the well-being of the majority.[5] According to the doctrine of philosophical liberalism, the very

2. Langan, "Defending Human Rights," 74.

3. Feinberg, *Social Philosophy*, 90.

4. O'Neill, *Christian Social Ethics*, 64–71.

5. Pinckaers, "Role of Virtue," 295.

"irreconcilability of our local and ethnocentric conceptions of the (common) good" leads to cherishing the liberties of the moderns, namely to pursue our own good in our own way.[6] In turn, such thinkers often regard individual liberty and equality as key to recognizing human dignity and as the top political goals. In our culture, this type tends to conceive human rights "in terms of specific freedoms or immunities enjoyed by the individual," such that they are often described as "negative" insofar as they "imply the correlative duty of non-interference (e.g., freedom of speech, of assembly, etc.)"[7] Nozick even claims that "negative liberties... fill up the space of rights."[8] Socio-economic rights such as the provision of basic needs (e.g., adequate nutrition, health care, potable water, and education) usually face relegation to an inferior sphere or get "dismissed as mere rhetorical license."[9] For instance, concern exists about how such rights may entail restrictions on the "natural right" of liberty, or defining who has the duty to ensure socio-economic rights.[10]

Martha Nussbaum defends a form of political liberalism, which she connects to her re-working of human rights theory in terms of capabilities.[11] However, unlike many adherents of philosophical liberalism, her theory of capabilities covers the terrain of both political-civil rights and socio-economic rights. The central capabilities also play a similar role as human rights by "providing the philosophical underpinning for basic constitutional principles."[12]

Nussbaum's approach centers on respect for the dignity of persons as choosers. This respect requires us to defend universally a wide range of liberties, plus their material conditions; and it requires us to "respect persons as separate ends, in a way that reflects our acknowledgement of the empirical fact of bodily separateness, asking how each and every life can have the preconditions of liberty and self-determination."[13] Capabilities mean what we are able to do and be, and thus, are distinct from actual functioning. They represent a quality of life assessment. To

6. O'Neill, "What We Owe," 29.

7. O'Neill, *Christian Social Ethics* course, 72.

8. Nozick, *Anarchy, State, and Utopia*, 238.

9. O'Neill, "What We Owe," 30.

10. Feinberg, *Social Philosophy*, 95

11. Nussbaum, *Women and Human Development*, 8.

12. Ibid., 97.

13. Ibid., 59–60.

develop a working list of functions that would appear to be of central importance in human life, Nussbaum asks: Is the person capable of this, or not? More specifically, she says, "We ask not only about the person's satisfaction with what she does, but about what she does, and what she is in a position to do (what her opportunities and liberties are). And we ask not just about the resources that are sitting around, but about how those do or do not go to work, enabling [each person] to function in a fully human way."[14]

Nussbaum's list of central human capabilities entails two levels of conception of the human being. The first level is the shape of the human form of life necessary for a life to be *human*, such as mortality, the human body, and cognitive capability. The second level is the basic human functional capabilities necessary for a *good* human life.[15] Attending to both of these levels, Nussbuam conceives of the central human capabilities as:

1. life, which entails being able to live a normal length of life;

2. bodily health, which includes adequate nourishment and shelter;

3. bodily integrity, which includes security against sexual assault and domestic violence;

4. senses, imagination and thought, which entails being able to use these in ways informed by an adequate education;

5. emotions, which entails being able to have attachments outside ourselves and not having our emotional development shattered by overwhelming fear and anxiety;

6. practical reason, which entails being able to form a conception of the good life and engage in critical reflection about the planning of one's life;

7. affiliation, which includes being capable of living with and toward others, being capable of empathy, justice, and friendship, and being capable of accepting treatment as one with dignity;

8. other species, which entails being able to live with concern for and in relation to the wider world of nature;

14. Ibid., 70–71.
15. Nussbaum, "Human Capabilities, Female Human Beings," 75–85.

9. play, which entails being capable of laughing, playing, and enjoying recreation; and

10. control over one's environment, both politically such as being able to participate, and materially such as being able to hold property.[16]

She claims that "practical reason and affiliation are central to the entire project: they suffuse all the other capabilities, making them fully human." The list entails a multiple realizability, which means its members can be more concretely specified in accordance with local beliefs and circumstances. Each one is central and thus should not be canceled out to get more of another.[17]

Roman Catholic Social Teaching offers another key type. Along with the official teaching documents, such as *Pacem in Terris* and *Economic Justice for All*, key contemporary thinkers include David Hollenbach and Bill O'Neill. Catholic tradition offers two warrants for human dignity. First, dignity arises from the person's transcendence over things in our ability to think, choose, hope, and make moral judgments. This warrant is accessible and plausible apart from doctrines of the Christian faith. Second, in contrast to most philosophical liberalism, our sense for human dignity arises from being made in the image of God and redeemed by Christ.[18] Further, the human person's dignity is interwoven with a social nature, recognizing our coming from another, our interdependence, interconnectedness, and orientation to friendship.

O'Neill explains that this type conceives of human rights "in terms of specific freedoms and entitlements, which must be presupposed if the dignity of all" is to be better recognized in society.[19] Hollenbach explains that this conception of rights requires respect for the spheres of freedom, need, and relationship.[20] The Catholic conception of the public or common good often gets explained primarily in terms of rights, which always involves correlative responsibilities or duties. Since equal rights often face unequal threats, then a duty exists to protect the most vulnerable.[21] This entails seeing the moral claims of the poor as just

16. Nussbaum, *Women and Human Development*, 78–80.

17. Ibid., 92, 77, 81.

18. Hollenbach, *Justice, Peace, and Human Rights*, 95.

19. O'Neill, *Christian Social Ethics*, 72.

20. Hollenbach, *Justice, Peace, and Human Rights*, 95.

21. Christianson, "Moral Claims," 99, 102.

entitlements. This type of human rights theory ensures both political-civil rights and socio-economic rights.[22] For instance, they argue that basic needs or subsistence function as the necessary conditions for one to adequately exercise their political-civil rights, i.e., liberty or political participation to design and implement policies that affect them and their dependents. Thus, these basic subsistence needs ought to be accorded the status of rights, i.e., socio-economic rights, if the claim to ensure political-civil rights has any adequate moral weight. For instance, O'Neill argues, "inasmuch as these conditions, or more precisely agential capabilities, are presumed in exercising practically rational agency, they are mutually implicative."[23]

O'Neill argues that human rights function as the deep or "narrative grammar of public reasoning" or the public discourse about policy. This contrasts with a view of human rights as properties of abstract sovereign selves, which often resonates with philosophical liberalism. Human rights function even more specifically as the narrative grammar of responding to the suffering of the world. In other words, O'Neill argues that communities restore human rights not simply by punishing perpetrators who violate laws, but more adequately by engaging the suffering and wounds of both victims and perpetrators in the mutual creation of a new civic narrative of respect for the concrete other.[24] I describe more of this thinking later in the chapter along with some implications.

The United Nations Declaration of Human Rights in 1948 attempted to arrive at a list of human rights consistent with various understandings of the human person and human dignity. They ground their rights on the recognition of our "inherent dignity." Their first article describes the human person as "free and equal in dignity" and "endowed with reason and conscience" with the assertion that we "should act towards one another in a spirit of brotherhood."[25] Although the UN does not ground human dignity in the image of God as in Catholic Social Teaching, the UN's list of rights is nearly synonymous with that tradition's list of rights.

22. Immaculate Heart, "Summary of Roman Catholic Rights."
23. O'Neill, "What We Owe," 34.
24. O'Neill, "Rights of Passage," 55–58.
25. UN Declaration of Human Rights, Preamble and Article 1.

HUMAN RIGHTS THEORY: LIMITS

My thesis argues that a virtue-based assessment of nonviolent peace-making is more adequate than a rules or strategy-based assessment. However, I have also argued that a virtue-based approach faces important limits, particularly for public discourse and policy. In turn, this chapter focuses on addressing those limits by supplementing virtue with aspects of human rights discourse. Before I elaborate on how human rights could function in this way, I want to clarify why human rights theory is not the center of my nonviolent peacemaking assessment.

First, in chapter 1, I analyzed the limits of a rules-based assessment. Human Rights theory often functions primarily as a set of rules, and thus, lends itself to the limits of a rules-based assessment of nonviolent peacemaking. The insufficiency of rules for forming persons and communities represents one of the most important limits. They certainly provide guidelines for times of uncertainty or for those lacking virtue. However, being aware of the right to political participation or to food is not sufficient to generate the kind of character that adequately interprets and applies these rights. On this point, Mary Midgely argues that rights contain "no pathways for comparing the nature of different claims and different ideals, nor for inventive compromise." She gives examples of this failure in the popular debates about abortion and euthanasia.[26]

In contrast, practices corresponding to a virtue-based assessment of nonviolent peacemaking provide room for the character development or the formation of persons and communities, which more wisely interpret, apply, and at times even revise notions of human rights. For instance, the virtue of prudence includes discerning how to get from principle or rule to application, that is, how to reach the end in a concrete situation.[27] Rules need virtues since rules alone lack the ability for good moral judgment. Our character shapes how we see and describe situations, which then determines judgment and decision. Good moral judgment must account for previously un-encountered events and circumstances, subtle differences in interaction (like tone or touch) and personal commitments. Virtues give us the wisdom to recognize the

26. Midgely, "Rights-Talk," 105.

27. Miller, *Interpretations of Conflict*, 227.

morally relevant issues, find the right activity, and also strengthen us to act on it.[28]

Relying on a more external-based motivation such as rights and duty develops persons less sustained in their peacemaking than relying primarily on a more integrated motivation such as virtue, which draws people to act out of a vision of human flourishing and an attraction to the good. Virtues function as a foretaste of this good, which rights merely point us toward. A virtue-based account recognizes the sets of core practices that correspond with each virtue. Thus, persons need virtue, not merely rules, to sustain moral activity.[29] Further, the lack of formation generated by a rules-based assessment explains why a list of human rights fails to sufficiently cultivate the imagination, creativity, or what John Paul Lederach calls the "artfulness" of peacebuilding.[30]

Contemporary Catholic Social Teaching relies primarily on a rights-based ethic for war and peace issues. Catholic Social Teaching tends to argue that nonviolence at times is unable to protect and promote certain human rights, such as the right to defense or the duty to defend the innocent. In turn, Catholic Social Teaching maintained the inadequate position that nonviolent peacemaking is only or primarily fit for individual persons and interpersonal relationships. Thus, this rights-based ethic also reinforced an emphasis on "just" war theory more than a broad range of nonviolent peacemaking practices, especially regarding government or state action in acute conflict situations. Those operating from this point of view often portray an inadequate imagination for nonviolent peacemaking, which in part contributed to most Catholic leadership often failing to adequately challenge political and military leadership on the preparation for war and use of war, i.e., disproportionate military spending, the atomic bomb in WWII, Vietnam, Iraq, and Afghanistan, etc. Only in the U.S. Bishops' 1993 document, which included a more prominent place for virtues, do they re-assess their position and at least invite serious consideration for a nonviolent ethic and nonviolent peacemaking practices in the social, governmental, and international realm of action.

Second, Martha Nussbaum argues that human rights discourse is unclear on many points. She explains that human rights theories differ

28. Kotva, *Christian Case for Virtue Ethics*, 31, 34.

29. Porter, *Recovery of Virtue*, 70.

30. Lederach, *Moral Imagination*, ix and 29.

on the basis of rights claims, such as rationality, sentience, or mere life. In turn, the basis of rights can affect the types of rights acknowledged, promoted, and prioritized, such as understanding rights as "side-constraints (negative) on goal-promoting action or instead as one part of the social goal (positive) that is being promoted."[31] For instance, some emphasize political-civil rights, such as the U.S., others social-economic rights, such as China, and even others the rights of peoples or environmental and development rights.[32] China's rejection of free speech and free association and some Islamic regimes' rejection of the right to change one's religion also illustrate different versions of rights.[33] These theories also differ on whether rights exist pre-politically or as artifacts of laws and institutions. They differ on whether rights only belong to individual persons or also to groups. Human rights theories also differ about the relationship between rights and duties, such as whether there is always someone with the duty to ensure the right and how to decide the responsible party. Finally, these theories differ on how to understand the objective of rights, such as a right to a type of treatment, to a level of achieved well-being, to resources, or to certain opportunities and capacities.[34] In light of this lack of clarity, Nussbaum proposes central capabilities as an alternative to human rights language, which I expand in the next section.

According to Johan Galtung, the lack of clarity in human rights discourse also arises in part due to the neglect of human needs discourse. Galtung, who is generally regarded as the founder of the discipline of peace and conflict studies, suggests a needs approach could focus on security, welfare, freedom, and identity needs. Such a needs approach is "fruitful in legitimizing the entry" onto the future agenda for human rights. For example, Galtung suggests the following rights would come into view with a needs approach: right to sleep, right not to be killed in war, right to access challenging work requiring creativity, and the right to social transparency, etc.[35]

31. Nussbaum, *Women and Human Development*, 97.

32. Brown, "Universal Human Rights," 115; Appleby, *Ambivalence of the Sacred*, 246.

33. Dunne and Wheeler, "Introduction," 11; Brown, "Universal Human Rights," 116.

34. Nussbaum, *Women and Human Development*, 97.

35. Galtung and Wirak, "On the Relationship," 17, 25b, 48. Nussbaum's capabilities approach is partially intended to address the neglect of human needs discourse, with-

The compliance gap between the declared commitments of governments to human rights and their compliance with these standards represents a third key limit to rights-based approaches. For instance, according to a 1997 report by Amnesty International, 123 of the 185 sovereign states still routinely practice torture. Furthermore, humanity has failed to banish the crime of genocide outlawed in 1950 from the practice of the world as illustrated by Rwanda in 1994 and Darfur in 2003. Some argue that this compliance gap arises due to the various views of the meaning and priority of certain rights.[36] For instance, in order to get a clearer understanding of these various views of human rights, Charles Taylor argues that engaging in moral theory requires considering people's conception of the good, because the good is what "gives the point of the rules which define the right."[37] However, others argue that closing the compliance gap requires forming ethical communities, which includes a cosmopolitan education in human rights.[38] Both of these arguments suggest the importance of critically and routinely reflecting on our conceptions of the good life or of human flourishing. Such reflection both continuously clarifies the meaning and priorities of human rights, and illuminates the virtues which constitute human flourishing and can form the kinds of ethical communities that more regularly comply with the declared commitments to human rights.

A fourth key limit of human rights theory arises from the *human* part of the phrase. The emphasis placed on 'human' often risks devaluing non-human life and the broader environment or cosmos as a whole. The virtue of solidarity, which arises from our sense of interdependence and interconnectedness, assists us in mitigating this devaluing. Also, the virtue of hospitality, which welcomes the other including non-humans, assists in mitigating an overemphasis on the human. These two virtues, solidarity and hospitality, are part of the related set of virtues which the virtue of nonviolent peacemaking uplifts.

---

out suffering the shortcomings of such discourse.

36. Dunne and Wheeler, "Introduction," 2–3.

37. Taylor, *Sources of the Self*, 89; O'Reardon, "Theorizing International Human Rights," 40.

38. Booth and Dunne, "Learning Beyond Frontiers," 323–25.

HUMAN RIGHTS DISCOURSE: CONTRIBUTIONS

In this section, I affirm the ways that some aspects of human rights discourse offer three important contributions to a virtue-based assessment of nonviolent peacemaking, especially for public discourse and policy. First, human rights presently have more moral traction than virtue in public discourse and policy. Second, they more easily move beyond the obstacle arising from the tendency to view virtue ethics as requiring too thick a conception of human flourishing, especially for increasingly diverse societies. Third, they can help us to see more clearly how the virtue of nonviolent peacemaking actually protects and ensures human rights, both enhancing the validity of nonviolent peacemaking practices for public discourse and policy, and assisting in measuring *some* ways that nonviolent peacemaking works. Many secondary contributions also arise from aspects of human rights discourse, which I describe below.

In general, virtues need rules, especially since most humans live in communities. Moral laws offer the ordering principles a community must embody to act in concert while each seeks their personal good and the common good.[39] Rules function as devices useful within the terrain of virtue. For instance, rules assist in the moral education of youth or for judges in the legal system. A rule functions as a summary of and an educative guide to virtuous choice, so that part of being virtuous entails "knowing when to use the rule and when to let it go."[40] Re-examining our rules provides one way to test our narratives against our ongoing experience.[41] For instance, the rule or duty of nonmaleficence assists the virtue of practical reasoning by requiring us to withstand the narratives of progressivism and provincialism.[42] Rules often provide guidance when limited time, bias, or frenzy may hinder good judgment. Finally, rules indicate certain concrete kinds of action or practices, which characterize particular virtues. Thus, rules depict or call us toward virtues. Rules serve the virtues by assisting us in both the acquisition and at times execution of the virtues.[43]

39. Porter, *Recovery of Virtue*, 70.

40. Nussbaum, "Comparing Virtues," 359.

41. Hauerwas, *Peaceable Kingdom*, 119.

42. Miller, *Interpretations of Conflict*, 235, 241–42. Progressivism tends to see a "march toward civilization" that fails to account for the suffering. Provincialism tends to construct a radical "otherness" recording only the excellences of one's tribe or nation.

43. Kotva, *Christian Case*, 35–36.

In the *Ambivalence of the Sacred*, Scott Appleby notes the historical development within each major religious tradition of "moral norms that enjoin care for the poor and oppressed, condemn violence under most if not all circumstances," and mandate reconciliation to enemies. Thus, he argues that religious intellectuals need to translate into popular religious idioms their vision of religion as a nonviolent and rights-bearing sacred trust. He describes this as moving from a first order religious language, which tends to be exclusivist, into a second order religious discourse, which would offer a more cross-cultural vocabulary. Appleby suggests human rights theory as this second order religious discourse.[44]

Catholic Social Teaching offers an example of this movement to what Appleby calls a "second order religious discourse." Although Catholic Social Teaching's rights-based approach to nonviolent peacemaking contains important limits, it also offers some key contributions for public discourse and policy. For Catholic Social Teaching, peace depends on a just political order, which recognizes the full range of human rights.[45] By emphasizing the need to respect the rights of others, such as by offering some form of defense or resistance when their life is threatened or dignity ignored, human rights indicate the urgency of claims and a way to focus the activity of nonviolent peacemaking. The defense of these rights in Catholic Social Teaching entails a strong presumption against using violence or war.[46] In 1979, Pope John Paul II argued that, "violence is evil," and that "violence is a lie, for it goes against the truth of our faith, the truth of our humanity. Violence destroys what it claims to defend: the dignity, the life, and the freedom of human beings. Violence is a crime against humanity, for it destroys the very fabric of society."[47] In turn, he exhorted persons to turn away from the paths of violence particularly by not following any leaders who "train you in the way of inflicting death . . . Give yourself to the service of life, not the work of death. Do not think that courage and strength are proved by killing and destruction. True courage lies in working for peace . . . Violence is the enemy of justice. Only peace can lead the way to true justice."[48]

44. Appleby, *Ambivalence of the Sacred*, 255, 279–80.
45. Whitmore, "Reception to Catholic Approaches," 514.
46. U.S. Bishops, "Harvest of Justice is Sown in Peace," Section 1.
47. Pope John Paul II, Homily at Drogheda, 18.
48. Ibid., 19–20.

In 1984, the Sacred Congregation for Doctrine of the Faith led by Cardinal Josef Ratzinger, who is now Pope Benedict XVI, argued that violence degrades the dignity of both the victims and the perpetrators.[49] Notably, Bell's attempt to link Christian virtue with "just" war rarely attends to human dignity.[50] In 1991 before the Gulf War, Pope John Paul argued that, "a peace obtained by arms could only prepare new acts of violence."[51] Before the Iraq War of 2003, Pope John Paul reiterates "war is always a defeat for humanity."[52] More recently in 2008, Pope Benedict reflecting on the cross of Christ explained, "What are the horrors of war, violence visited on the innocent, the misery and injustice that persecutes the weak, if not the opposition of evil to the Kingdom of God? And how does one respond to such evil if not with the unarmed love that defeats hatred, life that does not fear death?"[53] In a March 2009 visit to Cameroon in Africa, the Pope said, "genuine religion . . . rejects all forms of violence . . . not only on faith but on principles of right reason."[54] Later that month, the Pope connected discipleship to Jesus' way described as, "Jesus . . . the King of the Universe did not come to bring peace to the world through an army, but through refusing violence."[55] Therefore, supplementing a virtue-based account of nonviolent peacemaking with human rights discourse from Catholic Social Teaching suggests that *practices* of nonviolent peacemaking deserve a clear, ongoing emphasis in public discourse and policy, if such policy claims to aim at a justpeace.

Catholic Social Teaching's acknowledgement of social-economic rights along with political-civil rights reinforces the nonviolent peacemaking practice of the constructive program, which Gandhi called the main arm of nonviolence. This acknowledgement particularly enriches U.S. public discourse and policy, since the U.S. tends to focus on political-civil rights and has yet to ratify the International Covenant on Economic, Social, and Cultural Rights.[56] Therefore, the social-economic

---

49. Sacred Congregation, "Instruction," section xi, paragraph 7.
50. Bell, *Just War*.
51. Pope John Paul II, "War, a Decline for Humanity," 527, 530.
52. Pope John Paul II, "International Situation Today," 544.
53. Pope Benedict XVI, "Overcome Every Possible."
54. Benedict XVI, "Saving Message."
55. Zenit News, "Pontiff Calls."
56. Shah, "USA and Human Rights."

rights aspect further clarifies the importance and specific role of nonviolent peacemaking in U.S. public discourse and policy.

John Dear, S.J. argues that the human rights movement ought to join the global peace movement. He argues that war and the nuclear weapons, which sustain our culture of war, represent the ultimate violation of human rights. For instance, Dear explains that when the U.S. bombed Hiroshima, Nagasaki, Vietnam, Panama, Iraq, etc., and sold weapons to warring nations, the U.S. violated the basic human rights of ordinary people. Dear argues that when the U.S. used depleted uranium and poisoned the earth, such as in Basra, Kosovo, and Iraq, the U.S. violated the rights of generations to come. Many of the economic sanctions and torture in Iraq violated human rights. Exploding nuclear weapons for testing in Nevada and maintaining thirty thousand other nuclear weapons violate people's basic rights to live in good health, without being immersed in fear, and ultimately to live in peace.[57]

In accord with Catholic Social Teaching and Martin Luther King, Dear argues that war preparation in the form of the arms race and excessive military spending violates human rights by taking resources away from basic rights such as food, education, health, housing, jobs, and the right to life, which depends on many of these basic necessities.[58] Thus, this level of military spending perpetuates the gap between the rich and poor, which functions as one of the key factors contributing to more violence.[59] For instance, some countries spend more on military expenditure than on social development, communications infrastructure and health combined. In 2003, 80 percent of the countries in the developing world to which the U.S. sold arms have been categorized by the U.S. State Department as either undemocratic regimes or governments with major human rights violations. As noted earlier, the U.S. by far leads both global military spending at about 46 percent, and global arms sales.[60] Meanwhile, a 1998 UN report indicated that only $6 billion a year was needed to achieve basic education for all, and only $13 billion a year for basic health and nutrition.[61]

57. Dear, "Human Rights and Nonviolence."

58. Shah, "Arms Trade: A Major Cause," and "USA and Human Rights;" Dear, "Human Rights."

59. Whitmore, "Reception of Catholic," 514.

60. Shah, "Arms Trade is Big Business"; and "World Military Spending."

61. UNDP, "Human Development Report," 1998, 37.

With Dear, the U.S. Bishops argue that these excessive levels of military spending express a serious disorder in a world where millions lack the necessities of life. They suggest that wars around the globe today provide ample evidence that weapons exacerbate conflicts and fuel regional arms races. The arms race represents one of the "greatest curses on humanity and the harm it does to the poor is more than can be endured . . . Diverting scarce resources from military to human development is not only a just and compassionate policy, but it is also a wise long-term investment in global peace and national security."[62] Pope John Paul taught, "If development is the new name for peace, war and preparations for war are the major enemies of the integral development of peoples." If we take the "common good of all humanity as our norm . . . peace would be possible."[63]

Dear points out how great Christian exemplars of nonviolent peacemaking in the U.S., e.g., Martin Luther King and Dorothy Day, made the connections between human rights and nonviolence. Martin Luther King's virtue-based approach to nonviolence linked the struggle for civil rights and equality with the issues of poverty and ending the war in Vietnam. Inspired by Catholic Social Teaching, Dorothy Day's houses of hospitality linked the rights to housing and food with opposing war, nuclear weapons, and global poverty.[64]

According to Dear, the UN Declaration of Human Rights offers a blueprint toward a nonviolent world. He cites the rights to freedom from violence in Article 2, the rights to life, longevity and livability, along with freedom from torture in Article 3, and the duty to prefer nonviolence when asserting one's rights found in Article 29. Further, he argues that if more people promoted this declaration of human rights then more would arrive at the conclusion that humans "must renounce war and violence and become individuals, communities and nations of nonviolence."[65]

Along with Catholic Social Teaching, the UN Declaration of Human Rights includes the categories of both political-civil and socio-economic rights.[66] The United Nations explicitly arose with the deter-

---

62. US Bishops, "Harvest of Justice is Sown in Peace," section 2.5.2.

63. John Paul, *On Social Concern*, par. 10.

64. Dear, "Human Rights."

65. Ibid.

66. UN "Declaration of Human Rights."

mination to "save succeeding generations from the scourge of war."[67] Therefore, this version of human rights theory aims to contribute to the public significance and vision of what nonviolent peacemaking practices ought to entail.

O'Neill's conception of human rights as the "narrative grammar" of responding to the suffering and passion of the world also offers a contribution. His conception shows a more integral relationship between human rights and virtues, mediating the virtue of solidarity and hospitality into public discourse and policy, and arguing for the value of a specific nonviolent peacemaking practice, namely Truth and Reconciliation Commissions. Truth commissions also cultivate a more shared civic narrative, which helps address the concern about virtue being too embedded in a particular narrative for a diverse society.

O'Neill argues that in the South African Truth and Reconciliation Commission human "rights appear not as properties of abstract, sovereign selves, but rather as the grammar of victims' testimony." In this context, the testimony and public hearing function to help restore a sense for the victims' "civic and human dignity," and thus, cultivates a new civic narrative committed to human rights. The grammar of human rights functions as an implicit aim or narrative *telos* of citizens' public reasoning and testimony.[68] Human rights, understood as a narrative grammar, arise from the particular virtues that make this type of public discourse possible. These virtues, such as respect, recognition, civility, and reciprocity arise from and reinforce a "common faith" about inherent human dignity, which the Truth and Reconciliation Commissions restore and generate.[69] I would also add the virtue of reverence by which I mean one affirms the good and the potential for good or for conversion in all people. Valuing and participating in such testimony enables persons to cultivate the virtue of respect and to see more clearly how human rights preserve the conditions of our practical, discursive agency. In other words, the virtue of respect for the concrete other as a practically rational, discursive agent "implies respect for the necessary conditions of her exercising agency."[70] Hence, such respect implies recognition of

---

67. Charter of the United Nations, Preamble.
68. O'Neill, "What We Owe," 32–39.
69. O'Neill, "Violent Bear It Away," par. 31.
70. O'Neill, "Rights of Passage," 55–58.

right-claims to basic civil-political liberties, *and* to subsistence and basic security.

O'Neill argues that the human rights requirement for equal respect and recognition "justifies preferential treatment for those whose basic rights are most imperiled."[71] The attentiveness to those most threatened helps to indicate an urgency of claims or priorities for action as persons attempt to practice the virtues, particularly the virtue of nonviolent peacemaking. Further, this preferential treatment aspect of his human rights theory also helps to cultivate and is encompassed by the virtue of solidarity, which entails taking the victim's side as our own. Pope Paul IV described solidarity as the "indispensable basis for authentic justice and the condition for enduring peace."[72] O'Neill argues that the virtue of solidarity gets more specified in the virtue of hospitality, which performs a deeper interpretive function of the specific context allowing us to know who and how to welcome the other. Thus, in this context O'Neill explains that the virtue of hospitality is more a political obligation rather than a mere option, as philosophical liberalism suggests. The virtues of solidarity and hospitality represent two of the key virtues that get uplifted by assessing nonviolent peacemaking as a virtue. Therefore, O'Neill's conception of human rights theory helps indicate urgent claims, and mediate the "indispensable" virtue of solidarity and the virtue of hospitality into public discourse and policy.

Another example that amplifies O'Neill's insights about the close relationship between virtue and rights appears in philosopher David Putnam's work. While O'Neill argues that human rights necessarily entail certain virtues, such as respect and recognition, Putnam argues that rights theories necessarily entail the virtue of justice and of openness to truth or truth-seeking. For Putnam, moral action requires the disposition of seeking and accepting truth. In his view, comprehending and acting upon a rights theory requires this virtue.[73] Gandhi describes the virtue of nonviolent peacemaking or *Satyagraha* precisely as the only means or set of practices that realize the truth of our human equality and ultimate unity. Therefore, Putnam's argument about the necessity of the virtue of truth-seeking for human rights not only enhances our

71. O'Neill, "What We Owe," 35. See also Outka, *Agape* , 20. Cf. Dworkin, *Taking Rights*, 227.

72. Pope Paul IV, "Call to Action," 278.

73. Putnam, "Rights and Virtues," 96.

sense of virtue's import, but also amplifies the connection between en-suring human rights and the virtue of nonviolent peacemaking in public discourse and policy.

Martha Nussbaum's capabilities version of human rights theory both resonates well and offers some important contributions to a virtue-based assessment of nonviolent peacemaking. To develop this approach she initially addresses some of the limits of rights language in the follow-ing ways. First, she argues that her account of central capabilities takes clearer positions on the disputed issues mentioned above as limits to rights language. The central capabilities "state clearly what the motivat-ing concerns are and what the goal is." She argues we ought to think of rights as combined capabilities or as capacities to function. Thus, it becomes clear that people "don't really have the right to political partici-pation just because such language exists on paper: they really have this right only if there are effective measures to make people truly capable of political exercise." Further, she argues that economic and material rights face significant problems if understood as rights to resources or as a utility-based (satisfaction) analysis. The resources analysis faces the problem that "giving resources to people does not always bring dif-ferently situated people up to the same level of capability to function. The utility-based analysis faces the problem that traditionally deprived people may be satisfied with a very low living standard, believing that this is all they have any hope of getting."[74] A capabilities analysis looks at how people are enabled to live, and thus, contributes to a clear rationale for spending unequal amounts "on the disadvantaged, or creating spe-cial programs to assist their transition to full capability."[75]

Second, she argues that the language of capabilities also has an ad-vantage over rights language because it is "not strongly linked to one particular cultural and historical tradition as the language of rights is be-lieved to be."[76] In turn, capabilities language offers more public accessi-bility, which helps transcend the debate about rights and Westernization. The questions about what one is able to do and what opportunities we have for functioning arise across cultures.

Nevertheless, Nussbaum argues that rights language still plays four important roles in public discourse. First, rights language recalls that

74. Nussbaum, *Women and Human Development*, 99.

75. Ibid., 97–99.

76. Ibid., 99.

people have justified and urgent claims to certain types of treatment, regardless of how the world around them responds. Highlighting the justification for a certain type of treatment communicates more than a mere recognition of a person's basic capabilities, such as rationality or language. Second, in the area of state guaranteed rights, the language of rights places great emphasis on the importance and basic role of these spheres of ability. Rights language is more "rhetorically direct" than saying "able to do and to be." Third, rights language reinforces the emphasis on the ability to choose to function, which for Nussbaum represents the appropriate political goal, rather than simply actual functioning. Fourth, rights language preserves a sense of the terrain of agreement, while persons continue to deliberate about the proper type of analysis, such as resources, utility, or capabilities, at the more specific level.[77]

Nussbaum's capabilities approach resonates well with virtue ethics. Her argument about the central capabilities arises in the context of recognizing that humans enjoy common spheres of experience and that a corresponding virtue(s) perfects each sphere.[78] The spheres provide the terrain of a possible virtue, which would consist in whatever turns out to be choosing and responding well within that sphere. These "grounding experiences," such as bodily appetites or fear of death, provide a framework for cross-cultural comparisons of virtue and accounts of human flourishing.[79] In turn, Nussbaum argues that the capabilities provide a necessary focus for political planning, not as a complete account of human flourishing, but rather as "specifying the capacities that have value in any plan of life that persons may otherwise choose."[80] Just legislators should aim to promote "the capability to live a rich and fully human life." Nussbaum offers a sketch of a "thick vague conception of good human functioning," and provisionally identifies basic human functional capabilities.[81] The virtues encompass these capabilities and draw them to perfection. For instance, Nussbaum argues the capabilities of practical reason and affiliation are both central human powers, since "they suffuse all the other capabilities, making them fully human."[82] The virtue

77. Ibid., 100–101.

78. Keenan, "Proposing Cardinal Virtues," 714; and Crooker, "Functioning," 174–76.

79. Nussbaum, "Comparing Virtues," 352–53.

80. Nussbaum, *Women and Human Development*, 148.

81. Nussbaum, "Aristotelian Social Democracy," 217, 205.

82. Nussbaum, *Women and Human Development*, 92, 72.

of prudence encompasses and perfects the power of practical reason, which entails being able to form a conception of the good and critically reflect on the planning of one's life. Her description of affiliation indicates both the importance of a capability for friendship, which is central to virtue ethics, as well as associations with the virtues of respect, compassion, and justice. Nussbaum argues that capabilities make more room for the moral virtues normally associated with women, such as love, attention to others needs, and willingness to sacrifice. Capabilities also cultivate the moral abilities to perceive a situation and the needs of others, along with reasoning well about how to meet those needs. Therefore, she claims that her liberal account provides more richness than standard liberal proceduralist approaches.[83]

The capabilities include what kind of people we can become, not merely what we can do. "Who we are becoming" is a central area of concern for virtue ethics, more than specific acts. She explains that her list of central capabilities should be understood as combined capabilities. For Nussbaum, the combined capabilities include the internal capabilities combined with suitable external conditions to exercise the function.[84] The attention to developing the internal powers or capabilities is also a central area of focus for virtue ethics. Further, her particular attention to imagination and emotions as central capabilities resonates well with virtue ethics.

In sum, Nussbaum's capabilities version of human rights theory helps to illustrate the integral relationship between virtues and capabilities. Thus, her theory helps to mediate virtues with public discourse and policy. Further, the way capabilities more easily bypass the debate over rights and Westernization, suggests they would function more smoothly in global public discourse and policy. In turn, capabilities with their relationship to virtue also assist in overcoming the often-perceived limit that virtue is too strongly linked to a particular cultural or historical tradition. Her use of grounding or spheres of experience each perfected by virtue illustrates the cross-cultural potential. Finally, her attention to ensuring capabilities and to clarifying the rationale to provide especially for the disadvantaged helps to mediate the constructive program, which expresses the main arm or a core practice of the virtue of nonviolent peacemaking.

83. Nussbaum, *Women and Human Development*, 79, 245.
84. Ibid., 84–85.

Cahill challenges and extends the contribution of Nussbaum's approach by arguing that the categories of kinship and religion would enhance Nussbaum's list of central capabilities, which appears to reflect a liberal bias. Cahill's category of religion would further enhance the significance of engaging questions about a human *telos*, and thus, virtue ethics. By religion, Cahill means that all humans are open to a religious experience, i.e., we all "wonder about the origin of the world and an intelligent purpose behind its fortunes, about the human fate after death, about a larger order of reward and retribution for good and evil, about salvation from our wrongdoing and suffering, and about a unity of all persons and of the natural world in a dimension transcending history." Cahill argues that Nussbuam deals with kinship indirectly and in ways that "minimize its social content." Cahill acknowledges that Nussbaum's category of affiliation could include kinship, but Cahill argues that Nussbaum's explanation of affiliation tends to merely connote consensual relationships.[85] Therefore, the recognition of kinship as a corrective to affiliation reinforces the social dimension to being human and how that is integral to understanding human dignity.

Cahill's attention to kinship as a revision to Nussbaum's list of shared human experience opens up the recognition of our lives coming from another. In part, this resonates with Hannah Arendt's attention to our "natality" as potentially the central category of political thought.[86] The "being given" aspect to our human experience suggests the gift-ness of each person. Thus, our human dignity consists of something even more than being "choosers" as Nussbaum argues, or being rational, as many scholars have argued.

Further, this shared experience of "being gifts," implies the value of a central capability to live as gifts amongst other gifts. Nussbaum argues that each shared experience entails a virtue, or perhaps set of virtues, that perfects that sphere of experience. Cahill's attention to kinship contributes to understanding how the virtue of nonviolent peacemaking perfects a sphere of shared experience. The virtue of nonviolent peacemaking entails practices that realize the truth of our equal dignity and

---

85. Cahill, *Sex, Gender, and Christian Ethics*, 59–61. Cahill also notices that Nussbaum mentions infant development as a separate category of basic human experience, but Cahill argues that Nussbaum's approach "individualizes and desocializes the infant stage."

86. Arendt, *Human Condition*. She refers to "natality" both as the birth of each individual and as a capacity of beginning something new or to act.

shared unity with all being along with the conciliatory love that draws enemies toward friendship. Thus, this virtue functions as one of or the key virtue that perfects the sphere of experience suggested by being a gift and living out that giftedness amongst other gifts. The virtue of nonviolent peacemaking entails practices of valuing our lives and others' lives as gifts, offering our lives as gifts, defending the lives of others as gifts, without being possessive of any of our lives by ensuring our survival by any means or at any costs, such as by using violence. Thus, this virtue also perfects the shared experience of conflict, particularly acute conflict. Nonviolent peacemaking orients persons to engage and transform conflict. Therefore, the recognition of our shared experiences of being "gifts" and of facing conflict both amplifies the role of and strengthens the argument for assessing nonviolent peacemaking as a virtue relevant for public discourse and policy.

The contributions of human rights theory mentioned above by Dear, Catholic Social Teaching, O'Neill and Nussbaum help illuminate how nonviolent peacemaking actually promotes and ensures human rights, especially the right to life, more adequately than is often thought. All four sources facilitate our understanding of how the constructive program arm of nonviolent peacemaking promotes and ensures human rights, such as social and economic rights, especially for the most vulnerable. O'Neill argues that the nonviolent peacemaking practice of Truth and Reconciliation Commissions assist in cultivating a culture of promoting and ensuring human rights. Nussbaum's list of central capabilities, which correspond to common spheres of experience perfected by virtue, illustrates how a virtue-based assessment of nonviolent peacemaking helps enable persons and communities to promote and ensure the central capabilities.

Dear offers a more direct analysis, which aims to solidify the relationship between human rights, especially the right to life, and practices of nonviolent peacemaking. He gives numerous examples of how violence fails to protect human rights, especially the right to life. Supportive of Dear's aims to solidify the connection between nonviolence and respect for life, Hans Kung reflects on the movements toward a global ethic. For instance, Kung refers to the 1993 Chicago Declaration on a Global Ethic, which the InterAction Council of former Presidents of State and Prime Ministers confirmed. This council affirmed four direc-

tives, with the first one reading, "commitment to a culture of nonviolence and respect for life."[87]

Another piece of evidence to support Dear's argument that nonviolent peacemaking protects and ensures the right to life arises by comparing the contemporary cases of Algeria and India. Both of these countries
gained independence from European colonial powers around the same
time. However, India largely used nonviolence, while Algeria largely
relied on violence. Both Algeria and its opponent, France, suffered enormously more casualties with Algeria losing about 900,000. Further, the
relations between these two countries were strained almost to the present day. In contrast, the much more vastly populated India only lost a
few thousand, and relations with the British immediately entered an era
of relative cooperation and mutual benefit.[88]

Nagler offers more arguments for the way nonviolence protects life.
He argues that up through 1993, only one person had been killed and
three wounded in the whole history of the particular practice of nonviolent interposition, spanning about 100 years and tens of thousands of
volunteers. The practice of accompanying threatened persons in high-
conflict zones has functioned quite successfully in protecting life. For
instance, Nagler argues that no one killed a volunteer or accompanied
person between 1985 and 2001 in Central America, and suggests comparing that to the deaths of armed soldiers and guerrillas in that period.[89]

A recent Freedom House Study offers a further piece of corroborating evidence to how nonviolent peacemaking practices protect and
ensure human rights, particularly those associated with a durable democracy. In 2005, Adrian Karantnycky directed research analyzing 67
countries over the past 33 years that transitioned from an authoritarian
or tyrannical system. The central conclusion to this research suggests
that how such a transition occurs and the types of forces used to press
that transition significantly impacts the success or failure of democratic
reform. Further, their four principal findings include the following.
First, "People power" movements matter, because nonviolent civic
forces provided a major source of pressure for decisive change in most
transitions (50 of 67). Second, there is comparatively little positive effect
for freedom in "top-down" transitions launched and led by elites. Third,

87. Kung, *Global Ethic*, 109–11.

88. Nagler, *Hope or Terror?* 22.

89. Nagler, *Search for a Nonviolent Future*, 111.

the presence of strong and cohesive nonviolent coalitions functioned as the most important of the factors examined in contributing to freedom. Fourth, prospects for freedom significantly rise when the opposition to the old system does not use violence. Thus, they call for such policies as investing in civic life, coalition building, and nonviolent training.[90] Further, more recent research has demonstrated that nonviolent civilian resistance campaigns from 1900–2006 have been more than twice as effective than their violent counterparts.[91]

Therefore, supplementing a virtue-based assessment with certain aspects of human rights discourse enhances our appreciation for the capacity of nonviolent peacemaking to ensure human rights, particularly the right to life, and thus also enhances the validity of nonviolent peacemaking practices for public discourse and policy.

SUMMARY

Although rules-based assessments of nonviolent peacemaking in general and human rights theory in particular have important limits, certain aspects of human rights discourse offer significant contributions to a virtue-based assessment of nonviolent peacemaking. The three main contributions of human rights discourse include the following.

1. Human rights presently have more moral traction and thus assist in mediating virtue into public discourse and policy.

2. Human rights, especially as capabilities, more easily move beyond the obstacle arising from the tendency to view virtue ethics as representing too thick a conception of human flourishing.

3. They help us to see more clearly how the virtue of nonviolent peacemaking actually protects and ensures human rights. Thus, rights both enhance the validity of nonviolent peacemaking practices for public discourse and policy, and assists in measuring some ways that nonviolent peacemaking works.

First, human rights theory presently enjoys more moral traction, and thus assists in mediating virtue into public discourse and policy, especially for U.S. culture. For instance, O'Neill's conception of rights as a

90. Karatnycky, "How Freedom is Won: From Civic Resistance to Durable Democracy."

91. Chenoweth and Stephan, *Why Civilian Resistance Works.*

"narrative grammar" contributes by showing a more integral relation-ship between human rights and virtues, mediating the virtue of solidar-ity and hospitality into public discourse and policy. Likewise, Putnam suggests the virtue of truth-seeking as integral to human rights theory. Also, Nussbaum's capabilities version of human rights, along with Cahill's corrections, helps to illustrate the integral relationship between virtues and capabilities. Stassen's just peacemaking theory recognizes the importance of advancing human rights by naming it as a norma-tive practice. The attention to human rights as a normative or paradig-matic practice contributes to mediating the import of virtue into public discourse.

Human rights discourse enjoys more moral traction in part because it provides summaries of past decisions and offers minimum guidelines for the common good of a society. Thus, human rights assist those want-ing to live in society but perhaps not wanting to consciously become virtuous. However, these minimum guidelines also indicate certain ac-tions that depict and call us to the virtues. Thus, human rights assist those seeking virtue but just beginning to develop the virtues.

Second, certain conceptions of human rights theory more easily move beyond the obstacle arising from the tendency to view virtue eth-ics as suggesting too thick a conception of human flourishing. O'Neill's conception of human rights leads him to argue that truth commissions often function to create a more shared civic narrative, which helps ad-dress the concern about virtue being too embedded in one tradition for diverse societies. Nussbaum argues that the capabilities more easily transcend the debate about rights and Westernization, which allows it to function more smoothly in global public discourse and policy. In turn, capabilities with their integral relationship to virtue also assist in over-coming the often-perceived limit that virtue is too strongly linked to a particular cultural or historical tradition. Her insight about "grounding experiences" or shared spheres of experience that virtue perfects illus-trates the accessibility across traditions.

Third, human rights discourse helps us to see more clearly how the virtue of nonviolent peacemaking actually protects and ensures human rights. Thus, rights both enhance the validity of nonviolent peacemaking practices for public discourse and policy, and assists in measuring some ways that nonviolent peacemaking works. Catholic Social Teaching's emphasis on the need to respect the basic rights of all others indicates the urgency of claims and clarifies a way to determine the use of nonviolent peacemaking practices. Supplementing a virtue-based account of nonviolent peacemaking with human rights theory from Catholic Social Teaching indicates that practices of nonviolent peacemaking deserve the predominant emphasis in public discourse and policy, if such policy claims to aim at justpeace. Catholic Social Teaching, the UN, and Nussbaum's acknowledgement of social-economic rights along with the political-civil rights, reinforces the value of the nonviolent peacemaking core practice of the constructive program, which Gandhi called the main arm of nonviolence. The social-economic rights part of human rights discourse further clarifies the importance and specific role of nonviolent peacemaking in public discourse and policy, particularly in the U.S., which has not yet ratified the International Covenant related to such rights.

Dear uses human rights discourse to indicate how war and the preparation for war often violate basic human rights, and thus, why the peace movement and the practices of nonviolent peacemaking make more sense for a public policy concerned with ensuring human rights. The UN also makes a strong connection between their mission to end war and the ensuring of human rights. O'Neill's conception of human rights leads him to argue that the nonviolent peacemaking practice of Truth and Reconciliation Commissions can ensure and protect human rights.

In light of the contributions that aspects of human rights discourse offer a virtue-based assessment of nonviolent peacemaking, I turn in the next chapter to the fruits of this merging by examining deeper implications for the development of Catholic Social Teaching and for U.S. public policy. Toward this end, I draw out seven core practices of the virtue of nonviolent peacemaking suggested by this merging of rights and virtue ethics.

PART FOUR

The Fruits of Merging Virtue and Human Rights

7

Impact on Catholic Social Teaching and U.S. Policy

Core Practices

INTRODUCTION

IN THIS CHAPTER, I analyze the fruits of merging a virtue-based assessment of nonviolent peacemaking with aspects of human rights theory. First, I use official Catholic Social Teaching to illustrate a movement toward this type of merging. I primarily draw on recent official documents along with Pope John Paul II and Pope Benedict XVI. Second, I further this integration by arguing for a shift to a virtue-based approach to nonviolent peacemaking. I indicate seven core practices of nonviolent peacemaking that could now arise more clearly and more frequently in Catholic Social Teaching especially, but also in U.S. public discourse and policy.[1]

CATHOLIC SOCIAL TEACHING: TOWARD RIGHTS AND VIRTUE

Catholic Social Teaching functions as a tradition both of religious discourse and of unfolding such discourse into more publicly persuasive arguments for policy. Contemporary Catholic Social Teaching stands in a tradition of ethical discourse moving toward integrating human rights and virtue. In chapter one, I described Catholic Social Teaching's

---

1. Parts of this chapter were previously published in McCarthy, "Catholic Social Teaching," 136–50.

tendency toward rule-based assessments of nonviolent peacemaking. In chapter six, I explained further how this tendency gets expressed in a rights-based approach to confronting conflicts, especially acute conflicts. I then offered some initial assessments of the limits and contributions of aspects of human rights discourse, particularly in Catholic Social Teaching.

However, contemporary Catholic Social Teaching offers a gradually increasing re-cognition of the importance of virtue, especially since Vatican II, but also more clearly since the U.S. Bishops 1993 document *The Harvest of Justice is Sown in Peace*. They combined drawing more readily on the Bible, especially the Christian Scriptures which offers a clear resonance to virtue ethics, with the extending of the call to holiness to include the laity. In turn, Catholic Social Teaching increasingly questioned the possibility of a just war and increasingly valued the potential of nonviolent peacemaking practices for public policy. The particular practices of nonviolent peacemaking illustrated by Gandhi, Martin Luther King, and the many successful nonviolent movements of the 1980's, especially the Solidarity movement in Poland, also contributed to these positions arising in Catholic Social Teaching.

Pope John Paul II taught that peace is the fruit of solidarity, which he also described as a key virtue.[2] In this context, he increasingly taught about the expanding potential of nonviolence and the need to end war. According to Christianson, John Paul summarizes his teaching in his statement "violence, which under the illusion of fighting evil, only makes it worse."[3] Pope John Paul II argued in 1979 that, "violence is evil."[4] In turn, he exhorted persons to turn away from the paths of violence particularly by not following any leaders who "train you in the way of inflicting death . . . Give yourself to the service of life, not the work of death. Do not think that courage and strength are proved by killing and destruction. True courage lies in working for peace . . . Violence is the enemy of justice. Only peace can lead the way to true justice."[5] Pope John Paul also made key contributions to the Solidarity labor movement in

---

2. John Paul II, *On Social Concern*, no. 39–40; C. Curran, "Commentary on," 430.

3. Christianson, "Catholic Peacemaking," 23. See also John Paul II, *The Hundredth Year*, no. 23, 25, 52 and "War, a Decline for Humanity."

4. John Paul II, Homily at Drogheda, 18.

5. Ibid., 19–20.

Poland and thus, the general nonviolent movements that toppled communism in Eastern Europe.

In the *Challenge of Peace* document of 1983 by the U.S. Bishops, they focus on nuclear war, but they also offer reflections on the value of nonviolence and on developing nonviolent means of conflict resolution. Although a virtue-based ethic is not predominant in the document, they do acknowledge that some Christians since the earliest days have "committed themselves to a nonviolent lifestyle." They note that: "the objective (of nonviolence) is not only to avoid causing harm or injury to another creature, but, more positively, to seek the good of the other. Blunting the aggression of an adversary or oppressor would not be enough. The goal is winning the other over, *making the adversary a friend* (emphasis mine)."[6] The aim to make the adversary a friend clearly resonates with assessing nonviolent peacemaking as the virtue that realizes the good of conciliatory love.

After the wave of nonviolent revolutions in the 1980's, which included thirteen nations in 1989 comprising almost 30 percent of the world's population, the U.S. Bishops updated their thinking in the 1993 document.[7] They orient the document by discussing the theology, spirituality and ethics of peacemaking in section one. They remind readers that Jesus calls all people, especially Christians, to become peacemakers and that at the heart of our faith lies "the God of peace," (Rom 15:33) who desires peace for all people (Psalm 85; Isa 57:19). The Bishops argue that for the gift of peace to transform our world, it also requires "peaceable virtues, a practical vision for a peaceful world and an ethics to guide peacemakers in times of conflict." They offer a list of virtues, previously mentioned, because they argue "true peacemaking can be a matter of policy only if it is first a matter of the heart."[8] The vision of a peaceful world entails: "the primacy of the global common good for political life; the role of social and economic development in securing the conditions for a just and lasting peace; and the moral imperative of solidarity between affluent, industrial nations and poor, developing ones."[9]

With the virtues and practical vision in hand, the ethics to guide peacemakers in terms of conflict consist of the increasing importance of

6. U.S. Bishops, "Challenge of Peace," Section 111 and 223.

7. Nagler, "Movement Toward Peace in Crisis," 196.

8. U.S. Bishops, "Harvest of Justice," Introduction and Sect. I.

9. Ibid., Sect. I.A.2.

nonviolent peacemaking and the increasing questions about "just" war theory. Following *Challenge of Peace*, the Bishops begin by clarifying that the Christian vision of nonviolence is not passive, such as found in popular notions of a "non-resisting pacifism." Then they turn to the possibilities of nonviolent peacemaking for public policy. "Although nonviolence has often been regarded as simply a personal option or vocation, recent history suggests that in some circumstances it can be an effective public undertaking as well . . . One must ask . . . whether it also should have a place in the public order with the tradition of justified and limited war . . . Nonviolent strategies need greater attention in international affairs."[10]

In the midst of the Bishops' increasing questioning of "just" war theory, they consider the importance of character and a properly formed conscience:

> Moral reflection on the use of force calls for a spirit of moderation rare in contemporary political culture. The increasing violence of our society, its growing insensitivity to the sacredness of life and the glorification of the technology of destruction in popular culture could inevitably impair our society's ability to apply just-war criteria honestly and effectively in time of crisis. In the absence of a commitment of respect for life and a culture of restraint, it will not be easy to apply the just-war tradition . . . given the neglect of peaceable virtues . . . serious questions remain about whether modern war . . . can meet the hard tests set by the just war tradition.[11]

This increasing emphasis on virtues, character, conscience and vision in Catholic Social Teaching arises out of a tradition that acknowledges that all persons, not just political leaders, own responsibility for the common good. In this context, the Bishops shift to an agenda for peacemaking that includes: strengthening global institutions, securing human rights, assuring sustainable and equitable development, restraining nationalism and eliminating religious violence and, building cooperative security. In the final section on concluding commitments, the Bishops again return to discourse congenial to virtue, with language such as conversion and imagination: "At its heart, today's call to peacemaking is a call to conversion, to change our hearts, to reject violence, to love our enemies . . .

10. Ibid., Sect. I.B.1.
11. Ibid., Sect. I.B.2 and Sect. I.C.

To believe we are condemned in the future only to what has been in the past . . . is to underestimate both our human potential for creative diplomacy and God's action in our midst which can open the way to changes we could barely imagine . . . For peacemakers, hope is the indispensable virtue."[12]

Pope Benedict XVI also indicates a way of thinking that supports the trajectory of further integrating virtue ethics into Catholic Social Teaching. He wrote his first encyclical *Deus Caritas Est*, i.e., God is Love, in 2005. Reflecting on the centrality of love in Christian faith, Benedict argues that love can be commanded because God has first given love. In other words, the central theme of Christian ethics is about a response to a gift, an attraction to a good before and more than assent to a command, duty, rule, or right. Near the end of this encyclical Pope Benedict weaves this thinking into directly speaking of virtue:

> Faith, hope and charity go together. Hope is practiced through the virtue of patience, which continues to do good even in the face of apparent failure, and through the virtue of humility, which accepts God's mystery and trusts him even at times of darkness. Faith tells us that God has given his Son for our sakes and gives us the victorious certainty that it is really true: God is love! Love is possible, and we are able to practice it because we are created in the image of God. To experience love and in this way to cause the light of God to enter into the world . . .[13]

I have argued that nonviolent peacemaking represents a virtue entailing a set of paradigmatic practices, which realize the specific goods of conciliatory love as well as the truth of our equal dignity and ultimate unity. In 2007, Pope Benedict spoke about the gospel text "love your enemies." He described nonviolence for Christians as *"not mere tactical behavior* but a person's *way of being*, the attitude of one who is convinced of God's love and power, who is not afraid to confront evil with the weapons of love and truth alone. Loving the enemy is the nucleus of the 'Christian revolution,' a revolution *not based on strategies of economic, political or media power* (emphasis mine)."[14] When we combine his reflections on love in his encyclical, which prioritizes attraction to the good over command and rule, with his reflection on love of enemies and particularly

12. Ibid., Sect. III.B.

13. Pope Benedict, *God is Love*, par. 14, par. 39.

14. Pope Benedict, Midday Angelus, 2007.

nonviolence as a way of being rather than mere tactic or strategy, Pope Benedict further opens the conceptual space to understand nonviolent peacemaking as a virtue oriented to the good of conciliatory love.

However, the movement toward integrating virtue ethics still faces significant challenges or growing edges. I previously demonstrated how contemporary Catholic Social Teaching has relied primarily on a rules-based and more recently rights-based assessment of nonviolence. I mentioned earlier how even within the U.S. Bishops 1993 document, rights language has a significant, if not primary role. The term "virtue" is used only thirteen times, while the term "rights" is used over fifty times. In the vision of a peaceful world, they define the three key elements in terms of human rights. They understand the just war tradition in terms of a state's right and duty to defend against aggression as a last resort, and as aiming at the kind of peace that ensures human rights. They permit humanitarian intervention, i.e., using lethal force, in exceptional cases as a right and duty. They describe seriously considering nonviolent alternatives by national leaders as a moral obligation, or what Christianson calls a "*prima facie* public obligation."[15]

Yet, in the ethics section they promote nonviolence as being an "effective public undertaking" under some circumstances, and thus, "nonviolent strategies" deserve more attention. In this instance, nonviolence gets portrayed primarily as a strategy or tactic, precisely in the context of arguing for its increased role in public discourse and policy. Further, in the 2004 Compendium of the Social Doctrine of the Church, the priority of rights is even more pronounced without any mention of the phrase "peaceable virtues" or "nonviolence." The Compendium acknowledges the value of the "witness of unarmed prophets," but gives it little explication except to condition it on the defense of human rights.[16] The relationship between peaceable virtues, nonviolence and human rights needs further clarification and development in Catholic Social Teaching, particularly for public discourse and policy.

---

15. Christianson, "Catholic Peacemaking," 23.

16. Pontifical Council, *Compendium*, Chapter 11, paragraph 494, 496.

DEVELOPMENT OF CATHOLIC SOCIAL TEACHING
AND IMPACT ON U.S. POLICY

My project of a virtue-based assessment of nonviolent peacemaking supplemented by aspects of human rights offers particular contributions toward developing Catholic Social Teaching. These contributions consist of both a shift in understanding nonviolence, and a set of practices that arise more clearly and will more likely be sustained.

The shift in understanding consists in assessing nonviolent peacemaking as a virtue, which realizes the specific goods of a conciliatory love that draws enemies toward friendship, and truth, particularly the truths of the ultimate unity of all being and equal human dignity. Recognizing this virtue qualifies key virtues, such as justice, courage, and prudence, and uplifts to more prominence a certain set of related virtues, such as solidarity, humility, hospitality, mercy, empathy, and what the Muslims call *hilm* or calmness under provocation. Further, the integral relationship between virtue and human rights gets further illuminated by drawing on the particular works of O'Neill on rights as a narrative grammar, and Nussbaum on capabilities with Cahill's additions.

Taking my approach, the next document of Catholic Social Teaching would speak about peace and nonviolence by explaining nonviolent peacemaking as a virtue, how it qualifies key virtues and uplifts a set of related virtues. The integral relationship between virtue and human rights would get a substantial analysis drawing on thinkers such as O'Neill, Nussbaum, and Cahill. This would set the stage for naming and elaborating on a set of paradigmatic practices that correspond to the virtue of nonviolent peacemaking. I now turn to this set of practices as the second core contribution which my project offers to the development of Catholic Social Teaching.

A first practice arising more clearly and sustained more readily consists in celebrating the Eucharist with an explicit orientation to nonviolent peacemaking. Pope Benedict's reflections on the centrality of love, love of enemies, and Christian nonviolence included recognition of the central role of the Eucharistic practice. He argues that the Eucharist draws us into the dynamic of Jesus' self-giving, consists of God's own agape coming to us bodily, makes present the reality that love was first given, and constantly renewed the saints, i.e., our models of Christian virtue.[17] Pope Benedict explains further that love of enemies is the "nu-

17. Pope Benedict, *God is Love*, par. 13–14, 18.

cleus of the Christian revolution," which is a revolution of love not based on strategies or on definitively human resources, but on the gift of God.[18] The Eucharist draws us into this revolution of nonviolent love.

Fr. Cantalamessa and Rev. Emmanuel McCarthy have gone further in connecting the Eucharist and nonviolence. Fr. Cantalamessa, the Preacher to the Papal Household in 2005, affirmed the growing attention to the Eucharist as the sacrament of nonviolence and God's absolute no to violence.[19] Rev. Emmanuel McCarthy argues that the words "suffered and died" in the Eucharistic prayer are theologically correct, but pastorally insufficient. He suggests one of the options for the Eucharistic prayer include something like the following:

> On the night before He went forth to His eternally memorable and life-giving death, rejecting violence, loving His enemies, praying for His persecutors, He bestowed upon His disciples the gift of a New Commandment: "Love one another. As I have loved you so you also should love one another." Then he took bread . . . But, we remember also that he endured this humiliation with a love free of retaliation, revenge, and retribution. We recall His execution on the cross. But, we recall also that He died loving enemies, praying for persecutors, forgiving, and being superabundantly merciful to those for whom (retributive) justice would have demanded (retributive) justice.[20]

Rev. McCarthy argues that Jesus proclaimed at the Last Supper both to "do this in memory of me" and the "new commandment." Thus, we need to re-unite them in our Eucharistic prayer. So far, Fr. McManus, who is one of two or three of the top Catholic liturgists in the past century, Fr. Cantalamessa, and Rev. Ken Untener, the former Bishop of Saginaw, Michigan support Rev. McCarthy's suggestion.[21] I think a virtue-based, i.e., character formation focused, assessment of nonviolent peacemaking strengthens the argument for this core formation practice of Catholics and other Christians to follow the trajectory of Rev. McCarthy's insights on the Eucharistic prayer.

This practice of connecting the Eucharistic prayer with nonviolent peacemaking extends to the associated practices of prayer in general,

18. Pope Benedict, Midday Angelus.

19. Zenit News, "Eucharist is 'God's.'"

20. McCarthy, *Nonviolent Eucharistic Jesus*, 4–5.

21. Ibid., 6–7, 10.

but also to the practice of meditation. Jesus, Gandhi, Khan, and King all emphasized the practice of prayer or meditation. The practice of meditation is often more congenial than prayer for non-religious persons, although many religious persons also practice meditation. The virtue of nonviolent peacemaking not only uplifts the significance of these related practices, but also informs how and to what end(s). For instance, prayer and meditation would function to re-connect us with the source of our lives and with the interconnectedness of all being. These practices often generate solidarity and patience, as well as a capacity to locate and focus on the deeper issues, desires, wounds, and needs. When situations of conflict become particularly trying and long lasting, these practices nourish our energy and sustain us for the long haul.

Fasting often accompanies prayer or meditation. Fasting would function as a way of discernment as Khan illustrated well. Fasting would also function as a way of cultivating a sense of solidarity with the poor, hungry, and vulnerable, and thus, move us into the work of the constructive program. Further, Gandhi illustrated how fasting functions to stir the hearts, especially of loved ones, to transform their ways from violence toward nonviolent peacemaking. Policymakers more readily become the kinds of people who better see, imagine, and commit to policies oriented to nonviolent peacemaking when they engage in prayer, meditation, or fasting, *informed* by the virtue of nonviolent peacemaking.

The attention to formation that a virtue-based assessment offers raises a second core practice: training and education in nonviolent peacemaking. The U.S. Bishops have spoken generally about how our nation needs more research, education, and training in nonviolent means of resisting injustice, but a virtue-based assessment clarifies and enhances the implementation of the specific practices.[22]

Appleby makes the argument for stronger religious education in nonviolent peacebuilding, spiritual-moral formation as the key internal condition for moving beyond violence, and to professionalize religious peace builders.[23] Religious members need educating and training in the art and science of conflict resolution.[24] Hollenbach argues for educating the heart, especially in the virtues of courage and patience. He suggests such education would entail some immediate experience of the suffer-

---

22. U.S. Bishops, *Harvest*, Sec. I.B.1.

23. Appleby, *Ambivalence*, chapter 8.

24. Johnston, *Religion, the Missing Dimension of Statecraft*, 313.

ing of the victims of injustice, developing a prudence that understands the conflict and the change at work as well as the ability to live with complexity, involvement in a supportive community of peers and co-workers, acknowledging one's limits by deepening self-knowledge, and experience that some success in the struggle for a justpeace has been and remains possible by seeing and hearing the stories as well as meeting the people involved in these stories.[25]

Lederach suggests an emphasis on the moral imagination, which resonates well with a virtue-based assessment of nonviolent peacemaking. He defines the moral imagination as the "capacity to imagine something rooted in the challenges of the real world yet capable of giving birth to that which does not yet exist." Lederach argues that "transcending violence is forged by the capacity to generate, mobilize, and build the moral imagination." For Lederach, mobilizing the moral imagination consists in practicing four disciplines: capacity to imagine ourselves in a web of relationships that includes our enemies; the ability to sustain a paradoxical curiosity that embraces complexity without reliance on dualistic polarity; a belief in and pursuit of the creative act as always possible, permanently in reach, and always accessible; and acceptance of the inherent risk of stepping into the mystery of the unknown that lies beyond the far too familiar landscape of violence.[26]

Lederach offers a set of general implications of this training for peacebuilding. One implication entails that conflict professionals think of themselves as artists as well as professionals with technical expertise. Thus, training provides intentional space in both process and intervention designs for the artistic side and listening to the inner voice, with disciplines such as journaling, storytelling, poetry, painting, drawing, music, and dance. Another implication entails providing early and continual space for exploring questions of meaning and the journey such as: Who are we? What are we doing? Where are we going? What is our purpose? These questions get further emphasis with a virtue-based assessment. A final implication Lederach suggests entails requiring political, civic, religious, and education leaders to attend continuing education annually for one week in a School for the Moral Imagination. The class would include perceived enemies, such as political enemies, and a mix of people the leaders claim to serve. In class, they would talk openly

25. Hollenbach, *Justice, Peace, and Human Rights*, 220–24.

26. Lederach, *Moral Imagination*, ix, 5, 38.

and honestly about their hopes and fears. Teachers would mostly share stories of overcoming seemingly insurmountable odds to break out of injustice by using nonviolence. Teachers would make time available for other artistic disciplines.[27]

Other examples of training and educating for nonviolent peace-making include the development of Justice and Peace Studies programs and community-based or service-learning opportunities. Although growing, these and similar programs remain marginal in academia. They usually include the study of nonviolence but often could emphasize it more.[28] A virtue-based assessment uplifts this need for more emphasis in our education on nonviolent peacemaking, and suggests relevant courses toward developing "deep nonviolence," such as meditation or contemplation, and nonviolent communication.[29] Other educational projects include supporting alternatives to college ROTC and high school JROTC programs, such as Capt. Paul Chappell's Peace Leadership Program and the Leaders for Truth program for high schools.[30] Little Friends for Peace is an example of peacemaking education for children and youth, particularly those living in hostile neighborhoods.[31] More national and international education includes the movement to establish a National Peace Academy, analogous to the academies for the armed forces, and a substantial increase in resources for the U.S. Institute of Peace, which provides an Academy for International Conflict Management and Peacebuilding. The U.S. Institute of Peace Academy engages many government officials, including police and military members. Former ambassador Dr. Dane Smith argues that the administration should explore "giving USIP the mandate to take over much of the function of training in the peace-building field."[32] The U.S. State Department recently developed a Civilian Response Corps to provide civilian experts for deployment to regions at the risk of, in, or transitioning from conflict. However, while they draw on various fields of expertise for this Corps, they fail to include expertise in nonviolent resistance or move-

---

27. Ibid., 173–77.

28. Peace and Justice Studies, *Global Directory of Peace Studies*.

29. Rosenberg, *Nonviolent Communication*.

30. Chappell, "Peace Leadership Program"; Teach Peace Foundation, "Leaders Education."

31. Little Friends for Peace.

32. Smith, *U.S. Peacefare*, 21.

ment training.[33] Although, in the State Department's new Bureau of Conflict and Stabilization they do have some staff with expertise in this area. Another option to consider is establishing a U.S. Department of Peace to provide a clearer commitment to domestic peacemaking issues, civil society, and more serious value of the peacebuilding field.

The formation of communities committed to the virtue of non-violent peacemaking closely relates to the practice of training and education. These communities provide a fertile and sustaining space to encounter nonviolent peacemaking, to grow in the virtue of nonviolent peacemaking and its related virtues, and to experiment with or imagine practices of nonviolent peacemaking. The Community of the Ark, the Catholic Worker Houses, and the Peace Community of San Jose de Apartado, Colombia offer good examples.[34] Gandhi illustrated this practice with his ashrams, understood as training for *Satyagrahis*. One of the core practices for just peacemaking theory entailed forming grassroots peacemaking groups, particularly within Christian communities, but also within society in general.[35] Public policy at the local, state, national, and international level could also set up pilot-programs or experiment with the formation of nonviolent communities in the hope of drawing wisdom and practices eventually for the larger societies.

A third core practice arising more clearly in a virtue-based and human rights assessment of nonviolent peacemaking involves attention to religious or spiritual factors, especially for public discourse; and to learning about religion(s), particularly in the form of intra-religious or inter-religious dialogue. A virtue-based approach emphasizes conceptions of the good life, which persons in the major religious traditions have been reflecting on and enacting for hundreds of years.

However, religion has too often been a missing dimension in U.S. statecraft. Johnston argues that the "intellectual framework within which most Americans in this field are introduced to the scholarly literature of international relations" represents one of the causes. He explains that the school of political realism with its emphasis on states and military power has long dominated this intellectual framework, while the major competing theory, liberalism, with its emphasis on economic power, also often gives scant or distorted attention to religious factors. Johnston

---

33. Civilian Response Corps.

34. Shephard, *Community of the Ark*. Lozano, "I Am the Leader."

35. Friesen, "Encourage Grassroots."

offers a number of examples of the disregard for religious factors. He describes such failures of U.S. diplomacy during the past century in Palestine, Iran, Pakistan, Vietnam, Poland, Nicaragua, South Africa, and the Philippines.[36] Although 9/11 illuminated the religious factor, U.S. statecraft often continues to ignore or mis-read this factor. In the context of the Iraq war, many observers claim that the US failed adequately to understand the Sunni/Shia relationship.[37] A narrow focus on political rather than social reconciliation extended this mis-reading.

Appleby and Johnston elaborate on numerous examples of how the religious factor and religious actors function as a rich resource for peacemaking. For instance, religious actors functioned as activists in the Philippines, South Africa, and East Germany. They functioned as mediators in Rhodesia, Nicaragua, and Mozembique.[38] Appleby particularly argues that training religious actors as nonviolent peacemakers inculcates forgiveness and compassion as political virtues. Religious actors can also provide a stronger concept of reconciliation beyond the political realm.[39] The U.S. Institute of Peace initiated a religious peacemaking and interfaith dialogue workshop in Iraq.[40] Yet, the USIP receives inadequate funding from the federal budget at only about 40 million per year. The U.S. ought to assign religious attaches to certain diplomatic missions to monitor religious movements and maintain contact with religious leaders.[41] The U.S. government's Civilian Response Corps for acute conflict situations ought to also include expertise in religion and religious peacemaking.[42]

Constructive program or social uplift of one's own community represents a fourth core practice arising from a virtue-based and human rights assessment of nonviolent peacemaking. This practice includes a particular attention to the poor and marginalized. Jesus, Gandhi, and Khan all lived this focus on the poor and marginalized. One key implication of engaging this practice entails the fair trade movement finding

36. Johnston, *Religion*, 287–92.

37. Codevilla, "American Statecraft"; Shuster, "Iraq War Deepens Sunni-Shia Divide."

38. Johnston, *Religion*, 313.

39. Appleby, *Ambivalence*, chapters 4, 5, 8.

40. U.S. Institute of Peace, Iraq Program.

41. Luttwak, "Missing Dimension," 16.

42. Civilian Response Corps.

stronger support with its emphasis on the poor and easily exploited.[43] Nussbaum's central capabilities theory, extended by Cahill, represents a policy framework for actualizing the focus on the poor and marginalized found in the constructive program. The constructive program would enhance our commitment to the Millennium Development Goals, particularly since progress toward most of these goals is still not on target, and since recent spending cuts for the U.S. in FY 2011 included millions from this account.[44] For instance, world hunger has hit a record high at one sixth of the population (1 billion), while many in the developing world are richer than ever.[45] The Human Development Index, grounded in capabilities theory, receives more prominence in a virtue-based assessment, particularly compared to Gross Domestic Product or economic development.[46] A shift to the development of the human person supports uplifting the value of human security and global security at least alongside, if not of higher priority, than national security.[47]

Since a constructive program aims to construct and sustain peaceful societies, people and policymakers would take more seriously the Global Peace Index. According to the 2011 index, the U.S. ranks 82 out of 153 countries,[48] which seriously suggests that some U.S. policy shifts are needed. For instance, our high and disproportionate levels of domestic violent crime, military spending and arms sales represent just some areas in need of transformation. April 2011 budget cuts to FY 2011 included cuts to the Peace Corps, U.S. Institute of Peace, and a 73% cut to the conflict prevention Civilian Response Corps, now down to only $40 million.[49] While almost every agency got cut, the Pentagon got a $5 billion increase.[50] This activity occurs within the context of a U.S. foreign aid program, which became increasingly "securitized" during the past Bush Administration. "Securitization" describes a process of using foreign aid to advance the donor governments' national security. This

43. Fair Trade Federation; Fair Trade Certified.

44. UN, Millennium Development Goals: 2008 Progress Chart. Warrick, "Far-Reaching Cuts," A3.

45. BBC News, "World Hunger hits 1 Billion."

46. UNDP, Human Development Reports.

47. Axworthy, "Human Security."

48. Vision of Humanity, "Global Rankings 2011."

49. Stark, "Prevention in the New 2011 Budget."

50. Warrick and Rucker, "Far-Reaching Cuts," A3.

logic tends to perpetuate the idea that poverty is a problem if it creates security threats, so for instance the U.S. might not invest as much in Congo.[51] Further, the Institute of Economics and Peace offered the first rankings of each U.S. state's level of peacefulness, which revealed some clear regional differences and how $360 billion annually could be saved if we increased our peacefulness to Canada's level.[52]

A constructive program also clarifies that nonviolence functions essentially as a constructive endeavor. Stassen's ten practices of just peacemaking theory largely represent an example focusing attention on the constructive practices that make for peace, rather than simply on avoiding violence—or indeed justifying war. Attending to these practices would also improve the U.S. ranking on the Global Peace Index. Stassen argues that just peacemaking entails an ethics of normative practices rather than principles. Like Catholic Social Teaching, Stassen also speaks of the importance of nurturing moral character or a spirituality that includes courage, hope, patience, humility, etc. Thus, his theory resonates well with and moves us in the direction of a virtue-based ethic. Yet, when Stassen considers the relationship between Catholic Social Teaching and just peacemaking theory, he frames the key questions in terms of the just war tradition and strategic nonviolence, rather than considering a virtue-based assessment of nonviolence.[53]

I appreciate Stassen's emphasis on normative practices, but I think the virtue of nonviolent peacemaking, and its related set of virtues would enhance the just peacemaking theory. For instance, a virtue-based ethic would amplify the development of character and the kind of imagination, which engages and creatively applies, extends, and perhaps corrects the practices of just peacemaking theory. The particular virtue of nonviolent peacemaking that aims at conciliatory love and realizing the truth of the unity of all being, would amplify the just peacemaking practices of cooperative conflict resolution and acknowledging responsibility while seeking repentance. The constructive program highlighted by this virtue would also include ecological care, which Stassen recognizes as a key piece missing from the theory.[54] Further, as I will elaborate shortly, this virtue indicates the practice of civilian-based defense, which just peace-

51. Petrik, "Securitization of Official Development Aid."

52. Vision of Humanity, "U.S. Peace Index."

53. Stassen, *Just Peacemaking*, 16, 35, 202, 212–13; *Kingdom Ethics*, chapter 5.

54. Stassen, *Just Peacemaking*, 38.

making theory fails to address. Finally, I suspect the virtue of nonviolent peacemaking would create the kinds of people that better imagine alternatives to and further marginalize the use of violence permitted by the UN's responsibility to protect (R2P) agreement, which some authors of just peacemaking theory support.[55] The virtue of nonviolent peacemaking would similarly enhance Schlabach's just policing model, which to a lesser extent permits the use of violence.[56]

Conflict transformation, particularly in the form of Truth and Reconciliation Commissions, arises as a fifth core practice corresponding to the virtue-based and human rights assessment of nonviolent peacemaking. Conflict transformation often corresponds to the general insights of restorative justice. By conflict transformation I follow Lederach, who describes it as envisioning and responding "to the ebb and flow of social conflict as life-giving opportunities for creating constructive change processes that reduce violence, increase justice in direct interaction and social structures, and respond to real-life problems in human relationships."[57] Conflict is not held to be problematic and something merely to manage or resolve, but rather as a creative opportunity for personal, relational, structural, and cultural growth or transformation. Structural refers to how conflict impacts systems and structures— how relationships are organized, and who has access to power—from family and organizations to communities and whole societies. Cultural refers to how conflict changes such things as norms that guide patterns of behavior between elders and youth or women and men.[58] Conflict transformation arises more clearly in a virtue-based approach that is personal, relational and growth oriented.

The accent on reconciliation in conflict transformation resonates well with Pope John Paul's addition of forgiveness to the convoy concept of peace in Catholic Social Teaching, and with his message of "no justice

---

55. Ibid., 174. The two main elements of R2P are: 1) Each individual State has the responsibility to protect its populations from genocide, war crimes, ethnic cleansing, and crimes against humanity; 2) The international community through the United Nations also has the responsibility to use appropriate diplomatic, humanitarian, and other peaceful means to help protect populations from these tragedies. Should such means become inadequate then use of collective violence becomes an option. UN General Assembly, Sixtieth Session, pars. 138–39.

56. Schlabach, *Just Policing*, chapters 1, 4, and 5.

57. Lederach, *Little Book of Conflict Transformation*, 390–97.

58. Lederach, Neufeldt, and Culbertson, *Reflective Peacebuilding*, 18.

without forgiveness."[59] In 2000, the U.S. Bishops wrote a document supporting restorative justice.[60] Previously, I explained O'Neill's argument for the value of Truth and Reconciliation Commissions, particularly for integrating virtue and human rights. Christianson argues "Catholic Social Theory needs a theory of conflict and principles of conflict transformation and reconciliation."[61] Kenneth Himes acknowledges the underdevelopment in Catholic Social Teaching of alternative ways to achieve peace and particularly strategies for conflict resolution, calling for Catholic Social Teaching to give more attention to the themes of reconciliation, truth-telling, restorative justice and forgiveness, as well as to develop an ethic for resolving conflict, that goes beyond the strategy of dialogue.[62] Yet, when Himes alludes to developing an ethic for resolving conflict, he primarily points to more rules in the form of *jus post bellum* norms, rather than a virtue-based ethic with the virtue of nonviolent peacemaking.[63] A virtue-based ethic more adequately addresses the need to cultivate the character, which imagines various ways to achieve peace and respond to conflict. Further, my approach would particularly enhance the conflict transformation themes Himes mentions and sustain the persons in their practice. Dan Philpott begins to move in this direction by naming reconciliation's animating virtue as mercy, and offering six practices or ways to reconciliation and justice.[64]

Conflict transformation and particularly Truth and Reconciliation Commissions would greatly enrich contemporary policy discussions. For instance, policy leaders in the peacebuilding field sent a proposal to the incoming U.S. administration in late December 2008.[65] They pointed to the role of civil society in peacebuilding, conflict prevention, conflict resolution and negotiation, conflict management and stabilization.

59. Christianson, "Catholic Peacemaking," 24; John Paul II, "No Peace Without Justice."

60. U.S. Bishops, "Responsibility, Restoration."

61. Christianson, "Peacebuilding in Catholic Social Teaching."

62. Himes, "Peacebuilding as a Developing Norm in Catholic Social Teaching."

63. Often, but not always, *jus post bellum* norms emphasize rights language, war crimes tribunals, and the notion of ending conflict rather than virtue, reconciliation, such as Truth and Reconciliation Commissions, and the notion of conflict transformation. I suspect that the rules-based approach is, in part, responsible for this limit. For instance, see Orend, *War and International Justice*; "Justice After War"; *Morality of War*.

64. Philpott, "Lessons in Mercy," 11–14.

65. Schirch, "Building Bridges and Preventing Conflict."

However, the proposal lacked any mention of conflict transformation or even reconciliation. The author affirmed to me the value of conflict transformation but said that it remains out of the vocabulary or off the radar for many of the policy thinkers they address. A virtue-based assessment of nonviolent peacemaking would contribute to repairing this disconnect by clarifying the meaning and value of conflict transformation in general, and Truth and Reconciliation Commissions in particular.

Search for Common Ground offers an example of a U.S.-based global organization engaged in conflict transformation, which would get more attention and resources.[66] They have developed participatory theater as a form of conflict transformation. For instance, in the Democratic Republic of the Congo actors are trained to analyze a conflict, how to determine the positions and interests of those in the conflict, and what it means to transform it. After using active listening to engage various parties of the community, the actors perform in public presenting the reality of the community to the audience. Then they ask for comments and rewind the performance. As each scene is replayed, they ask for the audience to present alternative reactions by the characters so that the audience literally acts out a new future. The performance maintains its focus, emotions, and intensity in order to speak to the heads and hearts of the audience.[67]

Another key form of conflict transformation, which could include participatory theater, is Truth and Reconciliation Commissions. These commissions generally aim at establishing a public record of human rights abuses over a certain period of time in a particular country or related to a particular conflict. They hope to resolve or transform conflict from the past, and often to promote a more sustainable peace and justice. Such commissions often allow victims, their relatives, and perpetrators to have their story heard and to give evidence of human rights abuses within an official public forum. In turn, these commissions submit a final report with conclusions and recommendations.[68] Designers of these commissions may also include strong procedural safeguards as part of legitimizing the approach and coinciding with constitutional principles.

Only a few Truth Commissions have generally been recognized as occurring in the U.S., and *none* has been officially developed or even

---

66. Search for Common Ground.

67. Slachmuijlder, "Setting the Stage for Peace," 228.

68. Truth Commissions.

endorsed by the local or national justice system. However, about 35 commissions have occurred across the globe since 1974, including the most famous one in South Africa beginning in 1995.[69] In the U.S., one occurred in North Carolina in 2005 regarding a local massacre back in 1979. KKK members killed five people in the course of a demonstration. Four television crews captured the crime on film. The demonstrators had been promised a police escort. But the police failed to appear on the scene until the murderers had made good their escape. Two separate trials of all-white jurors acquitted the accused. Yet, a federal suit in 1985 found them liable for one death and required the City to pay a settlement. However, no apology or acknowledgement of wrongdoing arose.[70]

Rev. Johnson of Greensboro realized how the "powers" tend to resist recognizing general patterns of injustice by describing events as "isolated." In turn, they scapegoat individuals or small groups. When someone pushes to address the patterns in the U.S., the deeply traumatized dominant culture faces its own history of trauma. Johnson points to the patterns of prisoners and bond-servants escaping to the New World, and then inflicting their trauma on others, i.e., Native Americans and particularly in the institution of slavery. Therefore, in 2001 Rev. Johnson and other local residents initiated and implemented the Greensboro Truth and Reconciliation Project in the midst of official opposition from the city council and the white press. In 2006, the commission found that the police knew of these groups' plans to provoke a violent confrontation and the strong potential for violence. The findings launched a formal year of discussion and various initiatives, such as a living wage campaign.[71]

Other grassroots commissions occurred in Ohio in 2006 regarding poverty in the U.S., and in New York in 2010 on conscience in war.[72] Truth and Reconciliation Commissions have also been proposed in the U.S. for issues like torture, racism and structural injustice, such as Hurricane Katrina; sexism and patriarchy, and U.S. foreign policy in Central America.[73]

69. Truth Commissions.

70. Enns and Myers, *Ambassadors of Reconciliation*, 139.

71. Ibid., 142–47.

72. Poor People's Economic Human Rights Campaigns; Truth Commission on Conscience in War.

73. Hammond; Poverty Initiative; and Perry, "Time for a U.S. Truth Commission."

Truth and Reconciliation Commissions would enhance policies regarding Iraq and Afghanistan. In the 2003 Iraq War, to the limited extent that our policy considered reconciliation it focused on political reconciliation or compromise between political leaders and the formation of the rule of law. In contrast, some policy leaders argued for a more adequate reconciliation between persons, civil society groups, and with the U.S., as well as for the broader structural and cultural dimensions of conflict transformation.[74] In Afghanistan, the U.S. continues to emphasize military force and drone bombing after ten years of war, while social wounds deepen with Koran burnings, urination on dead Afghan bodies, and direct killing of civilians by U.S. soldiers. Finally, since these commissions can be designed to ensure accountability and actually contribute to creating the conditions for respecting human rights and the rule of law, they would enhance U.N. policy as at least a complement to the International Criminal Court, if not as an eventual substitute.

Unarmed civilian peacekeeping (UCP) or third party nonviolent intervention (TPNI) arises as a sixth core practice corresponding to a virtue-based and human rights assessment of nonviolent peacemaking. This practice entails an outside party intervening in a conflict as a non-partisan, with compassion for all parties, without violence, with the aims of defusing violence and of creating a space for reconciliation and peace building. Ramon Generoso of the Interfaith Center for a Culture of Nonviolence describes the proposal for local UCP as aiming "to empower civilians and communities through nonviolent direct action, both peacemaking and peacekeeping, that would enable them to assert peace within their communities, help enforce the ceasefire at the ground level, and help defuse small conflicts which could evolve into larger ones."[75] Lakey explains that TPNI (or UCP) often assists the struggle to continue, but with less violence and directly affects the field of physical conflict.[76]

The virtue-based and human rights assessment of nonviolent peacemaking cultivates the kinds of persons who would imagine, prepare for, enact and sustain UCP. The Nonviolent Peaceforce, which arose from reflecting on Gandhi's idea of *shanti sena* (peace army), offers a prime example of the UCP in practice. Other contemporary examples include the Balkan Peace Team (1994–2001), Christian Peacemaker Teams,

---

74. Kucinich, "12 Point Plan for Iraq."

75. Generoso, "Exploring Civil Society-led Third Party Nonviolent Intervention."

76. Lakey, "How to Develop Peace Teams."

Peace Brigades International (PBI), Witness for Peace, the Michigan Peace Team, and the Muslim Peacemaker Teams in Iraq.[77]

UCP often includes more specific practices such as interposition, accompaniment, proactive engagement with armed actors, interactive monitoring, documenting, rumor control, modeling nonviolent behavior, and sometimes includes connecting local persons to national and international resources, as well as providing safe places from violence or for dialogue.[78] Interposition refers to directly placing one's body between hostile parties. PBI provided an example of accompaniment when they sent international volunteers to El Salvador and Guatemala to walk with local human rights activists threatened with assassination. By instilling a sense of solidarity and a glare of publicity, they reduced the chance of assassination and all of the local activists survived while with PBI.[79]

The practice of UCP would contribute to present public discourse and policies in the following ways. First, the U.N. Peacekeeping forces are still largely based on military operations, although their scope of operations has been expanding.[80] Meanwhile the debate about using private military contractors, such as Blackwater, now Xe Services, to address the limits of U.N. Peacekeeping continues to hold significant traction.[81] The practice of UCP provides an alternative form of peacekeeping, which would change the debate. UCP would shift the ground of U.N. peacekeeping from military operations to civilian operations; shift the training from military virtues to the virtue of nonviolent peacemaking and its related set of virtues; offer the specific practices of nonviolent modeling, interposition, and proactive engagement with armed actors; and more adequately integrate the aim of reconciliation rather than primarily settling for keeping parties apart. The practice of UCP also offers a way to enrich and uphold the recent but unstable consensus on the Responsibility to Protect, and thus, potentially enhance its legitimacy.[82]

---

77. Schweitzer, "Human Security," 114–15; Christian Peacemaker Teams, Peace Brigades, Witness for Peace, Michigan Peace Team, Muslim Peacemaker Teams.

78. Nonviolent Peaceforce, "Mission"; Lakey, "How to Develop Peace Teams."

79. Lakey, "How to Develop Peace Teams." For other examples, see Nagler, *Is There No Other Way*, 238–72.

80. UN Department of Peacekeeping.

81. Isenberg, "Contractors vs. Genocide."

82. International Coalition, "Introduction to R2P."

Second, the U.S. government's development of a Civilian Response Corps to provide civilian experts for deployment to regions at the risk of, in, or transitioning from conflict deserves praise. However, the implementation of the originating directive faces bureaucratic roadblocks and takes a backseat, like so many other positive possibilities, to the wars in Iraq and Afghanistan.[83] Further, the Civilian Response Corps emphasizes stabilization with concern for U.S. national security interests, while drawing on expertise from policing and the rule of law.[84] A virtue-based approach to nonviolent peacemaking would enhance the policy of developing and implementing a Civilian Response Corps in the following ways. It would emphasize a justpeace with a broader concern for human security. It raises the value of civilian participation and intervention. It clarifies UCP and its more particular forms, as well as the practice of conflict transformation and the particular form of truth and reconciliation commissions. A virtue-based approach suggests that the Civilian Response Corps should also include experts in UCP and conflict transformation or restorative justice.

Third, UCP would offer some insights to the just policing model or to policing in general. One of these insights includes the creation of local peace teams as a supplement to and perhaps eventually a substitute for armed police. The Michigan Peace Team has in part initiated this idea of the local peace team. Also, the success of street outreach workers, such as the Street Outreach Team in Oakland California, which entails training and deploying unarmed, non-police, street-smart and street credible persons to patrol high violence areas, is a movement in this direction.[85] Similar programs exist in Boston, Chicago (Ceasefire), Providence, and DC (Homecomers).[86]

Civilian-based defense (CBD) arises as a seventh core practice that becomes clearer in a virtue-based and human rights approach. This practice entails using nonviolent resistance methods to defend against military invasion, occupation or *coups d'etat*. The resistors do not physically prevent invading troops from entering their territory. Yet, everyone participates in the resistance, taking responsibility for their defense

83. Feinstein, "Darfur and Beyond," 26; Bensahel, "Improving Capacity," 46.

84. Civilian Response Corps.

85. Grant, "Mayor's Street Outreach Program."

86. Scrimshaw, "Violence Virus"; Ceasefire.

rather than delegating it to an elite group.[87] Civilian-Based Defense resistance primarily entails non-cooperation with the opponent's orders and perhaps creation of a parallel government, to the point of making it inconvenient to nearly impossible for the occupying force to benefit or even stay.[88] The power of this practice is in part grounded in the notions that one who refuses to submit cannot be ruled, and the distinction between persons and their agenda. Nagler explains that the power of "resisting the latter [agenda] but resolutely acknowledging the humanity of the former [persons], develops an almost irresistible counterforce."[89]

A virtue-based assessment is particularly congenial to everyone's personal growth, such as the participation and taking fuller responsibility, which Civilian-Based Defense emphasizes. Further, a virtue-based assessment would be especially helpful in drawing our attention to developing the courage and solidarity to engage this practice, the commitment to maintain it the face of ongoing repression, the imagination to find ways not to cooperate, and the capacity to discriminate between the shared dignity of persons and their agenda. The recognition of shared dignity or humanity in Civilian-Based Defense also entails relating to the other as potential friends, i.e., with the conciliatory love that the virtue of nonviolent peacemaking enacts and aims toward.

Taking different forms Civilian-Based Defense arose a number of times in the past century and some governments recently incorporated it into their defense planning. Past examples include the 1923 resistance to Wolfgang Kapp's attempted *coup d'etat* in Germany,[90] the Norwegian and Danish resistance against German occupation during WWII,[91] the Czechoslovakian resistance against Soviet occupation in 1968,[92] and the Baltic countries in 1990–91.[93] Sweden, Austria, and Lithuania recently incorporated Civilian-Based Defense into their defense planning by

---

87. Nagler, *Is There No Other Way*, 252–53.

88. Roberts, "Introduction," 9.

89. Nagler, *Is There No Other Way*, 135–36.

90. Sharp, *Waging Nonviolent Struggle*, 91–100; Sternstein, "Ruhrkampf of 1923," 106–35.

91. Ibid., 135–42; Skodvin, "Norwegian Nonviolent Resistance," 136–53. On Denmark, see Bennett, "Resistance Against," 154–72.

92. Nagler, *Is There No Other Way*, 133–36; Sharp, *Waging Nonviolent Struggle*, 189–204.

93. Sharp, *Waging Nonviolent Struggle*, 277–86.

providing research and development funds to create nonviolent methods to prevent military occupation.[94]

Adam Roberts describes four possible stages toward a Civilian-Based Defense policy:

1. research and investigation;

2. general public education in nonviolent action and Civilian-Based Defense, with concentrated training and organizational preparations;

3. application of civilian defense in specific areas without complete abandonment of military defense policy; and

4. public commitment to Civilian-Based Defense.

Roberts elaborates on stage 3 as having potential application to resisting coup d'etats, especially military ones; resisting external aggression, particularly defending exposed parts that are difficult to defend militarily; dealing with guerrilla threats, either in allied countries or one's own territory; resisting blockades; and serving as a sanction for a military disarmament or disengagement agreement.[95]

The UN, the U.S., and the Catholic Church, particularly Catholic schools, could all develop and emphasize policy on funding research and investigation into Civilian-Based Defense (stage 1), as well as general public education in Civilian-Based Defense with concentrated training and organizational preparations (stage 2). In the U.S., moving toward a Civilian-Based Defense policy would help correct our enormously disproportional military budget and research funds allocated for the military, in order to free up funds for addressing root causes of violence, other social injustices, pollution, and human development.[96] For instance, the U.S. with the world's most powerful and expensive investment in the military also has cultivated one of the world's highest prison populations per 100,000 people.[97] In 1996, Zahn reported that 65% of all public research and development funding went to military use; and when we included private funds, the figure is still 30–40% compared to

94. Lakey, "How to Develop Peace Teams"; Sharp, *Waging Nonviolent Struggle*, 516.

95. Roberts, "Transarmament to Civilian Defence" 292–95.

96. Zahn, *Alternative to the Pentagon*, 1–14.

97. Vision of Humanity, "Global Peace Index: USA"; Zahn, *Alternative to the Pentagon*, 8–11.

Germany at 4% and Japan at 1%. He points out that others argue that the "brain drain" from civilian to military progress represents a significant factor in the decline of manufacturing jobs in the U.S. and in the production rate of goods.[98] Further, developing the State Department's new Bureau of Conflict and Stabilization or creating a U.S. Department of Peace could enhance the resources, skill, and will to increasingly move toward a Civilian-Based Defense policy in collaboration with the Departments of Homeland Security and Defense.

In 1983, the U.S. Bishops document *Challenge of Peace* mentions "popular defense" and calls for further research, education, and training by Catholic universities in peacemaking.[99] Yet, Catholic thinkers have produced little on Civilian-Based Defense, and what has been produced remains on the margins. A virtue-based assessment of nonviolent peacemaking would better cultivate the people interested in doing this activity and responding to this call. If Catholic schools of higher education gave priority to the virtue of nonviolent peacemaking, and similarly to prioritize research into corresponding practices like Civilian-Based Defense, then ROTC programs on campus would require serious reconstruction of their curriculum or the school should develop an analogous Peace Leadership Training Program; and ROTC should be given a diminished authority on campus, if not completely discontinued.

In sum, I have argued for seven core practices that arise more clearly and more frequently in our imagination, and more likely sustained with a virtue-based assessment of nonviolent peacemaking. These practices further the integration of virtue and rights, especially in Catholic Social Teaching, but also contribute to U.S. public discourse and policy. The seven practices include:

1. celebrating the nonviolent Eucharist, with secondary components of prayer, meditation, and fasting;

2. training and education in nonviolent peacemaking, with the secondary component of forming nonviolent peacemaking communities;

3. attention to religious or spiritual factors, especially in public discourse, and learning about religion, particularly in the form of intra-religious or inter-religious dialogue;

98. Zahn, *Alternative to the Pentagon*, 1–14. Cassidy, "Military Dollars."
99. U.S. Bishops, *Challenge of Peace*, sections 223–29.

4. the constructive program with its particular focus on the poor and marginalized;

5. conflict transformation and restorative justice, particularly in the form of Truth and Reconciliation Commissions;

6. unarmed civilian peacekeeping both in the form of international implementation and local peace teams; and

7. civilian-based defense.

SUMMARY

In this chapter I argued that Catholic Social Teaching illustrates a trajectory of thinking that integrates virtue and human rights in the assessment of nonviolent peacemaking. I furthered this integration for Catholic Social Teaching by arguing for the shift from a rights-based assessment to a virtue-based assessment of nonviolent peacemaking, which my project developed throughout. This shift indicated seven core practices of nonviolent peacemaking that would now arise more clearly and more frequently in the tradition of Catholic Social Teaching, but also with significant implications for U.S. public discourse and policy.

8

Case Study

Applying the Practices to Situations of Genocide—Sudan

INTRODUCTION

IN THIS CHAPTER, I continue to analyze the fruits of merging a virtue-based assessment of nonviolent peacemaking with aspects of human rights discourse. I apply this freshly merged approach and the particular core practices to the difficult contemporary case of genocide or mass atrocity, such as found in Sudan.[1] First, I describe key elements of the historical situation and some of the policy approaches to the conflict in Sudan. Second, I explore some potential implications arising from some of the core practices corresponding to the virtue of nonviolent peacemaking. Instead of making a detailed proposal for the particular situation in Sudan I am primarily raising questions and suggesting a repertoire of possible responses, which could also potentially hold for other similar situations. A detailed proposal for this ongoing conflict requires further research and closer on the ground contact.

SOME KEY HISTORICAL ELEMENTS
AND POLICY RECOMMENDATIONS

An international treaty outlawed genocide since 1948, but such acts continue to occur and have accounted for over 20 million deaths since then. The recent history of genocide reveals that the global community has offered very inconsistent responses. For instance, NATO's military

1. Following the UN's Responsibility to Protect principle described below, by mass atrocity I include genocide, war crimes, ethnic cleansing, and crimes against humanity.

intervention in Kosovo in 1999 indicated a willingness to more directly confront genocide. However, the 75 days of bombing increased the killings of the Kosovar population from 1,000 over the whole year before to another 10,000, including 500 Serbian civilians. The bombing also led to a massive forced migration of about 1.4 million, about 2/3 of the Kosovar population.[2] On the other hand the international community was reluctant to intervene to halt the mass killing in Rwanda during 1994 and in Darfur, Sudan primarily during 2004–2005. The recent endorsement of the responsibility to protect principle (R2P) by the U.N. in 2005 represents an important but relatively under-reported shift in policy. R2P redefines sovereignty as entailing both rights *and* responsibilities. This principle begins to resolve the historic tension between human rights and states' rights in favor of the person.[3]

Assessing the conflict in Sudan requires a look at the history. From the Egyptian invasion of 1821, the attractions of South Sudan to those further North were ivory and slaves. After the interlude of the rule of the Mahdi and his successor from 1885–1898, Sudan was ruled by a British-Egyptian condominium from 1899–1955. The British sought to avoid triggering more Islamic dissent and so concentrated their efforts in the north, with minimal attention to the South beyond security. Because of ethnic and religious divisions between the peoples of northern and southern Sudan, they sought to insulate the South from Islamic influence, for example by requiring northern Sudanese to obtain permits to travel to the South, and some other districts. The marginalization and inferior development of the South, West and East, coupled with the legacy of slavery and the treatment of their peoples by the ruling elites as second class citizens, sowed the seeds of future conflicts.

Since independence in 1956, Sudan has struggled with civil war between the north and south almost continuously. The All Africa World Council of Churches sponsored the talks in Addis Ababa that led to the only notable break in the fighting between the years of 1972–1983. The war resumed in 1983 when then President Nimeiri denounced the Addis agreement and introduced Sharia law. Since the military coup that brought Omar-al Bashir to power in 1989, groups from other peripheral areas of Sudan exposed the simmering conflict

2. Cortright, *Peace: A History*, 290.

3. Feinstein, "Darfur and Beyond," v–10.

and have entered further into conflict with the central government.[4] The major concerns of such groups included the government's policies that exploit local resources, impose religious and cultural beliefs on diverse populations, and pit local tribes and ethnic groups against each other for short-term political gain.

Darfur is one of these peripheral areas, which has seen violence and insecurity since the 1970's. Major incidents included a bitter conflict between the Arab and Fur in the late 1980s and an incursion by the Southern rebels in 1991. After relative calm since 1994, armed groups in Darfur launched a major uprising in February 2003 with the goal of equal representation in government and improved infrastructure. The government responded with armed Arab militias called *janjaweed*, which targeted the villages of the armed groups in Darfur.[5] These attacks displaced over 2.5 million and may have killed between 200,000–400,000 people.[6] In September 2004, U.S. Secretary of State Colin Powell accused the government of Sudan of committing "genocide."[7]

The 2005 Comprehensive Peace Agreement (CPA) did not directly include Darfur, yet it did contain elements that affect the whole of Sudan, such as elections, wealth sharing, and land. At the same time, promised international aid slowly trickled in.[8] In 2006, only one of three armed groups from Darfur signed the Darfur Peace Agreement (DPA) that would have brought a ceasefire and measures to reduce Darfur's political and economic marginalization. However, the conflict continued.[9] Although authorized in 2007, the hybrid AU/UN peacekeeping force (UNAMID) deployed very slowly. In July 2008 and again in 2010, the International Criminal Court's Prosecutor requested the arrest of Sudan's President al-Bashir for genocide, crimes against humanity, and murder.[10] In response to the first arrest warrant, al-Bashir ordered 13 foreign NGO's to leave Darfur.[11] In 2010, Darfur faced increasing

4. Hanson, "Sudan's Fractured Internal Politics."

5. Ibid.

6. Save Darfur Coalition, "Genocide in Darfur—Briefing Paper."

7. Slavin, "Powell Accuses Sudan of Genocide."

8. Hanson, "Sudan's Fractured."

9. Feinstein, "Darfur and Beyond," 44. Sontag and Mines, "Transformational Diplomacy," 10.

10. Maweni, "Sudan's President Omar."

11. Crilly, "President al-Bashir of Sudan Taunts the West."

violence compared to 2009, although not at the levels of 2003–05. In January 2011, Southern Sudan voted to become an independent state and southern Sudanese returned from the north in increasing numbers. There has since been tribal conflict in the South and the threat of further violence in north/south border areas, especially Abyei as shared oil resources and the exact border demarcation remain key challenges.

U.S. public discourse and policy recommendations regarding Darfur between 2006–2010 represented a wide range of ideas. In 2007, Feinstein of the Council of Foreign Relations recommended immediately strengthening the African Union mission in Darfur, readying an international armed force now, and enforcing the UN and Darfur Peace Agreement flight bans. He argued that if the international armed force included participation by China, then the Sudanese government would get some political cover to accept the force. Feinstein explained that enforcing the flight bans could also include economic sanctions on Khartoum leadership and taking over airports.[12] The Enough Project and the Save Darfur Campaign offered similar ideas in terms of increasing the pressure, such as pursuing the ICC's arrest warrants, increasing targeted sanctions, and expanding the arms embargo.[13]

Andrew Natsios, former U.S. special envoy to Sudan in 2006–7, and Scott Gration, the special envoy from 2009–2011, argued for engagement and normalization of U.S.-Sudan relations with a focus on implementing the CPA. Natsios argued that the ruling national party in Sudan will do anything to stay in power regardless of international pressure, because they recognized that if removed then they will face domestic retaliation and war crimes trials abroad.[14] Others also supported this focus on the CPA and called for deferring the arrest warrant for Bashir under the condition he implement the CPA.[15] China, the African Union, League of Arab States, and Non-Aligned Movement all supported the deferment of the arrest warrant due to concern that it would upset the peace process and negotiations.[16] A few experts continue to argue that the conflict requires a domestic political deal in Sudan with buy in from all parties. Thus, they suggest the U.S. ought to revisit the CPA to include

12. Feinstein, "Darfur and Beyond," 42–45.

13. Prendergast, Norris, and Fowler, "President Obama's."

14. Natsios, "Beyond Darfur."

15. Stares and Noyes, "Think Twice on Bashir."

16. Tong, "China Regretful."

more regions, or focus on discrete tasks such as monitoring CPA outcomes and funding research on the politics of land in Sudan.[17]

Others have argued that oil functions as a major driver of the conflict, which represents a more marginal position in the public discourse about Darfur. Eggbert Wesselink of the European Coalition on Oil in Sudan, Human Rights First, and Frederick W. Engdahl of the Center for Research on Globalization represent this position.[18] Engdahl argues that the struggle between China and the U.S. for control of oil resources functions as a key aspect to the conflict. China's national oil company is Sudan's largest foreign investor, while China takes 65–80 percent of Sudan's oil production. China expects to pass U.S. demand for oil import in a few years. Engdahl explains that the U.S., in part, covertly financed the long-simmering civil war to break the south, where the majority of oil fields exist, from the Islamic Khartoum-centered north. According to Engdahl, the U.S. also provided military aid, training, and weapons to Chad's president Idriss Deby, who worked with Chevron and who conspired in the initial military strike in 2003, which set off the conflict in Darfur. Engdahl claims that Deby provided soldiers and arms to Darfur rebels in conflict with the Khartoum government.[19] In the mid-2000's, U.S. development aid for Sub-Saharan Africa was decreased sharply, while military aid rose. U.S. Assistant Secretary of State for Africa, Walter Kansteiner, stated in 2002, "West Africa's oil has become of national strategic interest to us."[20]

APPLYING THE CORE PRACTICES

These issues certainly raise difficult concerns, which require urgent and wise responses. In the context of my project on a virtue-based assessment of nonviolent peacemaking, I want to primarily raise some

17. Hanson, "Sudan's Fractured."

18. Wesselink quoted in Staff Writers, "New Secret Oil Installations in Darfur"; Herbst, "Oil for China, Guns for Darfur;" Human Rights First; Morse, "War of the Future," and "Blood, Ink, and Oil"; Engdahl, "Darfur: Forget Genocide, There's Oil"; Center of Research on Globalization.

19. Engdahl, "Darfur: Forget Genocide." John Garang, who was trained at Fort Benning, Georgia, led the Sudan People's Liberation Army in the South until July 2005. Engdahl explains that many of the arms brought into Darfur come from private "merchants of death" such as Victor Bout, a former KGB operative convicted in 2011 of arms trafficking.

20. Engdahl, "Darfur: Forget Genocide, There's Oil."

questions and suggest a repertoire of responses regarding Sudan, which could apply to other situations of mass atrocity and genocide.

In general, the reality of massive human rights violations along with the slow and inadequate international response indicates again the limits of a rights-based approach and the need for an alternative, such as a virtue-based approach. I elaborated on this "compliance gap" regarding human rights earlier. Further, in *The New Republic* David Rieff argues that "human rightism" led pro-Darfuri armed intervention activists to perpetuate a "reductionist dichotomy of victims and abusers," which "has been the staple myth of humanitarian interventions."[21] My virtue-based approach supplemented by aspects of human rights discourse highlights seven core practices for Catholic Social Teaching geared toward public discourse and policy. What relevant analogies arise between these practices and the actual or potential responses to the case of Sudan?

Conflict transformation, particularly in the form of Truth and Reconciliation Commissions offers one relevant practice. This entails an emphasis on restorative justice, which focuses on the harms done to relationships and how to heal these relationships. Alex de Waal argues that a thread of restorative justice exists in Darfur. According to de Waal, when the people speak of justice they talk about returning to their homes, compensation, and being able to return to the life they lost. He views the ICC process as failing to address these components of justice.[22] Thabo Mbeki, head of an African Union panel on Darfur, says the ICC indictments will "do little to soothe the hatreds that have spawned rapes and massacres."[23] The level of distrust continues to affect policy and implementation of agreements, as the phrase "too many agreements dishonoured," is repeatedly invoked.[24] Daniel Akau, who lived in Sudan, argues that the many broken agreements occur in large part because of the failure to speak and address the truth about the deep-rooted causes of the civil wars and present conflicts, such as the policy of Arabization and the inequitable distribution of goods.[25] The wounds incurred from earlier conflicts between some Arab herdsman and some of the African

21. Rieff, "Moral Blindness: The Case Against Troops for Darfur," 14.

22. Waal, "Indicting Sudan's President for War Crimes."

23. Quoted in John Lewis, "Human Right in Darfur."

24. Fluehr-Lobban, "Religious Leaders and Conflict Management."

25. Akau, "Forgiveness and Reconciliatory Process in Sudan," 29–31.

farmers, which in large part arose from the lack of arable land and climate change, perpetuated the violence in Darfur.[26] Chol Mathiai wonders how any unified and peaceful Sudan can arise when there remain "no proper common grounds for its diverse cultures, religions, ethnic groups to meet; where bonds of marriage are rare, or where antagonism, intimidation, and animosity grow daily."[27] Many people of Darfur experience deep humiliation and react out of this throbbing wound, in some cases joining the armed resistance.[28]

The practice of conflict transformation would put these wounds and concerns into the center of the pursuit of justice in Sudan and Darfur. What shape could this practice take? How would this approach shift the tone of the discourse? The ICC arrest warrant further incited the fears in al-Bashir of facing retaliation if he relinquished power. This led to the expelling of the NGO's. What if accountability was re-framed, not excluded, so that healing became more central than both the threats and fears of retaliation and retribution? Perhaps, an ICC trial would still occur, but it certainly would not take center stage. Rather, a criminal trial would be a component of a larger, clearly articulated restorative justice process, which centered more on practices such as Truth and Reconciliation Commissions, smaller-scale practices of circles, family conferencing, or victim-offender conferencing. For instance, these circles could particularly focus on experiences of humiliation in order to mitigate resorting to direct violence, and on the generational differences at play particularly in Darfur. The circles could be complemented by participatory theater events similar to those used in the Democratic Republic of Congo. Such theater provides a space for the audience to literally act out a new future. In contrast to these conflict transformation approaches the punitive measures against rebel groups in Darfur tend to enhance their legitimacy and backfire.[29] The Darfur-Darfur Dialogue Consultation, which deployed to Darfur in 2008, works on local-level reconciliation and represented a positive sign in the practice of conflict transformation. However, the consultation has had limited support.[30]

26. Faris, "Real Roots of Darfur."
27. Quoted in Fluehr-Lobban, "Religious Leaders."
28. Braun, *Darfur Now: Six Stories, One Hope.*
29. Knopf, "Post-Referendum."
30. Dewall, "Part Two: Mediation."

However, British leaders implemented a policy of insulating the South from Northern Islamic influence, and neglected development needs in the South from 1899–1956. These strategies factored into the ongoing civil wars in Sudan since their independence in 1956. What role should the British have in being accountable for and in healing the discord in Sudan? The factor of climate change, particularly decreasing arable land, in the conflict between some Arab herdsman and some African farmers reveals a wider global responsibility.[31] Further, the struggle for oil control, particularly by large powers such as the U.S. and China, along with the infiltration of weapons and military aid also reveals a wider global responsibility. Since the U.S. is the largest human contributor to global warming, climate change, arms sales, and oil consumption, what role might the U.S. and even China have in being accountable for and in healing the discord in Sudan? These questions suggest the value of seriously considering a larger, more international Truth and Reconciliation Commission.

All adequate conflict transformation practices involve the structural level of injustices; and thus, closely relates to another core practice of the virtue of nonviolent peacemaking, i.e. the constructive program. The struggle for land exemplifies the relevance to Darfur of the constructive program, with its emphasis on uplifting the poor and marginalized. For instance, this practice would make the wealth sharing and land reform components of the Comprehensive Peace Agreement a top priority. However, concern arises that this agreement (and the Darfur Agreement) not only left out certain regions (or key groups), but also primarily functions as a pact between elites. How would the voices and needs of the poor and marginalized be included in the agreement or a revised version of it? Is there an indigenous way to engage and empower the poorer people, as Gandhi used the spinning wheel in India? In response to the threat power approach of the ICC arrest warrant al-Bashir removed 13 NGO's, which primarily harmed the poorest. The virtue of nonviolent peacemaking illuminates why the practices of both conflict transformation's integrative power approach and the constructive program mutually implicate each other.

The practice of the constructive program also further draws our attention to the factor of climate change and ecological damage in the conflict, such as poisoned water sources, and competition for the decreasing

31. Faris, "Real Roots of Darfur."

arable land.[32] In the midst of the land struggle, the central government generally supported the Arab herdsman politically and often supplied arms, such as to the *janjaweed*, who largely did the killing in Darfur. Further, this underlying factor of climate change in the conflict ought to lead the major industrialized countries, with our factories, power plants, automobiles, and reliance on oil, especially in the U.S. to recognize our involvement and the need to constructively change our style of living.[33]

Emphasis on uplifting the poor and marginalized, including the factor of ecological damage draws our attention to two other aspects of U.S. involvement in the conflict: oil and military aid. The practice of the constructive program would challenge the levels of U.S. military spending and arms sales, particularly to Sudan and more recently to South Sudan along with other poor regions of the world exacerbating these conflicts. This challenge is especially salient when development aid lags far behind or was even decreasing while military aid increased to such regions. The constructive program would also raise questions about who benefits (financially, politically, etc.) from continuing to rely heavily on oil, and the military power/technology to control it. Is the quest for "stability, security, and (even) human rights" more about providing Nussbuam's central capabilities to the people, especially the poor and marginalized; or more about maintaining/seizing the oil, military prowess and profit for the elite?[34]

The practice of constructive program resonates well with former British Ambassador to Sudan, Alan Goulty's wise suggestion to offer "more to the people of Darfur than simply a return to their villages and subsistence agriculture." Rather, any response must include "imaginative moves to create new employment and livelihoods, including for former rebel soldiers, a new agreement on land rights, and the provision of education and health services, especially for women."[35]

The core practice of attending to the role of religious and spiritual factors, particularly in the form of intra-religious dialogue also offers some insight for Sudan. The conflict in the Darfur region primarily involves Muslims. Religion functions as a core component of the identities for many but is not the primary factor in the conflict. What forms

32. Lewis, "Human Right in Darfur."
33. Faris, "Real Roots of Darfur."
34. Gration, "Current Status," June 2009.
35. Goulty.

of intra-religious dialogue could occur to draw on Islamic sources for peacemaking, such as Khan? Who are the religious leaders in these parties who could facilitate these processes? What religious leaders from outside the Darfur area could be resources for encouraging this development? What kind of atmosphere would be created if major religious leaders simply as a sign of solidarity regularly visited and even stayed for weeks in Darfur and the broader Sudan? Professor Carolyn Fluehr-Lobban working for the U.S. Institute of Peace argues that in Sudan "there has never been a mass-based peace movement, nor have religious leaders been positioned to be agents (not voices, but agents) for peace, nor have they confronted effectively or morally the chronic militarism that has fueled and perpetuated the wars that have plagued the country and decimated parts of it."[36] Attending closely to religious factors, policymakers would recognize the role of the Sudan Council of Churches in the southern Sudan peace process and give stronger weight to their call for holistic or restorative justice measures.[37] Further, the U.S. State Department deployed members of its Civilian Response Corps to Darfur, but as mentioned earlier, this set of experts should but does not include religious experts.[38]

As the attention to religious factors in Darfur would draw policy toward sources like Khan, the practice of training and education in the virtue of nonviolent peacemaking also arises. The strategy of armed resistance by various groups in Darfur gives the government cover and even legitimacy in some eyes to respond with violence. What forms of training and education might be developed in Darfur, which would cultivate the capacity to generate, mobilize, and build the moral imagination that transcends violence as Ledarch suggests?[39] Would there be a role for initiating small communities around the practices of nonviolent peacemaking? What would be the impact of mass distributing readings or radio broadcasts about Khan, Gandhi and even some of Sharp's detailed strategies of non-cooperation? What if the Civilian Response Corps included not only religious experts but experts in nonviolent peaceamking practices who were equipped to train others?

36. Fluehr-Lobban, "Religious Leaders and Conflict Management."

37. Lewis, "Human Right in Darfur."

38. Sontag and Mines, "Transformational Diplomacy in Darfur," 10–13.

39. Lederach, *Moral Imagination*, 5.

The practice of training in nonviolent peacemaking brings us to the difficult question about confronting immediate killing and the deployment of armed peacekeeping forces, such as the African Union and U.N. Much of the policy discussion around this issue called for deploying more and more armed forces along with tactics such as enforcing a no-fly zone or using private military firms.[40] What could the core practices of unarmed civilian peacekeeping or civilian-based defense suggest for this issue? For instance, the Nonviolent Peaceforce represents an international, civilian, non-partisan UCP force trained in interposition, accompaniment, creating safe spaces for living and for dialogue, proactive engagement with armed actors, interactive monitoring, documenting, rumor abatement, and modeling nonviolence.

Responding to an invitation from Sudanese organizations, the Nonviolent Peaceforce deployed a field team to the region of Mundri and Western Equatoria State in Southern Sudan in May 2010. In March 2012, the Nonviolent Peaceforce was up to eight field teams across Southern Sudan. Each team entails eight-twelve persons consisting mostly of Sudanese nationals. The teams focus on protection of civilians from violence, prevention of escalation, and peacebuilding. The protection element includes creating safe spaces, especially where armed intervention would be counterproductive or an overreaction. The safe spaces also allow meaningful dialogue to take place. They also offer workshops and training events to the communities on an ongoing basis. Living and working in the communities they protect cultivates the capacity to react flexibly, with trust from the community, and with context-appropriate responses. They focus particularly on protecting women and children, and have formed five all-women teams of peacekeepers to help identify sexual and gender-based violence. The Nonviolent Peaceforce has offered protection in refugee camps; been asked by the UN Refugee Agency to send three teams to Jongeli responding to expressed genocide intentions; and helped 40,000 internally displaced persons return after one killing sparked a crises of killings, home burnings and IDP's. Prevention entails working with partners, including state representatives, to develop an early warning and response program. For the Nonviolent Peaceforce, the peacebuilding element focuses on local solutions to local problems.

---

40. Feinstein, "Darfur and Beyond," 20.

They don't intervene directly in peace talks, but do help establish Peace Committees comprised of key actors from opposing communities.[41]

Could there be an increased role for the Nonviolent Peaceforce in accompanying women who are often threatened or raped as they venture off looking for firewood and water? Could they accompany local aid workers and human rights workers from various nongovernmental organizations and from Sudan? Could they create safe spaces for meaningful dialogue, such as in Darfur between the youth and older generation? Could they enhance the monitoring and documenting of peace accords, which groups like the Civilian Response Corps engage? Should substantial international financial resources be directed toward the Nonviolent Peaceforce?

Local peace teams represent another form of unarmed civilian peacekeeping, which the Nonviolent Peaceforce in part cultivates by using mostly Sudanese nationals. However, since the situation in Darfur involves Muslims, what are the prospects of equipping a set of (initially) small, local Muslim Peacemaker Teams? These arose in Iraq to address their civil strife. If complemented by the practice of drawing on religious sources of peacemaking, such as Khan's professionally trained peace army called the Servants of God, then the prospects would be further enhanced.

The practice of civilian-based defense requires more organization and training of local civilians, which limits its immediate effectiveness for any large-scale military incursion or coup. However, engaging the process would still be worthwhile as a way to provide an enticing vision and to integrate the smaller, local UCP teams. Sharp argues that historical evidence suggests that the non-cooperation component of civilian-based defense has been and could be valuable in situations of genocide, particularly at certain stages.[42]

The issue of capacity, not only with civilian-based defense, but also with UCP presents an important concern for the prospects of engaging such practices today in Sudan. Even if the Nonviolent Peaceforce and other similar groups may not provide enough personnel for all the relevant spots in Sudan or in Darfur at this historical moment, they could

41. Nonviolent Peaceforce, "Sudan Project: Strategy."

42. Sharp, *Civilian-Based Defense*, 84–85. He refers to examples from WWII when Germany recognized the need for the population it intended to exterminate to actually cooperate for control to be maintained.

still be increasingly considered for certain areas. Financial support for the Nonviolent Peaceforce and other similar organizations functions as a key obstacle to developing an existing, and relatively eager collection of would-be participants. In contrast, the global financial support for preparing armed forces ranges much higher than unarmed peacekeeping, especially in the U.S. For instance, the deployment of armed UN peacekeeping troops often struggles more with generating participation and the political will from various actors, and less with financial support.[43]

The shift from strategy-based or rules-based assessments of nonviolent peacemaking to a virtue-based assessment indicates a value in and commitment to becoming nonviolent peacemakers. Thus, *if* policymakers rely on or partially use armed intervention in Sudan at this historical moment, they would *also* take the following initiatives. Rather than describing our violence as "legitimate," "necessary," or "just," they would publicly recognize the use of violence as a tragedy. Thus, they would create spaces to mourn publicly the use of violence from *all* actors and our lack of development of nonviolent peacemaking practices. They would remind us of the heroes of nonviolent peacemaking, such as Gandhi, King, etc. and call us again to become those kinds of people. They would exponentially and with urgency increase our investment in developing the core nonviolent peacemaking practices, such as unarmed civilian peacekeeping and civilian-based defense. Further, they would more likely re-invigorate and sustain a commitment to addressing not just contributing factors, but the deep root causes of the violent conflict, which too often generates genocide or mass atrocity.

These initiatives should not function as "permission" to threaten or use violence as long as policymakers follow them later. Rather they indicate how a community and policymakers actually committed to the virtue of nonviolent peacemaking would respond if some chose violence. In fact, it would be quite difficult to ever turn to violence if a community acknowledged and committed itself to the virtue of nonviolent peacemaking. Further, the conceptualization of violent activity as "humanitarian intervention," needs to be reexamined. Even the founding Commission and core documents of the Responsibility to Protect Principle have recognized the limits and danger of this terminology.[44]

43. Feinstein, "Darfur and Beyond," 21.
44. Gossip, "Good News," 68.

Further, the acknowledgement of *human* excellence consisting in cultivating the virtue of nonviolent peacemaking suggests using the more precise notion of "armed" rather than "humanitarian" intervention for violent activity. This more precise usage is particularly significant in light of the various types of intervention described in the core practices of nonviolent peacemaking.

SUMMARY

In this final chapter I applied this freshly merged approach and the core practices to a difficult contemporary situation of genocide or mass atrocity. The seven core practices, which arise more clearly and are more likely sustained with a virtue-based assessment of nonviolent peacemaking, raise some key questions and suggest a repertoire of possible responses to the conflict in Sudan and other situations of mass atrocity. The application of these practices to this case is significant because Sudan typifies a situation that often yields a broader consensus for armed intervention, including the use of armed "peacekeepers." In this final chapter, I have offered some initial challenges to the tendency toward such a consensus.

Conclusion

THIS BOOK EXPLORED TWO interrelated questions. What is a more adequate way to assess nonviolent peacemaking compared to the more common rule-based or strategy-based assessments? What is a more fruitful way to mediate or persuade others in public discourse to increasingly implement nonviolent peacemaking practices not only in our public life but also particularly in public policy? I argued that a virtue-based assessment of nonviolent peacemaking enhanced by aspects of human rights discourse largely resolves the limits of a rule-based or strategy-based assessment of nonviolent peacemaking for U.S. public discourse and policy.

Initially, I assessed the limits of both the rules-based and strategy-based approaches to nonviolent peacemaking. Using major components of Catholic Social Teaching and moral philosopher James Childress as representatives of the rules-based type, I argued for the following key limits. First, nonviolence is often portrayed as having little constructive to add beyond refraining from violence. Thus, there is a serious truncating of the imagination in terms of practices of nonviolent peacemaking. Therefore, nonviolence is often associated with lacking a practical ethic for conflicts, especially between groups, or with passivity. Further, the main question in rule-based assessments of nonviolence tends to be about whether to use violence or not, rather than what practices might serve to guide our peacemaking initiatives and to indicate a genuine commitment to peace. Thus, merely following the rules often means that the "just" war criteria become the standard of moral reasoning about acute conflict.

Second, in Christian tradition, the rule-based assessment often gets played out in a tendency to blur the boundaries between nonresistance and nonviolent peacemaking on the one hand, and nonviolent peacemaking and limited ("just") war theory on the other. This blurring often yields an understanding of nonviolence as the absence or reduction of conflict. Such a notion of conflict often creates an overemphasis on dialogue and a devaluing of nonviolent struggle, especially if the aim includes transforming structural violence. Further, this blurring often excludes parts of humanity from the life practice of nonviolence, i.e. only for individuals or for extraordinary people.

Third, rules-based assessments offer an inadequate attention to developing virtue. The virtues are too often narrowly conceived as habits to follow rules. For instance, the key virtue of prudence becomes primarily a habit to obey the rule(s) rather than directing the moral agent to integrate and develop a range of moral virtues. Further, this limit yields inadequate attention toward the significance of the kinds of persons or groups interpreting and applying the rules.

Using Gene Sharp and Peter Ackerman as representatives of the strategy-based type, I argue for the following key limits. First, they have an overemphasis on consequences, and utilitarian moral reasoning. This method of moral reasoning yields an inadequate attention to integrating a virtue ethic, which results in a narrow view of prudence; a shift away from personal integration and transformation; maintaining a moral character primarily motivated by fear of punishment; insufficient attention to the formation of kinds of communities needed to envision, strategize, and sustain nonviolent struggle; inadequate assessments of particular nonviolent movements; a disconnect of means and more distant or less visible ends; and easier slippage into practices of injustice and violence. The preference satisfaction element of utilitarian reasoning in the U.S. reinforces both an overemphasis on and distortion of self/national interest in our approaches to acute conflict. Second, they emphasize wresting power from the other, which entails viewing conflict as adversarial; being highly reliant on the framing found in military language; and de-valuing the nonviolent practice of taking on the suffering in the situation. This limit includes a lack of resistance to using humiliation, which entails an emphasis on aggressiveness rather than assertiveness; ignoring the strengths, truth, or dignity of the opponent; and a de-emphasis on empathy, healing, and reconciliation. Third, they are embedded in western liberalism's narrow framing of moral reasoning options and view of the person, which entails an emphasis on self-interest, choice, procedural skills, and negative freedom.

I began the process of addressing these limits by exploring virtue-based assessments arising in Christian tradition. I illustrated the consistent testimony in the Gospels of Jesus' way of nonviolent peacemaking, as well as the predominance of peacemaking practices in Paul's writings and other early Christians in the scriptures. Next, I primarily drew on Spohn's argument that virtue ethics functions as the best way to appropriate the moral vision and practices of Jesus. Following this line of thinking, I made the argument not only that the practices of nonviolent peacemaking found in the models of Jesus and the broader scriptural witness ought to be assessed in a virtue-based ethic, but also that nonviolent peacemaking ought to be assessed as a distinct and central virtue.

In this light, I explored how the analogical imagination working with the scriptural witness has functioned in cultivating contemporary Christian practices of nonviolent peacemaking. I then described examples of three contemporary Christian theorists' virtue-based assessments of nonviolent peacemaking: Bernard Haring, Stanley Hauerwas, and Lisa Sowle Cahill. A unique contribution that Haring offered was the description of nonviolence itself as a virtue, which realizes the good of conciliatory love that works to turn enemies into friends and sinners into saints. Hauerwas argued that the centrality of nonviolence is the hallmark of the Christian moral life. He also argued that the virtue of peacemaking may see new opportunities not otherwise present in assessments of conflict, but nurturing this virtue requires communities of forgiveness and reconciliation. Cahill argued that a rule-governed ethic fails to account sufficiently for pacifism, and that a conversion-governed or virtue ethic is more conducive. She also argued that nonviolence and the unwillingness to harm arise out of a converted community life made up of the essential Christian virtues, such as forgiveness and compassion.

Next, I considered how assessing nonviolent peacemaking as a distinct virtue impacts other virtues and their paradigmatic practices, especially from a Christian perspective. I argued that the virtue of nonviolent peacemaking would qualify prominent virtues, such as justice and courage, as well as uplift a set of particular virtues, which do not often get the same attention when nonviolent peacemaking is assessed as primarily a rule or a strategy. For instance, virtues that would get a stronger priority and some qualification include humility, solidarity, hospitality, and mercy.

I showed by analogy how Christian practices of nonviolent peacemaking extend to and are enhanced by those beyond the Christian community, such as Gandhi and Khan. First, they demonstrate that a virtue-based approach functions within some other religious traditions and cultures, and even within a religiously plural society. With their realization of the Truth grounding all major religions, they willingly worked across and learned from various traditions. Second, their approach certainly resonates with the Christian virtue-based emphasis on conciliatory love and drawing enemies toward friendship, as well as on the priority of the poor and marginalized. Gandhi particularly emphasized Jesus' practices of nonviolence as par excellence. Gandhi also assessed nonviolence as the greatest virtue, but he extends the object or distinct good of this virtue to expressing the truth, which entails human equality and the ultimate unity of all being. Gandhi offers a recasting of the priority of the poor and marginalized with language of the constructive program, as the main arm of nonviolence. Third, both Gandhi and Khan regularly engaged in the practice of fasting. Fourth, they each promoted the practice of forming peace teams or armies. Khan illustrated that extremely violent persons in the midst of a violent culture contain the potential for transforming into disciplined practitioners of nonviolence. Fifth, they demonstrated how a virtue-based approach impacts public discourse and policy.

Then I illustrated how these three religiously grounded assessments of nonviolent peacemaking could function in U.S. public discourse and policy formation. To this end, I described and assessed the predominant methods of moral reasoning, i.e. rules-based and utilitarian-based methods, in U.S. public discourse and policy, particularly around issues of acute conflict and peace work. I argued that the mere incorporation of virtue in these two methods leads to a limited or distorted conception of virtue and in the kind of virtues emphasized. To illustrate this claim, I analyzed the role of the U.S. military.

To address these limits, I argued for a virtue-based approach by drawing on the example of Martin Luther King, who drew from both Christianity and Gandhi. King illustrates how such an approach functions well in U.S. public discourse and policy by both ensuring more human rights and being strategically effective. King's discourse and campaigns illustrate that the virtue of nonviolent peacemaking should not be conceived as private or merely for religious persons, but is appropriately conceived as a publicly accessible and civic virtue. I then argued that a contemporary illustration of how to move towards this kind of virtue-based approach is by supporting the Nonviolent Peaceforce, particularly as compared to the impact of some key elements in the U.S. military.

I expanded on the potential of a virtue-based approach by explaining how the role of virtue in U.S. public discourse and policy should be enhanced and qualified by the virtue of nonviolent peacemaking. I argued for enhancing the role of virtue in the following ways. First, the U.S. ought to equally emphasize the development of moral agency or rational deliberation, i.e. the virtue of prudence, in all persons not primarily in leadership or the elites. Second, public discourse ought to emphasize more the questions "who are we becoming?" and "who ought we to become?" which entails explicitly engaging our vision of human excellence or our *telos*. Third, policymakers ought to explicitly name the virtue(s), which a certain strategy or policy aims to or would likely cultivate in the people. For instance, I argued that the virtue of nonviolent peacemaking would qualify recent U.S. National Security Strategies in terms of our goals, how we speak about "enemies," and regular practices to serve as an indicator of a genuine commitment to a justpeace. Finally, this virtue would also qualify the virtues of justice and courage, while uplifting other key virtues for U.S. public discourse and policy.

However, I ended this discussion by naming some key limits of such a virtue-based assessment of nonviolent peacemaking in U.S. public discourse and policy. First, virtue ethics and the thicker vision of human excellence it implies faces not impossibility but difficulty making headway into a public discourse and policy that largely depends on rules or utilitarian forms of moral reasoning. Second, in a heavily pluralist society such as the U.S., a variety of virtues, understandings of the virtues, paradigmatic practices for the virtues, and visions of human excellence exist. Thus, extensive dialogue and patience is necessary. Third, a virtue-based approach functions well when a significant number of people want to be virtuous or at least care about who they are becoming, and that people who do care have developed a minimum level of virtue in order to adequately participate in and organize a society. For now there still may be significant numbers of people who do not fall into one or both of these categories.

I addressed these key limits of a virtue-based assessment of nonviolent peacemaking by exploring certain aspects of human rights discourse as a way to supplement a virtue-based assessment. After describing some general characteristics of human rights theory, I briefly examined some key limits of human rights discourse, in order to indicate more clearly why it functions to supplement rather than replace a virtue-based assessment. First, human rights lend themselves to the limits of a rules-based assessment, as illustrated in key parts of Catholic Social Teaching. Second, human rights discourse is often unclear on many points, such as the basis of rights claims, whether rights are pre-political or artifacts of laws and institutions, whether rights only belong to individual persons or also to groups, etc. Third, the human rights approach suffers from a compliance gap between the declared commitments of governments to human rights and their compliance with these standards. Fourth, the emphasis placed on 'human' often does, or at least risks devaluing non-human life and the broader environment or cosmos as a whole.

Next, I analyzed the contributions that certain aspects of human rights discourse offer to a virtue-based assessment for public discourse and policy. I drew especially on Martha Nussbaum, William O'Neill, John Dear, and Catholic Social Teaching. I argued for three key contributions of human rights discourse. First, they presently have more moral traction than virtue in public discourse and policy, and thus, assist in mediating virtue into public discourse and policy, especially for U.S. culture. I drew on O'Neill's conception of human rights as a "narrative grammar" and Nussbaum's capabilities version of human rights to illustrate how this mediation of virtue occurs. Second, certain conceptions of human rights theory more easily move beyond the obstacle arising from the tendency to view virtue ethics as suggesting too thick a conception of human flourishing. O'Neill's arguments about Truth Commissions and Nussbaum's work on capabilities and "grounding experiences" illustrate this point.

Third, human rights help us to see more clearly how the virtue of nonviolent peacemaking actually protects and ensures human rights. Thus, attending to rights both enhances the validity of nonviolent peacemaking practices for public discourse and policy, and assists in measuring some ways that nonviolent peacemaking works. Catholic Social Teaching's emphasis on the need to respect the basic rights of all others indicates the urgency of claims and clarifies a way to determine the use of nonviolent peacemaking practices. Supplementing a virtue-based account of nonviolent peacemaking with human rights theory from Catholic Social Teaching indicates that practices of nonviolent peacemaking deserve the predominant emphasis in public discourse and policy, if such policy claims to aim at a justpeace. Catholic Social Teaching, the U.N., and Nussbaum's acknowledgement of social-economic rights along with the political-civil rights, reinforces the value of the nonviolent peacemaking core practice of the constructive program, which Gandhi called the main arm of nonviolence. The social-economic rights part of human rights theory further clarifies the importance and specific role of nonviolent peacemaking in U.S. public discourse and policy, which has not yet ratified the International Covenant related to such rights.

With these contributions I analyzed the fruits of merging a virtue-based assessment of nonviolent peacemaking supplemented by aspects of human rights discourse. I argued that my approach offers particular contributions toward developing Catholic Social Teaching, which has implications for U.S. public discourse and policy. These contributions consist of both a shift in understanding nonviolence, and a set of core practices that arise more clearly and will more likely be sustained.

The shift in understanding consists in assessing nonviolent peace-making as a virtue, which realizes the specific goods of a conciliatory love that focuses on drawing enemies into friendship, and truth, particularly the truths of the ultimate unity of all being and equal human dignity. Recognizing this virtue qualifies key virtues and uplifts a certain set of related virtues to more prominence, such as solidarity, humility, hospitality, mercy, empathy, and what the Muslims call *hilm* or calmness under provocation. The integral relationship between virtue and human rights would also get more substantial analysis in Catholic Social Teaching.

The shift in understanding sets the stage for naming and elaborating on a set of paradigmatic practices that correspond to the virtue of nonviolent peacemaking and its related set of virtues. I argued for seven core practices of nonviolent peacemaking that now arise more clearly and will more likely be sustained in the Catholic Social Teaching tradition especially, but also to different degrees have significant implications for U.S. public discourse and policy. These practices include:

1. celebrating the nonviolent Eucharist, with secondary components of prayer, meditation, and fasting;

2. training and education in nonviolent peacemaking, with the secondary component of forming nonviolent peacemaking communities;

3. attention to religious or spiritual factors, especially in public discourse, and learning about religion, particularly in the form of intra-religious or inter-religious dialogue;

4. the constructive program with its particular focus on the poor and marginalized;

5. conflict transformation and restorative justice, particularly in the form of Truth and Reconciliation Commissions;

6. unarmed civilian peacekeeping both in the form of international implementation and local peace teams; and

7. civilian-based defense.

Finally, I applied this freshly merged approach and the particular practices to the difficult contemporary situation of genocide or mass atrocity, such as Sudan. I primarily raised questions and suggested a repertoire of possible responses, which would also potentially hold for other similar situations. The application of these practices to this case is significant because Sudan typifies a situation that often yields a broader consensus for armed intervention, such as the use of armed "peacekeepers."

A number of further questions worth pursuing arise in light of this research. First, what mechanisms would integrate some of these core practices? Would it be necessary to prioritize the practices and if so, how would one do so? Second, what further implications exist for police training and for the just policing model? Further, what implications exist for the conceptualization and perhaps even existence of "just" war theories, including notions of "humanitarian intervention"? Third, although I have suggested some possible ways these practices could impact situations such as Sudan, a further question is would they actually have such an impact? To answer this would require closer on the ground contact, extending the practices where they exist, actually piloting some appropriate version of the practices not already in place, and than doing the research to analyze their impact. Fourth, to what extent could this virtue-based approach function in cultures where other key religious traditions predominate, such as Jewish and Buddhist? Fifth, could these practices actually become a substitute for armed intervention, and if so to what extent could they function in this way?

I hope the reader enjoyed and experienced a challenge by this book. I look forward to the ongoing dialogue about these recommendations and opportunities. I hope this book inspired and offered a way for us to move significantly closer to life of peacemaking and justice-making as well as to King's "Beloved Community." The adventure continues . . .

Wings of Hope
be with you!

Bibliography

ABC News. "US Army Battles Rising Suicide Rate," February 1, 2008. http://www.abc
.net.au/news/stories/2008/02/01/2151706.htm.

Abu-Nimer, Mohammed. "Conflict Resolution in an Islamic Context: Some Conceptual Questions." *Peace and Change* 21 (1996) 22–40.

————. *Nonviolence and Peace Building in Islam: Theory and Practice.* Gainesville: University Press of Florida, 2003.

Ackerman, Peter, and Jack Duvall. *A Force More Powerful: A Century of Non-Violent Conflict.* New York: Palgrave, 2000.

Ackerman, Peter, and Christopher Kruegler. *Strategic Nonviolent Conflict: The Dynamics of People Power in the Twentieth Century.* Westport, CT: Praeger, 1994.

Akau, Daniel. "Forgiveness and Reconciliatory Process in Sudan: Speaking the Unspeakable." *Peace Power: Journal of Nonviolence and Conflict Transformation* 2.2 (2006) 29–31.

"Amish and the Plain People." http://www.800padutch.com/amish.shtml.

Appleby, Scott. *The Ambivalence of the Sacred: Religion, Violence, and Reconciliation.* Lanham, MD: Rowman & Littlefield, 2000.

Aquinas, Thomas. *Summa Theologiae.* Translated by Fathers of the English Dominican Province. New York: Benziger, 1947–48.

Associated Press, "Child Abuse Rises when Dad is at War," July 31, 2007. http://www
.msnbc.msn.com/id/20056362/.

Axworthy, Lloyd. "Human Security: An Opening for UN Reform." In *The United Nations and Global Security*, edited by R. Price, and M. Zacher, 245–60. New York: Palgrave Macmillan, 2004.

Bacevich, Andrew. *The New American Militarism: How Americans Are Seduced by War.* New York: Oxford University Press, 2005.

BBC News, "World Hunger hits 1 Billion," June 19, 2009. http://news.bbc.co.uk/2/hi/ europe/8109698.stm.

Bell, Daniel. *Just War as Christian Discipleship: Recentering the tradition in the Church rather than the State.* Grand Rapids: Brazos, 2009.

Bellah, Robert N. *Beyond Belief: Essays on Religion in a Post-Traditionalist World.* Berkeley: University of California Press, 1991.

Benedict XVI, Pope. "God Is Love" (2005). http://www.vatican.va/holy_father/benedict_
xvi/encyclicals/documents/hf_ben-xvi_enc_20051225_deus-caritas-est_en.html.

————. Midday Angelus, 2007. http://www.catholicpeacefellowship.org/nextpage.
asp?m=2308.

————. "Overcome Every Possible Temptation to Racism, Intolerance and Exclusion." Speech at Castel Gandolfo, Italy, August 31, 2008. http://www.zenit.org/article-
23395?l=english.

———. Sacred Congregation for the Doctrine of Faith. "Instruction on Certain Aspects of the Theology of Liberation." Aug. 6, 1984; section xi, paragraph 7.Online: http://www.newadvent.org/library/docs_df84lt.htm.

———. "The Saving Message of the Gospel Needs to be Proclaimed." Speech in Cameroon, Africa, March 17, 2009. http://www.zenit.org/article-25389?l=english.

Bennett, Jeremy. "The Resistance Against the German Occupation of Denmark 1940–5." In *The Strategy of Civilian Defence*, edited by Adam Roberts, 154–72. London: Faber & Faber Limited, 1967.

Bensahel, N., O. Oliker, and H. Peterson. "Improving Capacity for Stabilization and Reconstruction Operations." RAND Corporation, 2009. http://www.rand.org/pubs/monographs/2009/RAND_MG852.pdf.

Berkman, John. "Recent Theological Developments." Presentation at Faith and Reason Institute conference on *Catholic Virtues, American Virtues*, Washington DC, February 2–3, 2001. http://www.frinstitute.org/rrvirtue2.html#sess2.

Bhattacharyya, Buddhadeva. *Evolution of the Political Philosophy of Gandhi*. Calcutta: Calcutta Book House, 1969.

Bing, Tony. "Albert Camus: The Plague and An Ethic of Nonviolence," Charles Lecture Series, Earlham College, 1998. http://www.earlham.edu/~tonyb/bing_charles1.html.

Booth, Ken, and T. Dunne. "Learning Beyond Frontiers." In *Human Rights in Global Politics*, edited by T. Dunne and N. Wheeler. New York: Cambridge University Press, 1999.

Bordin, Jeffery. "On the Psychology of Moral Cognition and Resistance to Authoritative and Groupthink Demands during a Military Intelligence Analysis Gaming Exercise." Paper presented at the *Joint Services Conference on Professional Ethics*, Springfield, Virginia, 2002. http://www.usafa.af.mil/jscope/JSCOPE02.

Boulding, Kenneth. *Three Faces of Power*. Newbury Park, CA: Sage, 1989.

Braun, Ted. *Darfur Now: Six Stories, One Hope*. Burbank, CA: Warner Home Video, 2008.

Brendt, Hagen. *Non-Violence in the World Religions*. London: SCM, 1998.

Brown, Chris. "Universal Human Rights: A Critique." In *Human Rights in Global Politics*, edited by T. Dunne and N. Wheeler. New York: Cambridge University Press, 1999.

Brown, Richard. *An Introduction to the New Testament*. New York: Doubleday, 1997.

Butler, Judith. *Precarious Life: The Powers of Mourning and Violence*. New York: Verso, 2006.

Bush, George, "Bush Says its Time for Action." CNN archives, November 6, 2001. http://archives.cnn.com/2001/US/11/06/gen.attack.on.terror/.

———. "President Extends Holiday Greetings, Thanks." *American Forces Press Services*, December 22, 2008. http://www.defenselink.mil/news/newsarticle.aspx?id=52438.

———. "State of the Union Address." January 30, 2002. http://archives.cnn.com/2002/ALLPOLITICS/01/29/bush.speech.txt/.

———. "U.S. National Security Strategy." 2006. http://georgewbush-whitehouse.archives.gov/nsc/nss/2006/http://georgewbush-whitehouse.archives.gov/nsc/nss/2006/sectionII.html.

Cahill, Lisa Sowle. *Love Your Enemies: Discipleship, Pacifism, and Just War Theory*. Minneapolis: Augsburg, 1994.

Cassidy, K., and Bean, K., "Military Dollars and Public Sense." In *The Nonviolent Activist* (April–May 1992) 4–7.

Catechism of the Catholic Church. New York, NY: Doubleday, 1995. http://www.vatican
.va/archive/ccc_css/archive/catechism/p3s1c1a5.htm.

Catholic Worker Communities. http://www.catholicworker.org.

Ceasefire. http://www.ceasefirechicago.org/.

Chappell, Paul. "Peace Leadership Program: Make a Career of Humanity." Nuclear
Age Peace Foundation, Santa Barbara, CA. http://www.wagingpeace.org/menu/
programs/peace-leaders/plp_booklet.pdf.

Chenowerth, E., and M. Stephan. *Why Civilian Resistance Works.* Chichester, NY:
Columbia University Press, 2011.

Childress, James. "Contemporary Pacifism: Its Major Types and Possible Contributions
to Discourse about War." In *The American Search for Peace: Moral Reasoning,
Religious Hope, and National Security,* edited by George Weigel and J. Langan.
Washington, DC: Georgetown University Press, 1991.

————. *Moral Responsibility in Conflicts: Essays on Nonviolence, War, and Conscience.*
Baton Rouge: Louisiana State University Press, 1982.

————. "Nonviolent Resistance: Trust and Risk-Taking Twenty-Five Years Later."
Journal of Religious Ethics 25.2 (1997) 213–20.

Chin, Jane. "Child Abuse and Neglect, Another Casualty of War," July 31, 2007. http://
www.chinspirations.com/mhsourcepage/child-abuse-and-neglect-another-
casualty-of-war.

Christian Peacemaker Teams. http://www.cpt.org/.

Christianson, D., et al. "Moral Claims, Human Rights and Population Policies."
Theological Studies 35 (1974) 83–113.

Christianson, D. "Catholic Peacemaking, 1991–2005: The Legacy of Pope John Paul II."
The Review of Faith and International Affairs 4 (2006) 21–28.

————. "Peacebuilding in Catholic Social Teaching: A Response to Kenneth Himes
O.F.M." Presented at Catholic Peacebuilding Network conference, April 15,
2008. http://cpn.nd.edu/papers_2008CPN/Peacebuidling%20in%20Catholic%20
Social%20teaching%20-%20Christiansen%20Response.pdf.

Civilian Response Corps. http://www.civilianresponsecorps.gov/.

Clymer, Jeffrey. *America's Culture of Terrorism: Violence, Capitalism, and the Written
Word.* Chapel Hill: University of North Caroline Press, 2003.

CNN. "U.S. Marine Guilty of Wrongful Sexual Contact in Japan." May 9, 2008.
http://www.cnn.com/2008/WORLD/asiapcf/05/09/japan.usmarine/index
.html?eref=rss_topstories.

————. CNN Heroes, "Former Addict Gives Homeless Veterans a Second Chance."
February 20, 2009. http://www.cnn.com/2009/US/02/19/heroes.roy.foster/index
.html#cnnSTCText.

Codevilla, Angelo. "American Statecraft and the Iraq War." *Claremont Review of Books*
7.4 (2007). http://www.claremont.org/publications/crb/id.1481/article_detail.asp.

Cortright, David. *Peace: A History of Movements and Ideas.* New York: Cambridge
University Press, 2008.

Crilly, Rob. "President al-Bashir of Sudan Taunts the West as Aid Agencies Warn of
Crisis." *The Times,* March 9, 2009. http://www.timesonline.co.uk/tol/news/world/
africa/article5869590.ece.

Crooker, David. "Functioning and Capability: The Foundations of Sen's and Nussbaum's
Development Ethic." In *Women, Culture, and Development: A Study of Human*

Capabilities, edited by M. Nussbaum and J. Glover, 153–98. New York: Oxford University Press, 1995.

Curran, Charles E. *Catholic Social Teaching: 1891–Present: A Historical, Theological, and Ethical Analysis*. Washington, DC: Georgetown University Press, 2000.

Curran, Charles E., Kenneth R. Himes, and Thomas A. Shannon. "Commentary on *Sollicitudo Rei Socialis*." In *Modern Catholic Social Teaching*, edited by Kenneth R. Himes et al., 415–35. Washington, DC: Georgetown University Press, 2004.

Dalton, Frederick. *The Moral Vision of Cesar E. Chavez: An Examination of his Public Life from an Ethical Perspective*. Thesis, Graduate Theological Union, 1998.

Darfur-Darfur Dialogue and Consultation. http://www.dddc.org/about.shtml.

Dear, John. "Human Rights and Nonviolence: The Christian Theology and Movement for Peace," July 2003. http://www.johndear.org/nonviolence/human_rights.htm.

DeLuce, Dan. "US Army Base Shuts Down After Rise in Suicides." *Truthout* May 29, 2009. http://www.truthout.org/052909A.

Department of the Army. "Army Training and Leader Development." Washington, DC, January 13, 2006. http://www.sexualassault.army.mil/files/AR%2035 0-1_13%20 Jan%2006.pdf.

Dewall, Alex. "Part Two: Mediation in the Political Marketplace," World Peace Foundation, Feb. 29, 2012. http://sites.tufts.edu/reinventingpeace/2012/02/29/part-two-mediation-in-the-political-marketplace/.

Donahue, John. "The Good News of Peace." *The Way: Contemporary Christian Spirituality* 22 (1982) 88–99.

Douglas, James. *The Non-Violent Cross: A Theology of Revolution and Peace*. 1968. Reprint, Eugene, OR: Wipf & Stock, 2006.

Dunne, Tim, and Nicholas Wheeler. "Introduction." In *Human Rights in Global Politics*, edited by Tim Dunne and Nicholas Wheeler. New York: Cambridge University Press, 1999.

Easwaran, Eknath. *A Man to Match his Mountains: Badshah Khan, Nonviolent Soldier of Islam*. Petaluma: Nilgiri, 1984.

Elie, Paul. "A Man for All Reasons." *The Atlantic Monthly*, November 2007. http://www.theatlantic.com/magazine/archive/2007/11/a-man-for-all-reasons/6337/.

Engdahl, Frederick William. "Darfur: Forget Genocide, There's Oil." *Asia Times Online*, May 25, 2007. http://www.globalpolicy.org/component/content/article/206/39764 .html.

———. Center of Research on Globalization. http://www.globalresearch.ca/index .php?context=va&aid=12300.

Enns, Elaine, and Ched Myers. *Ambassadors of Reconciliation: Diverse Christian Practices of Restorative Justice and Peacemaking*. 2 vols. Maryknoll, NY: Orbis, 2009.

European Coalition on Oil in Sudan. http://www.ecosonline.org/.

Fair Trade Certified. http://www.transfairusa.org/.

Fair Trade Federation. http://www.fairtradefederation.org/.

Faris, Stephan. "The Real Roots of Darfur." *The Atlantic Monthly*, April 2007. http://www.theatlantic.com/doc/200704/darfur-climate/.

Feinberg, Joel. *Social Philosophy*. Newark: Prentice Hall, 1973.

Feinstein, Lee. "Darfur and Beyond: What is Needed to Prevent Mass Atrocities." *Council Special Report* of the Council of Foreign Relations 22 (2007) 1–62. www.cfr.org/content/publications/attachments/DarfurCSR22.pdf.

Fletcher, Michael. "Bush Attacks Party of 'Cut and Run,'" *Washington Post*, September 29, 2006, A12. http://www.washingtonpost.com/wpdyn/content/article/2006/09/28/AR2006092801844.html.

Fluehr-Lobban, Carolyn. "Religious Leaders and Conflict Management in Deeply Divided Societies: Between Terror and Tolerance." Paper at The Vail Symposium, Denver, CO, April 16–18, 2008.

Foster, Gregory. "One War at a Time: The Case for Selective Conscientious Objection." *America*, November 17, 2008.

Friedman, Maurice. "Hasidism and the Love of Enemies." In *Peace is the Way*, edited by Walter Wink, 118–23. Maryknoll, NY: Orbis, 2000.

Friends Committee on National Legislation. "How is the Federal Government Spending our Income Tax Dollars?" http://www.fcnl.org/budget/Taxes10coin_chart.pdf.

Friesen, Duane. "Encourage Grassroots Peacemaking Groups and Voluntary Associations." In *Just Peacemaking*, edited by Glen H. Stassen, 3rd ed., 201–14. Cleveland, OH: Pilgrim Press, 2008.

Galtung, Johan. "Cultural Violence." *Journal of Peace Research* 27 (1990) 291–305.

Galtung, John, and Anders Wirak. "On the Relationship Between Human Rights and Human Needs." Paper, no. 71, 1978. http://www.transcend.org/galtung/papers/On%20the%20Relationship%20Between%20Human%20Rights%20and%20Human%20Needs.pdf.

Gandhi, Mohandas. *All Men Are Brothers*. New York: Continuum, 1980.

———. *The Collected Works of Mahatma Gandhi*. Ahmedabad: Navajivan, 1967–84._

———. *Constructive Program: It's Meaning and Place*. India: Navajivan, 1945.

———. Epigrams of Gandhiji, Democracy section. http://www.mkgandhi.org/epigrams/d.htm.

———. *Gandhi's Experiments with Truth: Essential Writings by and about Mahatma Gandhi*. Edited by Richard Johnson. Lanham, MD: Lexington, 2005.

———. *Gandhi on Non-violence: Selected Texts from Gandhi's "Non-Violence in Peace and War."* Edited by Thomas Merton. New York: New Directions, 1965.

———. *The Gandhi Reader: A Sourcebook of his Life and Writings*, edited by Homer A. Jack. Bloomington: Indiana University Press, 1956. Gandhian Institute Bombay, Sarvodaya Mandal and Sarvodaya Ashram, Nagpur. http://www.mkgandhi.org/momgandhi/chap28.htm and http://www.mkgandhi.org/momgandhi/chap21.htm.

———. *Harijan 4*, March 28, 1936.

———. *Hindu Dharma*. Ahmedabad: Navajivan, 1960.

———. *Mohandas Gandhi: Essential Writings*. Edited by John Dear. Maryknoll, NY: Orbis, 2002.

———. *The Selected Works of Mahatma Gandhi*. Edited by Shriman Navayan. Ahmedabad: Navajivan, 1957.

———. *Young India*. December 31, 1931.

Gandhi, Rajmohan. *Ghaffar Khan: Nonviolent Badshah of the Pakhtuns*. New Delhi: Penguin, 2004.

Garamone, Jim. "The March to Marine." *American Forces Press Service*. http://usmilitary.about.com/od/marinejoin/l/blbasic.htm.

Generoso, Ramon. "Exploring Civil Society-led Third Party Nonviolent Intervention for Peacekeeping Work in Support of the Mindanao Ceasefire: A Report on the Visit of David Grant, Liaison Officer to the UN, Nonviolent Peaceforce." http://www.freewebs.com/iccn/exploringtpni.html.

Gewirth, Alan. *The Community of Rights*. Chicago: University of Chicago Press, 1996.
———. "Rights and Virtues." *The Review of Metaphysics* XXXVIII/4 (1985) 739–62.
Gier, Nicholas. "Toward a Hindu Virtue Ethics." In *Contemporary Issues in Constructive Dharma*, edited by R. D. Sherma and A. Deepak, 2:151–62. Hampton, VA: Deepak Heritage, 2005. http://www.class.uidaho.edu/ngier/hinduVE.htm.
———. *The Virtue of Nonviolence from Gautama to Gandhi*. New York: State University of New York Press, 2004.
Gilligan, James. *Violence: Reflections on a National Epidemic*. New York: Vintage, 1997.
Girard, Rene. "The Bible's Distinctiveness and the Gospel." In *Girard Reader*, edited by James Williams, 145–76. New York: Crossroad, 1996.
———. "Mimesis and Violence" and "The Surrogate Victim." In *Girard Reader*, 9–19.
Goleman, Daniel. *Emotional Intelligence*. New York: Bantam, 1996.
Gossip, Ronald. "The Good News: The ICC and the R2P Principle." In *Peace Movements Worldwide: Peace Efforts That Work and Why*, edited by M. Pilisuk and M. Nagler, 3:60–72. Santa Barbara, CA: Praeger, 2011.
Goulty, Alan. Interview. Washington DC, March 11, 2011.
Grant, Kevin. "Mayor's Street Outreach Program." Part of Measure Y. Oakland, CA, 2004. http://measurey.org/index.php?page=mayor-s-street-outreach.
Gration, Maj. Gen. Scott. "Special Envoy to Sudan." U.S. Department of State. http://www.state.gov/s/sudan/index.htm.
Grossman, Lt. Col. David. *On Killing: The Psychological Cost of Learning to Kill in War and Society*. Boston: Little, Brown, 1995.
Gula, Rich. *Reason Informed by Faith*. New York: Paulist, 1989.
Haas, Richard. "Forward." In "Darfur and Beyond: What is Needed to Prevent Mass Atrocity," by Lee Feinstein. *Council Special Report* of the Council of Foreign Relations 22 (2007) 1–62. www.cfr.org/content/publications/attachments/DarfurCSR22.pdf.
Hammond, Rev. Fred. Mar. 22, 2008. http://serenityhome.wordpress.com/2008/03/22/truth-commission-in-mississippi/.
Hanson, Stephanie. "Sudan's Fractured Internal Politics." *Backgrounder* for Council of Foreign Relations, March 4, 2009. http://www.cfr.org/publication/18519/sudans_fractured_internal_politics.html.
Harak, Simon. *Virtuous Passions: The Formation of Christian Character*. Mahwah, NJ: Paulist 1993.
Haring, Bernard. *The Healing Power of Peace and Nonviolence*. Middlegreen, Slough, England: St. Paul, 1986.
———. *The Law of Christ*. Westminster, MD: Newman, 1961.
———. *Theology of Protest*. Toronto: Doubleday Canada, 1970.
———. *Virtues of an Authentic Life*. Liguori, MO: Liguori, 1997.
———. *What Does Christ Want*. Staten Island, NY: Society of St. Paul, 1968.
Harrington, Daniel. "The Gospel According to Mark." In *The New Jerome Biblical Commentary*, edited by Raymond Brown et al., 601–18. Englewood Cliffs, NJ: Prentice Hall, 1990.
Hastings, Michael. "Another Runaway General: Army Deploys Psych Ops on U.S. Senators." *Rolling Stone*, February 23, 2011. http://www.rollingstone.com/politics/news/another-runaway-general-army-deploys-psy-ops-on-u-s-senators-20110223?page=1.

Hauerwas, Stanley. "A Christian Critique of Christian America." In *The Hauerwas Reader*, edited by John Berkman and Michael Cartwright, 459–80. Durham, NC: Duke University Press, 2001.

———. *Christians Among the Virtues: Theological Conversations with Ancient and Modern Ethics*. Notre Dame: Notre Dame University Press, 1997.

———. *The Peaceable Kingdom: A Primer in Christian Ethics*. Notre Dame: Notre Dame University Press, 1983

———. "Peacemaking: The Virtue of the Church." In *The Hauerwas Reader*, edited by John Berkman and Michael Cartwright, 318–26. Durham, NC: Duke University Press, 2001.

———. "Should War Be Eliminated?: A Thought Experiment." In *The Hauerwas Reader*, edited by John Berkman and Michael Cartwright, 392–425. Durham, NC: Duke University Press, 2001.

Hays, Richard. *Moral Vision of the New Testament: Community, Cross, New Creation: A Contemporary Introduction to Christian Ethics*. New York: Harper Collins, 1996.

Herbst, Moira. "Oil for China, Guns for Darfur." *Business Week*, March 14, 2008. http://www.businessweek.com/globalbiz/content/mar2008/gb20080314_430126.htm.

Hibbs, Thomas. "Interpretations of Aquinas's Ethics Since Vatican II." In *The Ethics of Aquinas*, edited by Stephen J. Pope, 412–25. Washington, DC: Georgetown University Press, 2002.

Himes, Kenneth. "Peacebuilding as a Developing Norm in Catholic Social Teaching." Presented at Catholic Peacebuilding Conference, Notre Dame University, April 15, 2008, session V, panel 1. Online Audio: http://cpn.nd.eu/2008CPNConference%20-%20Post-Program.shtml.

Hollenbach, David. *The Common Good and Christian Ethics*. New York: Cambridge University Press, 2002

———. *The Global Face of Public Faith*. Washington, DC: Georgetown University Press, 2003

———. *Justice, Peace, and Human Rights: American Catholic Social Ethics in a Pluralistic World*. New York: Crossroad, 1988.

Human Rights First. http://www.stoparmstosudan.org/index.asp.

Immaculate Heart of Mary Parish Social Justice Committee. "Summary of Roman Catholic Rights, enumerated in *Pacem in Terris* by Pope John XXII." http://www.ihmsjc.org/roman_catholic_human_rights.htm.

International Coalition for the Responsibility to Protect. "An Introduction to R2P." http://www.responsibilitytoprotect.org/index.php/pages/2, and http://www.responsibilitytoprotect.org/index.php/united_nations/398?theme=alt1.

Isenberg, David. "Contractors vs. Genocide." *Middle East Times*, August 8, 2008. http://www.cato.org/pub_display.php?pub_id=9586.

John XXIII, Pope. "*Pacem in Terris*: Peace on Earth." In *Catholic Social Thought: The Documentary Heritage*, edited by David O'Brien and Thomas Shannon. Maryknoll, NY: Orbis, 1992.

John Paul II, Pope. Homily at Drogheda, Ireland, September 29, 1979. http://www.vatican.va/holy_father/john_paul_ii/homilies/1979/documents/hf_jp-ii_hom_19790929_irlanda-dublino-drogheda_en.html.

———. "The Hundredth Year." 1991. Online:http://www.vatican.va/holy_father/john_paul_ii/encyclicals/documents/hf_jp-ii_enc_01051991_centesimus-annus_en.html.

———. "The International Situation Today." *Origins* 32.33 (January 30, 2003) 543–45

———. "No Peace Without Justice, No Justice Without Forgiveness." January 1, 2002. http://www.vatican.va/holy_father/john_paul_ii/messages/peace/documents/hf_jpii_mes_20011211_xxxv-world-day-for-peace_en.html.

———. "Rich in Mercy," November 30, 1980. http://www.vatican.va/edocs/ENG0215/_INDEX.HTM.

———. "On Social Concern," December 30, 1987. http://www.vatican.va/holy_father/john_paul_ii/encyclicals/documents/hf_jpii_enc_30121987_sollicitudo-rei-socialis_en.html.

———. "War, a Decline for Humanity." *Origins* 20.33 (January 24, 1991) 525–31.

Johnson, Chalmers. "737 U.S. Military Bases = Global Empire." *AlterNet*, February 19, 2007. http://www.alternet.org/story/47998/.

Johnston, Douglas. *Religion, the Missing Dimension of Statecraft*. New York: Oxford University Press, 1994.

Karatnycky, Adrian. "How Freedom is Won: From Civic Resistance to Durable Democracy." June 1, 2005. http://www.freedomhouse.org/research/specreports/civictrans/FHCIVICTRANS.pdf.

Kay, Randi and Estrada, Ismael. "Female Veterans Report More Sexual, Mental Trauma." *CNN*, March 3, 2008. http://www.cnn.com/2008/US/03/19/women.veterans/index.html.

Keenan, Jim, and Daniel Harrington. *Jesus and Virtue Ethics: Building Bridges Between New Testament Studies and Moral Theology*. Lanham, MD: Rowman & Littlefield, 2002.

———. *Moral Wisdom: Lessons and Texts from the Catholic Tradition*. Lanham, MD: Rowman & Littlefield, 2004

———. "Proposing Cardinal Virtues." *Theological Studies* 56 (1995) 709–29.

———. "Ten Reasons why Thomas Aquinas is Important for Ethics Today." *New Blackfriar* 75.884 (1994) 354–63.

———. "Virtue Ethics." In *Basic Christian Ethics: An Introduction*, edited by Bernard Hoose, 84–94. London: Chapman, 1997.

———. "The Virtue of Prudence (IIa IIae 47–56)." In *The Ethics of Aquinas*, edited by Stephen J. Pope, 259–71. Washington, DC: Georgetown University Press, 2002.

Kelsay, John. Conversation at the Society of Christian Ethics Conference, 2008.

Keteyian, Armen. "Suicide Epidemic Among Veterans." *CBS News*, November 13, 2007. http://www.cbsnews.com/stories/2007/11/13/cbsnews_investigates/main3496471.shtml.

Khan, Abdul Ghaffar, "Address to Muslims," Delhi, October 10, 1969, quoted in P. S. Ramu, *Badshah Khan: Indo-Pakistan Relations*. Delhi: S. S., 1991.

———. *My Life and Struggle: Autobiography of Badshah Khan*. Delhi: Hind Pocket, 1969.

Khan, Khan Abdul Wali. "Life and Thought of Badshah Khan." In *Khan Abdul Ghaffar Khan: A Centennial Tribute*, 1–21. New Delhi: Har-Arnand, 1995.

Kilner, Captain Pete. "Military Leaders to Justify Killing in Warfare." Paper presented at *Joint Services Conference on Professional Ethics*, Washington, DC, 2000. http://www.usafa.af.mil/jscope/JSCOPE00.

Kimelman, Reuven. "Nonviolence in the Talmud." In *Roots of Jewish Nonviolence*, edited by Allan Solomonow, 24–49. Nyack, NJ: Jewish Peace Fellowship, 1985.

King, Martin Luther, Jr. "A Testament of Hope." In *A Testament of Hope: Essential Writings of Martin Luther King Jr.*, edited by James M. Washington, 313–30. New York: Harper Collins, 1986.

———. "Beyond Vietnam: A Time to Break the Silence." Speech given at Riverside Church in NYC, April 4, 1967. http://www.hartford-hwp.com/archives/45a/058. html.

———. "Letter From a Birmingham Jail." In *A Testament of Hope: Essential Writings of Martin Luther King Jr.*, edited by James M. Washington, 289–302. New York: Harper Collins, 1986.

———. "My Trip to the Land of Gandhi." In *A Testament of Hope: Essential Writings of Martin Luther King Jr.*, edited by James M. Washington, 23–30. New York: Harper Collins, 1986.

———. "Pilgrimage to Nonviolence." In *A Testament of Hope: Essential Writings of Martin Luther King Jr.*, edited by James M. Washington, 35–40. New York: Harper Collins, 1986.

———. "Stride Toward Freedom." In *A Testament of Hope: Essential Writings of Martin Luther King Jr.*, edited by James M. Washington, 417–90. New York: Harper Collins, 1986.

———. "Tribute to Gandhi," (1958). *Peacework Magazine* 368 (September 2006). http:// www.peaceworkmagazine.org/node/229.

———. "Where Do We Go From Here?" In *A Testament of Hope*, 518–44.

Knopf, Peyton. "Post-Referendum Sudan: Prospects for Peace." Council of Foreign Relations conference call, February 17, 2011.

Koontz, Theodore. "Christian Nonviolence: An Interpretation." In *The Ethics of War and Peace: Religious and Secular Perspectives*, edited by Terry Nardin, 169–96. Princeton: Princeton University Press, 1996.

Kossel, Clifford. "Natural Law and Human Law." In *The Ethics of Aquinas*, edited by Stephen J. Pope, 169–93. Washington, DC: Georgetown University Press, 2002.

Kotva, Joseph J. *The Christian Case for Virtue Ethics*. Washington, DC: Georgetown University Press, 1996.

Kucinich, Dennis. "12 Point Plan for Iraq." Introduced to Congress on January 9, 2007. http://kucinich.us/12-pt_Plan_Iraq.pdf.

Kung, Hans. *A Global Ethic for Global Politics and Economics*. New York: Oxford University Press, 1997.

Lakey, George. "How to Develop Peace Teams: The Light Bulb Theory." http://www .trainingforchange.org/light_bulb_theory.

Langan, John. "Defending Human Rights: A Revision of the Liberal Tradition." In *Human Rights in the Americas: The Struggle for Consensus*, edited by Alfred Hennelly and J. Langan, 69–101. Washington, DC: Georgetown University Press, 1982.

Larrow-Roberts, Nikolas, and John Perkins. "Breaking Out of the Culture of Violence: An Oral History with Former Economic Hit Man John Perkins." In *Peace Movements Worldwide: Peace Efforts That Work and Why*, edited by M. Pilisuk and M. Nagler, 3:327–39. Santa Barbara, CA: Praeger, 2011.

Lederach, John Paul. *The Little Book of Conflict Transformation*. Intercourse, PA: Good Books, 2003

———. *Moral Imagination: The Art and Soul of Building Peace*. New York: Oxford University Press, 2005.

Lederach, John Paul, Reina Neufeldt, and Hal Culbertson. *Reflective Peacebuilding: A Planning, Monitoring, and Learning Tool Kit.* Notre Dame: Kroc Institute University of Notre Dame, 2007. http://kroc.nd.edu.

Lewis, John. "Human Right in Darfur; Winners and Losers in the Search for Justice." *Africa Files*, 2009. http://www.africafiles.org/article.asp?ID=20950.

Little Friends for Peace. www.lffp.org.

Love, Maryann Cusimano. "Emerging Norms of Peacebuilding in Key Political Institutions." Panel at Catholic Peacebuilding Network Conference, April 13–15, 2008. http://cpn.nd.edu/2008CPNConference%20-%20Post-Program.shtml.

Lozano, Elizabeth. "I am the Leader, You are the Leader: Nonviolent Resistance in the Peace Community of San Jose de Apartado, Colombia." In *Peace Movements Worldwide: Peace Efforts That Work and Why*, edited by M. Pilisuk and M. Nagler, 3:93–109. Santa Barbara, CA: Praeger, 2011.

MacIntyre, Alasdair. *After Virtue: A Study in Moral Theology.* 2nd and 3rd ed. Notre Dame: Notre Dame University Press, 1984, 2007.

MacNair, Rachel. "Perpetration-Induced Traumatic Stress." In *Peace Movements Worldwide: Players and Practices in Resistance to War*, edited by M. Pilisuk and M. Nagler, 2:263–70. Santa Barbara, CA: Praeger, 2011.

———. *Perpetration-Induced Traumatic Stress: The Psychological Consequences of Killing.* Lincoln, NE: Praeger/Greenwood, 2005.

Marshall, Christopher. *Beyond Retribution: A New Testament Vision for Justice, Crime, and Punishment.* Grand Rapids: Eerdmans, 2001.

Marshall, T. H. *Citizenship and Social Class.* Concord, NH: Pluto, 1992.

Martin, Brian. "Gene Sharp's Theory of Power." *Journal of Peace Research* 26.2 (1989) 213–22.

Maweni, Rumbidzai. "Sudan's President Omar Hassan al-Bashir Indicted by the ICC: What's Next?" *Citizens for Global Solutions* (July 14, 2008). http://www.globalsolutions.org/issues/sudans_president_omar_hassan_al_bashi_indicted_icc_what_s_next.

McCain, John. "Not Tet: Iraq is Not Vietnam." Speech made to Senate on Apr. 7, 2004. http://www.nationalreview.com/document/mccain200404080912.asp.

McCarthy, Eli. "Catholic Social Teaching: Integrating the Virtue of Nonviolent Peacemaking." In *Peace Movements Worldwide: History and Vitality of Peace Movements*, edited by M. Pilisuk and M. Nagler, 1:136–50. Santa Barbara, CA: Praeger, 2011.

McCarthy, Emmanual Charles. *The Nonviolent Eucharistic Jesus: A Pastoral Approach.* Wilmington, DE: Center for Christian Nonviolence. http:http://www.centerforchristiannonviolence.org/data/Media/NV_Eucharist_PastoralApproach_01d.pdf.

McCord, Ethan. "Wikileaks' Collateral Murder: U.S. Soldier Ethan McCord's Eyewitness Story." United National Peace Conference Media Project. Albany, NY: Sanctuary Media, July 2010. http://www.mediasanctuary.org/movie/1810.

Metta Center for Nonviolence Education, in Glossary. http://www.mettacenter.org/?p=37.

Michigan Peace Team. http://michiganpeaceteam.org/.

Midgely, Mary. "Rights-Talk Will Not Sort Our Child-Abuse: Comment on Archard on Parental Rights." *Journal of Applied Philosophy* 8.1 (1991) 103–14.

Miller, J. Joseph. "Squaring the Circle: Teaching Philosophical Ethics in the Military." *Journal of Military Ethics* 3 (2004) 199–215.

Miller, Mark. *Why the Passion: Bernard Lonergan On the Cross as Communication.* PhD diss., Boston College, 2008.

Miller, Richard. *Interpretations of Conflict: Ethics, Pacifism, and the Just-War Tradition.* Chicago: University of Chicago Press, 1991.

Minnow, Martha. *Between Vengeance and Forgiveness: Facing History after Genocide and Mass Violence.* Boston: Beacon, 1998.

Mirror Neurons. http://www.mettacenter.org/definitions/mirror-neurons.

Mitchell, Greg. "The U.S. Soldier Who Killed Herself After Refusing to Take Part in Torture." September 15, 2010. http://www.thenation.com/blog/154649/us-soldier-who-committed-suicide-after-she-refused-take-part-torture.

Mohamed, Yasien. "The Evolution of Early Islamic Ethics." *American Journal of Islamic Social Sciences* 18.4 (2001) 89–132.

Moore, Specialist Jason. "Ambush in Mogadishu." Interview by CNN/Frontline. http://www.pbs.org/wgbh/pages/frontline/shows/ambush/rangers/moore.html.

Morse, David. "Blood, Ink, and Oil: The Case of Darfur." *Common Dreams*, July 21, 2005. http://www.commondreams.org/views05/072 1–26.htm.

———. "War of the Future, Oil Drives the Genocide in Darfur." *Common Dreams*, August 19, 2005. http://www.commondreams.org/views05/081 9–26.htm.

Muñoz-Rojas, Daniel, and Jean-Jacques Frésard. *The Roots of Behaviour in War: Understanding and Preventing IHL Violations.* Geneva: International Committee of the Red Cross, 2004.

Muslim Peacemaker Teams. http://www.mpt-iraq.org/.

Nagler, Michael. Class notes of Introduction to Nonviolence, 164a at University of Cal Berkeley, Fall 2006.

———. *Hope or Terror? Gandhi and the Other 9/11.* Minneapolis, MN: Great River Nonviolent Communication, 2006.

———. *Is There No Other Way? The Search for a Nonviolent Future.* Berkeley: Berkeley Hills, 2001.

———. "The Movement Toward Peace in Crisis." In *Peace Movements Worldwide: Peace Efforts That Work and Why,* edited by M. Pilisuk and M. Nagler, 3:194–203. Santa Barbara, CA: Praeger, 2011

———. *The Search for a Nonviolent Future: A Promise of Peace for Ourselves, our Families, and our World.* Maui: Inner Ocean, 2004.

Nanda, B. R. *Mahatma Gandhi: A Biography.* Woodbury, NY: Barron's, 1965.

Nardin, Terry. *The Ethics of War and Peace: Religious and Secular Perspectives.* Princeton, NJ: Princeton University Press, 1998.

National Peace Academy. http://www.nationalpeaceacademy.us/.

National Priorities Project, "Discretionary Budget FY 2010." http://nationalpriorities.org/en/resources/federal-budget-101/charts/discretionary-spending/discretionary-budget-fy2010/.

Natsois, Andrew. "Beyond Darfur: Sudan's Slide Toward Civil War." *Foreign Affairs* (May/June 2008). http://www.foreignaffairs.com/articles/63399/andrew-natsios/beyond-darfur

Negroponte, John. "Testimony Statement: Deputy of State Negroponte Stresses Increased Role of Civilian Agencies is Critical to National Security." U.S. Senate Committee on Foreign Relations, July 31, 2008. http://www.africom.mil/getArticle.asp?art=1962.

New Revised Standard Version. Edited by Wayne Meeks. New York: Harper Collins, 1993.

Niebuhr, Reinhold. *Christianity and Power Politics*. New York: Charles Scribner's Sons, 1940.

———. *Love and Justice*. Edited by D. B. Robertson. Louisville: Westminster John Knox, 1957.

Nonviolent Peaceforce. http://nonviolentpeaceforce.org.

———. "Convening Event." www.nvpf.org/en/conveningevent.

———. "Core Training." www.nonviolentpeaceforce.org/en/coretraining.

———. "Frequently Asked Questions." www.nvpf.org/en/faq.

———. "Mission." www.nonviolentpeaceforce.org/en/mission.

———. "Sudan Project: Strategy." http://www.nonviolentpeaceforce.org/fieldwork/all-projects/sudan-project.

———. "Who We Are." www.nvpf.org/en/whoweare.

Nozick, Robert. *Anarchy, State, and Utopia*. Oxford: Basil Blackwell, 1974.

Nussbaum, Martha: "Aristotelian Social Democracy." In *Liberalism and the Good*, edited by R. B. Douglas et al., 203–52. New York: Routledge, 1990.

———. "Comparing Virtues." *Journal of Religious Ethics* 21 (1993) 345–67.

———. "Non-Relative Virtues: An Aristotelian Approach." In *Ethical Theory: Character and Virtue, edited by* Peter A. French et al., 32–53. Notre Dame: University of Notre Dame Press, 1988.

———. *Women and Human Development: The Capabilities Approach*. Cambridge: Cambridge University Press, 2001.

Obama, Barack. "U.S. National Security Strategy," 2010. http://www.whitehouse.gov/sites/default/files/rss_viewer/national_security_strategy.pdf.

Office of Management and Budget, "Department of Defense." http://www.whitehouse.gov/omb/factsheet_department_defense/.

O'Neill, William. *Christian Social Ethics* graduate course at Graduate Theological Union, class notes Spring 2006.

———. *The Ethics of Our Climate: Hermeneutics and Ethical Theory*. Washington, DC: Georgetown University Press, 1994

———. "No Amnesty for Sorrow: The Privilege of the Poor in Christian Social Ethics." *Theological Studies* 55 (1994) 638–56.

———. "Rights of Passage: The Ethics of Forced Displacement." *Journal of Society of Christian Ethics* 27 (2007) 113–36.

———. "What We Owe to Refugees and IDP's: An Inquiry into the Rights of the Forcibly Displaced." In *Refugee Rights: Ethics, Advocacy, and Africa*, edited by David Hollenbach, 27–52. Washington, DC: Georgetown University Press, 2008.

———. "The Violent Bear It Away: Just War and U.S. Military Policy in the Eyes of Catholic Teaching." *Journal of Religion and Society* 4 (2008) 80–91.

———. "Visions and Revisions: The Hermeneutical Implications of the Option for the Poor." In *Hope and Solidarity: John Sobrino's Challenge to Christian Theology* edited by Stephen J. Pope, 31–43. Maryknoll, NY: Orbis, 2008.

O'Reardon, Donal. "Theorizing International Human Rights: Two Perspectives Considered." In *Human Rights and Military Intervention*, edited by A. Mosely and R. Norman, 34–49. Burlington, VT: Ashgate, 2002.

Orend, Brian. "Justice After War." *Ethics of International Affairs* 16 (2002) 43–56.

———. *The Morality of War*. Peterborough: Broadview, 2006.

———. *War and International Justice: A Kantian Perspective*. Ontario: Wilfrid Laurier University Press, 2000.

Pace Bene. "Four Steps: Center, Articulate, Receive, Agree." http://paceebene.org/nonviolent-change-101/tools-nonviolent-living/nonviolent-journey/four-steps.

Paul IV, Pope. "A Call to Action on the 80th Anniversary of *Rerum Novarum*." In *Catholic Social Thought: A Documentary Heritage*, edited by David O'Brien and T. Shannon, 263–86. Maryknoll, NY: Orbis, 1992.

Peace and Justice Studies Association and International Peace Research Association Foundation, *Global Directory of Peace Studies and Conflict Resolution Programs*, 7th ed., 2007. http://www.peacejusticestudies.org/globaldirectory/preface.pdf.

Perkins, Pheme. "Paul and Ethics." *Interpretation* 38 (1984) 268–80.

———. "The Rejected Jesus and the Kingdom Sayings." *Semeia* 20 (1981) 79–94.

Perry, Robert. "Time for a U.S. Truth Commission." *The Consortium*, February 17, 1997. http://www.thirdworldtraveler.com/Terrorism/US_TruthCommission.html.

Petrik, Jaroslav. "Securitization of Official Development Aid: Analysis of Current Debate." Paper presented at 2008 International Peace Research Conference, 14–19 July, Leuven, Belgium, Conflict Resolution and Peace-Building Commission. http://soc.kuleuven.be/iieb/ipraweb/papers/Securitization%20of%20Official%20Development%20Aid.pdf.

Pilgrim, Walter. *Uneasy Neighbors: Church and State in the New Testament*. Minneapolis: Fortress, 1999.

Pinckaers, Servais. "Ethics and the Image of God." In *The Pinckaers Reader: Renewing Thomistic Moral Theology*, edited by John Berkman and Craig Steven Titus, 130–43. Washington, DC: Catholic University of America Press 2005.

———. "The Role of Virtue in Moral Theology." In *The Pinckaers Reader: Renewing Thomistic Moral Theology*, edited by John Berkman and Craig Steven Titus, 288–303. Washington, DC: Catholic University of America Press 2005.

———. *Sources of Christian Ethics*. Washington, DC: Catholic University Press, 1995.

Philips, D. "Casualties of War, Part I: The Hell of War Comes Home." *The Gazette*, July 25, 2009. http://www.gazette.com/articles/iframe-59065-eastridge-audio.html.

Philpott, Dan. "Lessons in Mercy: Justice and Reconciliation in the Aftermath of Atrocities." *America*, May 4, 2009. http://www.americamagazine.org/content/article.cfm?article_id=11623.

Ponder, Joe. "Suicide and Homelessness at Epidemic Levels Among Former US Troops." *Pensito Review*, November 13, 2007. http://www.pensitoreview.com/2007/11/13/veterans-suicide-homelessness-epidemic/.

Pontifical Council for Justice and Peace. *Compendium of the Social Doctrine of the Church*. Libreria Editrice Vaticana, 2004. http://www.vatican.va/roman_curia/pontifical_councils/justpeace/documents/rc_pc_justpeace_doc_20060526_compendio-dott-soc_en.html.

Poor People's Economic Human Rights Campaign. "National Truth Commission." July 1 5–17, 2006. http://old.economichumanrights.org/ntc_report1.shtml.

Pope, Stephen, "Overview of the Ethics of Thomas Aquinas." In *The Ethics of Aquinas*, edited by Stephen J. Pope, 30–56. Washington, DC: Georgetown University Press, 2002.

Porter, Jean. *Nature as Reason: A Thomistic Theory of the Natural Law*. Grand Rapids: Eerdmans, 2005.

———. *The Recovery of Virtue: The Relevance of Aquinas for Christian Ethics*. Louisville: Westminster John Knox, 1990.

———. "The Virtue of Justice (IIa IIae, qq. 5 8–122)." In *The Ethics of Aquinas*, edited by Stephen J. Pope, 272–86. Washington, DC: Georgetown University Press, 2002.

Powers, Rod. "How to Survive Military Basic Training." http://usmilitary.about.com/od/joiningthemilitary/a/basictraining.htm.

Poverty Initiative, April 13, 2007. http://www.povertyinitiative.org/events/event_pages/4-1 3-07_truth_commission/ 4-1 3-07_truth_commission_main.html.

———. Graduate Theological Union, April 10, 2008. http://www.indybay.org/news items/2008/04/09/18491813.php.

Prendergast, J., et al. "President Obama's Immediate Sudan Challenge-Letter." January 22, 2009. http://www.enoughproject.org/publications/president-obama-immediate-sudan-challenge.

Putnam, David. "Rights and Virtues: Toward an Integrated Theory." *The Journal of Value Inquiry* 21.2 (1987) 87–99.

Qur'an. Translated by Abdullah Yusuf Ali. Elmhurst, NY: Tahrike Tarsile Qur'an, 1999.

Rawls, John. *A Theory of Justice*. Cambridge: Harvard University Press, 1999.

Reuters News, "Mental Illness Common Among Returning US Soldiers." March 12, 2007. http://www.reuters.com/article/healthNews/idUSTON27935120070312.

Rieff, David. "Moral Blindness: The Case Against Troops for Darfur." *The New Republic* 234.21/22 (2006) 13–16.

Roberts, Adam. "Introduction." In *The Strategy of Civilian Defence*, edited by Adam Roberts, 9–16. London: Faber & Faber Limited, 1967.

———. Transarmament to Civilian Defence." In *The Strategy of Civilian Defence*, edited by Adam Roberts, 291–301. London: Faber & Faber Limited, 1967.

Ruddick, Sara. *Maternal Thinking: Toward a Politics of Peace*. Boston: Beacon, 1995.

Rynne, Terrance. *Gandhi and Jesus: The Saving Power of Nonviolence*. Maryknoll, NY: Orbis, 2008.

Sacred Congregation for the Doctrine of Faith. "Instruction on Certain Aspects of the Theology of Liberation." August 6, 1984. http://www.newadvent.org/library/docs_df84lt.htm.

Sappenfield, Mark. "New Military Goals: Win the Peace." *Christian Science Monitor*, December 16, 2005. http://www.csmonitor.com/2005/1216/p01s02-usmi.html.

Save Darfur Coalition, "The Genocide in Darfur—Briefing Paper." June 2008. www.savedarfur.org/pages/background.

Sawatsky, Jarem. *Justpeace Ethics: A Guide to Restorative Justice and Peacebuilding*. Eugene, OR: Cascade, 2008.

Schaeffer-Duffy, Claire. "Regime Change without Bloodshed." *National Catholic Reporter*, November 15, 2002. http://www.natcath.org/NCR_Online/archives/111502/111502g.htm.

Schirch, Lisa. "Building Bridges and Preventing Conflict: A Memo to the New Administration." 3D Security-Initiative, Alliance for Peacebuilding, and Global Partnership for the Prevention of Armed Conflict, December 28, 2008. http://3dsec.sockhead.com/sites/3dsecurity.org/files/3D%20AfP%20and%20GPPAC%20Memo%20to%20Obama%20Admin%20December%2028%202008.pdf.

Schlabach, Gerald. *Just Policing, Not War: An Alternative Response to World Violence*, edited by Gerald Schlabach. Collegeville, MN: Liturgical, 2007.

Schneiders, Sandra. "The Foot Washing (John 13: 1–20): An Experiment in Hermeneutics." *Ex Auditu* 1 (1985) 135–46.

Schottroff, Luise. "'Give to Caesar What Belongs to Caesar and to God What Belongs to God': A Theological Response off the Early Christian Church to Its Social and Political Environment." In *Love of Enemy and Nonretaliation*, edited by Willard Swartley, 223–57. Louisville: Westminster John Knox, 1992.

Schweitzer, Christine. "Human Security: Providing Protection Without Sticks and Carrots." In *Peace Movements Worldwide: Players and Practices in Resistance to War*, edited by M. Pilisuk and M. Nagler, 2:108–19. Santa Barbara, CA: Praeger, 2011.

Scrimshaw, Susan. "The Violence Virus." *Boston Globe* Op-Ed, April 22, 2007. http://www.nonviolenceinstitute.org/2007/04/chicago_street_.html.

Search for Common Ground. http://www.sfcg.org/sfcg/sfcg_core.html.

Second Vatican Council. "Dogmatic Constitution of the Church." November 21, 1964. http://www.vatican.va/archive/hist_councils/ii_vatican_council/documents/vat-ii_const_19641121_lumen-gentium_en.html.

———. "Pastoral Constitution on the Church in the Modern World." December 7, 1965. http://www.vatican.va/archive/hist_councils/ii_vatican_council/documents/vat-ii_cons_19651207_gaudium-et-spes_en.html.

Sen, Amartya. *Development as Freedom*. New York: Knopf, 1999.

Shah, Anup. "The Arms Trade is Big-Business," November 9, 2008. http://www.globalissues.org/article/74/the-arms-trade-is-big-business.

———. "Arms Trade: A Major Cause of Suffering." www.globalissues.org/issue/73/arms-trade-a-major-cause-of-suffering.

———. "World Military Spending," Mar. 1, 2008. Chart: Information from Stockholm International Peace Research Yearbook, 2010 (U.S. Figures from Center for Arms Control and Non-Proliferation, May 2010). http://www.globalissues.org/article/75/world-military-spending, http://www.sipri.org/yearbook/2010/05/05A.

———. "The USA and Human Rights," August 21, 2002. http://www.globalissues.org/article/139/the-usa-and-human-rights.

Shanker, Thom. "Despite Slump, U.S. Role as Top Arms Supplier Grows." *NY Times*, Sept. 6, 2009. http://www.nytimes.com/2009/09/07/world/07weapons.html.

Sharp, Gene. *Civilian-Based Defense*. Princeton: Princeton University Press, 1990.

———. *Gandhi as Political Strategist*. Boston: Porter Sargent, 1979.

———. "People 'Don't Need to Believe Right.'" *National Catholic Reporter* 20 (September 7, 1984) 11.

———. *The Politics of Nonviolent Action*. Boston: Porter Sargent, 1973.

———. "Principled Non-Violence: Options for Action," Paper presented at Kroc Institute of Notre Dame, September 2006. http://www.aeinstein.org/lectures_papers/KROC_OPTIONS_BELIEVERS.pdf.

———. *Social Power and Political Freedom*. Boston: Porter Sargent, 1980.

———. "The Technique of Non-Violent Action." In *The Strategy of Civilian Defense* edited by Adam Roberts, 87–105. London: Faber & Faber, 1967.

———. *Waging Nonviolent Struggle: 20th Century Practice and 21st Century Potential*. Boston: Porter Sargent, 2005.

Shelling, Thomas. "Forward." In *Strategic Nonviolent Conflict*, by P. Ackerman and C. Kruegler. Westport, CN: Praeger, 1994.

Shepard, Mark. *The Community of the Ark*. http://www.markshep.com/nonviolence/Ark.html.

———. "Soldiers of Peace Narayan Desai and Shanti Sena, the 'Peace Army.'" http://www.markshep.com/nonviolence/GT_Sena.html.

Shue, Henry. *Basic Rights: Subsistence, Affluence, and U.S. Foreign Policy*. Princeton: Princeton University Press, 1996.

Shuster, Mike. "Iraq War Deepens Sunni-Shia Divide." *National Public Radio*, February 15, 2007. http://www.npr.org/templates/story/story.php?storyId=7411762.

Singh, Radhey Shyam. *The Constructive Programmes of Mahatma Gandhi*. New Delhi: Commonwealth, 1991.

Skodvin, M. "Norwegian Nonviolent Resistance During the German Occupation." In *The Strategy of Civilian Defence*, edited by A. Roberts, 162–81. London: Faber & Faber, 1967.

Slachmuijlder, Lena. "Setting the Stage for Peace: Participatory Theater for Conflict Transformation in the Democratic Republic of Congo." In *Peace Movements Worldwide: Peace Efforts That Work and Why*, edited by M. Pilisuk and M. Nagler, 3:226–30. Santa Barbara, CA: Praeger, 2011.

Slavin, Barbara. "Powell Accuses Sudan of Genocide." *USA TODAY*, Sept. 9, 2004. http://www.usatoday.com/news/washington/200 4–0 9–09-sudan-powell_x.htm.

Slote, M. "Virtue Ethics and Democratic Values." *Journal of Social Philosophy* 24.2 (1993) 38–49.

Smith, Dane. *U.S. Peacefare*. Santa Barbara, CA: Praeger ABC-CLIO, 2010.

Smock, David R. *Perspectives on Pacifism: Christian, Jewish and Muslim Views on Non-Violence*. Washington, DC: U.S. Institute of Peace, 1995.

Sobrino, Jon. *The Principle of Mercy: Taking the Crucified People from the Cross*. Maryknoll, NY: Orbis, 1994.

Sontag, E., and K. Mines. "Transformational Diplomacy in Darfur." *State Magazine*, June 2007. http://www.scribd.com/doc/32412131/State-Magazine-June-2007.

Spohn, William. *Go and Do Likewise: Jesus and Ethics*. New York: Continuum, 2003.

Staff Writers. "New Secret Oil Installations in Darfur." *African Online News*, September 14, 2009. http://www.afrol.com/articles/21316.

Stanford Encyclopedia of Philosophy. "Virtue Ethics." July 18, 2007. http://plato.stanford.edu/entries/ethics-virtue/.

Stares, P., and A. Noyes. "Think Twice on Bashir." *Newsweek*, March 5, 2009. http://www.newsweek.com/id/187870.

Stark, Alex. "Prevention in the New 2011 Budget." April 13, 2011. http://fcnl.org/issues/ppdc/prevention_in_the_new_2011_budget.

Stassen, Glen, editor. *Just Peacemaking: The New Paradigm for the Ethics of Peace and War*. 3rd ed. Cleveland: Pilgrim, 2008.

———. *Just Peacemaking: Transforming Initiatives for Justice and Peace*. Louisville: Westminster John Knox, 1992.

———. "Transforming Initiatives of Just Peacemaking Based on the Triadic Structure of the Sermon on the Mount." Paper at Society of Biblical Literature, Matthew group, 2006. http://www.sbl-site.org/assets/pdfs/Stassen_Transforming.pdf.

Stassen, Glen, and David Gushee. *Kingdom Ethics: Following Jesus in Contemporary Context*. Downers Grove, IL: Intervarsity, 2003.

Steim, Judith. "Contemporary Theories of Non-violent Resistance." PhD diss., Columbia University, 1969.

Sternstein, W. "The Ruhrkampf of 1923: Economic Problems of Civilian Defence." In *The Strategy of Civilian Defence*, edited by A. Roberts, 128–61. London: Faber & Faber, 1967.

Stohlberg, Sheryl Gay. "Bush Speech Criticized as Attack on Obama." *New York Times*, May 16, 2008. http://www.nytimes.com/2008/05/16/world/middleeast/16prexy.html?fta=y.

Swartley, Williard. *Covenant of Peace: The Missing Peace in New Testament Theology and Ethics.* Grand Rapids: Eerdmans, 2006.

Taylor, Charles. *Sources of the Self: The Making of Modern Identity.* Cambridge: Harvard University Press, 1989.

Teach Peace Foundation. "Leaders Education and Training: Program of Instruction." 2008–2011. http://www.teachpeace.com/leaderspoi.htm.

Tessman, Lisa. *Burdened Virtues: Virtue Ethics for Liberatory Struggles.* New York: Oxford University Press, 2005.

Thompson, Mark. "Why Are Army Recruiters Killing Themselves?" *Time*, April 2, 2009. http://www.time.com/time/magazine/article/0,9171,1889152,00.html.

Tillmann, Fritz. *The Master Calls: A Handbook of Christian Living.* Baltimore: Hellicon, 1960.

Toit, Andre Du. "The Moral Foundations of the South African TRC: Truth as Acknowledgment and Justice as Recognition." In *Truth v. Justice: The Morality of Truth Commissions*, edited by Robert Rotberg and Dennis Thompson, 122–42. Princeton, NJ: Princeton University Press, 2000.

Tong, Xiong. "China Regretful, Worried about Sudan President Arrest Warrant." *China View*, March 5, 2009. http://news.xinhuanet.com/english/2009-03/05/content_10946492.htm.

Tooke, Joan. *The Just War in Aquinas and Grotius.* London: SPCK, 1965.

Traina, Christina. *Feminist Ethics and Natural Law: The End of Anathemas.* Washington, DC: Georgetown University Press, 1999.

Truth Commission on Conscience in War. New York City, NY, 2010. http://conscience inwar.org/about/.

Truth Commissions Digital Collection n.d., United States Institute of Peace. http://www.usip.org/library/truth.html.

Tutu, Desmond. *No Future Without Forgiveness.* New York: Doubleday, 1999.

United Nations. "Charter of the United Nations, Preamble." San Francisco, June 26, 1945. http://www.un.org/aboutun/charter/preamble.shtml.

———. "Convention on the Prevention and Punishment of the Crime of Genocide." December 9, 1948. http://www.unhchr.ch/html/menu3/b/p_genoci.htm.

———. "Declaration of Human Rights." 1948. http://un.org/Overview/rights.html

———. Department of Peacekeeping. http://www.un.org/Depts/dpko/dpko/.

———. Development Program, Human Development Reports. http://hdr.undp.org/en/.

———. "Human Development Report," 1998. http://hdr.undp.org/en/media/hdr_1998_en_chap1.pdf.

———. "International Covenant on Economic, Social, and Cultural Rights." 1976. http://www2.ohchr.org/english/law/cescr.htm.

———. Millennium Development Goals, 2000. http://www.un.org/millenniumgoals/.

———. Millennium Development Goals: 2008 Progress Chart. http://www.un.org/millenniumgoals/2008highlevel/pdf/newsroom/MDG_Report_2008_Progress_Chart_en_r8.pdf.

U.S. Air Force. "Core Values," Jan. 1, 1997. http://www.usafa.af.mil/core-value/cv-mastr.html.

U.S. Army. "Soldier Life: Living the Army Values." http://www.goarmy.com/life/living_the_army_values.jsp.

U.S. Catholic Bishops. "Challenge of Peace: God's Promise and Our Response." In *Catholic Social Thought: A Documentary Heritage*, edited by David O'Brien and T. Shannon, 492–571. Maryknoll, NY: Orbis, 1992. http://www.usccb.org/sdwp/international/TheChallengeofPeace.pdf.

————. "The Harvest of Justice is Sown in Peace." November 17, 1993. http://www.usccb.org/sdwp/harvest.shtml.

————. "Hill Notes- February 2012." http://www.usccb.org/about/justice-peace-and-human-development/catholic-social-ministry-gathering/upload/2012Hill-Notes-International-Assistance-with-Chart.pdf.

————. Bishop Gregory. "Statement on Iraq." Feb. 26th, 2003. http://www.usccb.org/sdwp/international/iraqstatement0203.shtml.

————. Bishop Gregory. "Statement on War with Iraq." Mar. 19th, 2003. http://www.usccb.org/sdwp/peace/stm31903.shtml.

————. "Responsibility, Rehabilitation, and Restoration: A Catholic Perspective on Crime and Criminal Justice." November 15, 2000. http://www.usccb.org/sdwp/criminal.shtml.

U.S. Department of Defense. "Quadrennial Defense Review," February 2010. http://www.defense.gov/news/d2010usdprolloutbrief.pdf.

————. "National Defense Strategy," June 2008, 7. http://www.defenselink.mil/pubs/2008NationalDefenseStrategy.pdf.

U.S. Institute of Peace. "Iraq Program," Mar. 31, 2009—Apr. 4, 2009. http://www.usip.org/in_the_field/iraq/.

U.S. Marines Corps. "First to Fight." http://www.marines.com/main/index/making_marines/culture/traditions/first_to_fight.

————. "Core Values." http://www.marines.com/main/index/making_marines/culture/traditions/core_values.

U.S. Navy. "Personal Development." http://www.navy.com/about/during/personaldevelopment/honor/.

U.S. State Department. "Sudan: A Critical Moment, A Comprehensive Approach." October 19, 2009. http://www.savedarfur.org/pages/sudan-policy-review.

Vatican Today. "Christians Need to Understand their Faith in Order to Help Others to God." Feb. 24, 2012. http://thecatholicspirit.com/news/from-the-vatican/vatican-today-february-24-2012/.

Vision of Humanity. "Global Peace Index: USA," 2010. http://www.visionofhumanity.org/gpi-data/#/2010/scor/US/detail.

————. Global Rankings 2010. http://www.visionofhumanity.org/gpi-data/#/2010/scor.

————. Global Rankings 2011. http://www.visionofhumanity.org/gpi-data/#/2011/scor.

————. "U.S. Peace Index." April 6, 2011. http://www.visionofhumanity.org/info-center/us-peace-index/.

Vogt, Christopher. "The Common Good and Virtue Ethics." *Theological Studies* 68 (2007) 394–417.

Waal, Alex de. "Indicting Sudan's President for War Crimes." National Public Radio, March 9, 2009. http://www.ssrc.org/blogs/darfur/2009/03/09/alex-on-the-kojo-nnamdi-show.

Waldrep, Christopher, and M. Belliesiles, editors. *Documenting American Violence: A Sourcebook*. New York: Oxford University Press, 2006.

Walters, Gregory J. "MacIntyre or Gewirth? Virtue, Rights, and the Problem of Moral Indeterminacy." In *Philosophical Theory and the Universal Declaration of Human Rights*, edited by William Sweet, 183–200. Ottawa: University of Ottawa Press, 2003.

Warrick, Joby, and Philip Rucker. "Far-reaching Cuts." *Washington Post*, April 13, 2011, A3.

Weber, Thomas. "Nonviolence Is Who? Gene Sharp and Gandhi." *Peace and Change* 28 (2003) 250–70.

Wensveen, Luke van. *Dirty Virtues: The Emergence of Ecological Virtue Ethics*. Amherst, MA: Humanity, 2000.

Whitmore, Todd. "The Reception of Catholic Approaches to Peace and War in the United States." In *Modern Catholic Social Teaching*, edited by K. Himes, 493–521. Washington, DC: Georgetown University Press, 2004.

Wink, Walter. "Beyond Just War and Pacifism: Jesus' Nonviolent Way." *Review and Expositer* 89 (1992) 197–214

———. *Engaging the Powers: Discernment and Resistance in a World of Domination*. Minneapolis: Augsburg, 1992.

———. "Facing the Myth of Redemptive Violence." *Ekklesia*, November 16, 2007. http://www.ekklesia.co.uk/content/cpt/article_060823wink.shtml.

Wolfendale, Jessica. "Developing Moral Character in the Military: Theory and Practice." Presented at International Symposium for Military Ethics, Springfield, VA, January 24–25, 2007. http://isme.tamu.edu/ISME07/Wolfendale07.html.

Wright, N. T. "Kingdom Come: Public Meaning of the Gospels." *Christian Century* June 17, 2008. http://www.christiancentury.org/article.lasso?id=4862.

———. "Paul and Caesar: A New Reading of Romans." In *A Royal Priesthood: The Use of the Bible Ethically and Politically*, edited by Craig Bartholemew, 173–93. Carlisle, UK: Paternoster, 2002. http://www.ntwrightpage.com/Wright_Paul_Caesar_Romans.htm.

Yoanna, Michael de, and M. Benjamin. "Coming Home: The Army's Fatal Neglect." *Salon News*, April 8, 2009. http://www.salon.com/news/special/coming_home/2009/04/08/tape/.

Young, Iris Marion. *Justice and The Politics of Difference*. Princeton, NJ: Princeton University Press, 1990.

Zahn, Franklin. *Alternative to the Pentagon: Nonviolent Methods of Defending a Nation*. Nyack, NY: Fellowship, 1996.

Zenit News Service. "Eucharist is 'God's Absolute No to Violence.'" March 11, 2005. http://www.zenit.org/article-12485?l=english.

———. "Pontiff Calls Volunteers Peace Workers: Addresses Youth of Italy's Civil Service." March 29, 2009. http://www.zenit.org/rssenglish-25513.

Zinn, Howard. *Passionate Declarations: Essays on War and Justice*. New York: Harper Collins, 2003.

Zunes, Stephen. "The Origins of People Power in the Philippines." In *Nonviolent Social Movements: A Geographical Perspective*, edited by Stephen Zunes et al., 129–57. Malden, MA: Blackwell, 1999.

Index